December - 1979

Merry Christmas Steve!

Love
Jim & Cheryl

DECEPTION
IN · WORLD · WAR · II

Charles Cruickshank

DECEPTION
IN · WORLD · WAR · II

Oxford   New York   Melbourne   Toronto
OXFORD UNIVERSITY PRESS
1979

Oxford University Press, Walton Street, Oxford OX2 6DP

OXFORD LONDON GLASGOW NEW YORK TORONTO MELBOURNE
WELLINGTON KUALA LUMPUR SINGAPORE JAKARTA HONG KONG
TOKYO DELHI BOMBAY CALCUTTA MADRAS KARACHI
NAIROBI DAR ES SALAAM CAPE TOWN

British Library Cataloguing in Publication Data

Cruickshank, Charles Grieg
  Deception in World War II.
  1. World War, 1939–1945 – Campaigns
  2. Strategy 3. Deception
  I. Title
  940.54′012   D744   79–40615
  ISBN 0–19–215849–X

Set, printed and bound in Great Britain by
Fakenham Press Limited,
Fakenham, Norfolk

CONTENTS

ILLUSTRATIONS

PREFACE

This book is based on official papers in the Public Record Office and the National Archives of the United States. The photographs of dummy equipment and deceptive devices come from files in the Public Record Office and the National Archives, and from the Imperial War Museum collection. So far as I am aware they are now reproduced for the first time. Transcripts and facsimiles of Crown copyright records in the Public Record Office appear by permission of the Controller of Her Majesty's Stationery Office.

I wish to thank the Modern Military Branch of the National Archives for generous help over a period of years. I am also indebted to the presiding genii of the Langdale Room in the Public Record Office whose service is matched only by the efficiency of the new electronified records delivery system, which it is a joy to use; and to my editor, Adam Sisman, who has laboured far beyond the call of duty.

Finally, if anywhere in this account of multidimensional make-believe I give substance to shadow, or *vice versa*, credit my error to the skill of the deceptionists. They builded better than they knew.

NOVEMBER 1978   C.G.C.

INTRODUCTION

Deception in war is the art of misleading the enemy into doing something, or not doing something, so that his strategic or tactical position will be weakened.

A deceptive operation embodies all the signs of a real assault. It makes the enemy believe that pretended hostile activities are genuine. It induces a false sense of danger in one area, forcing him to strengthen his defences there, and therefore to weaken them somewhere else where the real attack is due.

Cover is a form of deception which leads the enemy to decide that genuine hostile activities are harmless. It induces a false sense of security by disguising the preparations for a real attack, so that when it comes the enemy will be taken by surprise.

The use of so-called 'Chinese soldiers' – dummy figures which can be animated to attract enemy fire and divert attention from a real attack elsewhere – is a simple example of overt deception. A rumour campaign suggesting to the enemy that troops embarking to invade a tropical country are in fact bound for the Arctic is an equally simple example of a cover operation.

At the other end of the spectrum, a deceptive plan may involve months of careful preparation, the movement of thousands of troops, hundreds of aircraft, and scores of warships, all in order to convince the enemy that a major assault is being mounted. A plan of this magnitude can alter the whole strategic balance of a campaign. A cover plan may be on the same scale, designed to conceal real preparations for a massive assault.

The perfect deception plan is like a jigsaw puzzle. Pieces of information are allowed to reach the enemy in such a way as to convince him that he has discovered them by accident. If he puts them together himself he is far more likely to believe that the intended picture is a true one. An almost endless variety of such pieces can be offered to the enemy. During the Second World War techniques of deception used by the Allies included the display of real and dummy aircraft, tanks, guns, vehicles, and encampments; fictitious radio traffic between non-existent military formations; carefully drafted rumours for circulation both in Britain and overseas; calculated indiscretions which British diplomats in neutral countries would let drop at their dinner parties; the display of a divisional sign on a handful of vehicles to support the existence of a whole non-existent division; the dropping of propaganda leaflets in enemy and enemy-occupied countries; and above all the fragments of information leaked to the enemy through German agents controlled by the Allies, which in practice was the key to the success of most of the Allied deception plans. These are just some of the standard pieces in the typical deception jigsaw. Colour was often added through an individual ploy, which could only be used once: for example, the use of a double to suggest that General Montgomery was in the Mediterranean area, when all the time he was in Britain; or the corpse that was floated ashore on a Spanish beach with a briefcase carrying phoney documents.

Many of the official papers on which this book is based became available for study for the first time in 1977 and 1978. The British and American Chiefs of Staff had ruled in 1945 that little should be revealed about deception after the War. Sir Winston Churchill wrote in 1951 that 'it would not be proper even now to describe all the methods employed to mislead the enemy ...'[1] Virtually nothing was said about deception by the various Commanders-in-Chief in their formal printed despatches, by the official historians (who had access to all the papers), and by the leading participants in their autobiographies. Probably all were inhibited by the ruling of the Chiefs of Staff. When the British files covering the period were released in 1971 under the new 'thirty-year rule', those dealing with cover and deception were withheld.

The account in the following pages is therefore the first to make full use of the official documents. It attempts a dispassionate appraisal of what was accomplished in the field of cover and deception – which may seem to be rather less dramatic and decisive than is suggested by some earlier accounts written without the benefit of the papers.

1 DECEIVING THE INVADER

Between the two World Wars the British Armed Forces had neglected the art of deception. The Americans, sceptical about its usefulness, had paid it even less attention. As late as December 1943, the Allied High Command found it necessary to prepare a memorandum reminding commanders that there was nothing new in the idea of military deception, and demonstrating how it could play a decisive part in winning a campaign. Some of the examples cited to prove the case – the Trojan Horse and the pretended retreat of the Norman cavalry during the Battle of Hastings – may have increased the scepticism of some. But the author of the memorandum also pointed out that the capture of Narvik and Bergen in 1940 by German soldiers concealed in seemingly harmless merchant ships was a modern example of the Trojan Horse ploy. He ventured to add that although deception had until then been relatively unexplored by the British (maybe a diplomatic understatement), they were far ahead of their American allies in this field – which was perhaps why the American General Bull refused to issue the memorandum.[1]

Thus, when the Munich crisis of September 1938 forced the British Armed Services to take stock of their position, it was found that little had been done to develop even the simplest forms of deception. A year later the Declaration of War saw several government departments engaged in uncoordinated efforts to make up for lost time. The department with most at stake was the Air Ministry.

The principal means of deception open to the RAF was the

fake or dummy aerodrome, which, it was hoped, the Germans would take for the real thing and on which they would then waste their bombs. Early in 1939 the Air Ministry had woken up to the fact that, although there had been much discussion of the part dummy aerodromes could play in the coming war, no policy had been decided. They looked up the precedents of 1914–18. Then dummy airfields and flare paths had been used to divert bombing raids and to exaggerate the number of operational aerodromes. However, it would be much more difficult and costly to provide a convincing imitation of the more modern RAF stations than it had been to simulate the primitive installations of the First World War.

On the other hand, it was now intended that permanent RAF stations in Britain should have 'satellites' to which aircraft would be dispersed; and it would be relatively easy to build imitations of these simpler satellite aerodromes. Unfortunately, the different RAF Commands did not see eye to eye on this issue. On behalf of Fighter Command, Air Chief Marshal Sir Hugh Dowding argued that the substance should be provided before the shadow. He felt that no dummies should be built until Fighter Command had all the real aerodromes it needed. He was also worried about the danger to civilians if dummy aerodromes were to be built near centres of population.

Bomber Command, represented by Air Vice Marshal Douglas Evill, were more forthcoming. 'Parent' aerodromes and their satellite 'children' should have nearby 'night dummies' – lighting-effects which at night would simulate an aerodrome in a stretch of open country; and all satellites should have 'day dummies' – an arrangement of fake runways and hangars which daytime enemy raiders would take for the real thing, being rather more conspicuous from the air. For Coastal Command, Air Chief Marshal Sir Frederick Bowhill welcomed the idea of dummies in principle, but was unenthusiastic about the day version. Potential enemies knew exactly where Britain's permanent aerodromes were and they would have no difficulty in pinpointing them by day, dummy or no dummy. In any case, he thought that the few enemy air attacks would be directed at industry, not at aerodromes. Nevertheless, he agreed that night dummies would be invaluable.[2]

In June 1939 it was decided that there should be daylight dummies of all satellite stations, and night dummies of all aerodromes, permanent *and* satellite, east of the line running Southampton–Birmingham–Perth. Because of the cost there would be no large buildings on the daytime dummies. They would have to depend for realistic effect on imitation huts, tents, and vehicles. They would be manned by servicemen, and were not to be sited near populous districts.[3]

At the end of August, with War only a few days away, the Air Ministry realized that they had bitten off more than they could chew. Commands were still busy putting themselves on a war footing, and essential preparations came first. For the time being it was decided that all the day dummies and satellite night dummies should be postponed; the deception programme would have to be restricted to dummy flare paths and fake lighting-effects to protect permanent aerodromes.[4]

This was a chore which the RAF had not been expecting. The Commander-in-Chief of Bomber Command, Air Chief Marshal Sir Edgar Ludlow-Hewitt, suggested that the whole matter of dummy aerodromes should be placed in the hands of 'a retired officer of drive and initiative', who would work on behalf of all three Commands. He disagreed with the assessment provided earlier by his subordinate Evill. Night dummies had only a limited value. In moonlight, aerodromes could be identified by their hangars, and on dark nights they could avoid detection by careful blackout schemes. The Luftwaffe would quickly spot the night dummies and realize that their real targets were elsewhere. He preferred well-planned daytime dummies. The new satellites would have few permanent buildings. So there would be no need to erect costly imitation hangars on the dummies intended to simulate them.[5]

The Air Ministry agreed that someone should be appointed

to act for the three Commands. The job went to Colonel Sir John Turner, then the Air Ministry's Director of Works. He was to evolve schemes to deceive enemy aircraft, and to advise on deception other than camouflage, which remained the responsibility of the Ministry of Home Security. In the middle of 1940 his responsibilities were widened to cover all deception schemes, including the construction of decoys for the protection of industrial undertakings and other vital points.[6]

Colonel Turner's Department – so-called to hide its purpose – concentrated first on facilities for the RAF. The earliest night dummy landing-strips used obsolete paraffin flares which could not be switched off when friendly aircraft were in the neighbourhood; Bomber Command claimed that the danger these posed to the RAF outweighed their deceptive effect on the Luftwaffe.[7] It was therefore essential to introduce electrically-lit dummies – 'Q sites' as they were called – as quickly as possible. The first became operational in June 1940. The flare paths were provided with lights to indicate obstructions, as fictitious as the runway itself, automobile lamps to represent aircraft headlamps, and a special signal to warn off friendly aircraft trying to land. The lights were controlled from an underground shelter connected by telephone to the parent station five or six miles away.[8]

The rules of the game were simple. When the parent station was attacked the operators attempted to induce the enemy aircraft to bomb the dummy. The lights were switched on when enemy aircraft were reported to be approaching – if they came on while the aircraft were overhead the raiders would see through the trick. The illusion that the dummy was live was heightened when an operator emerged from the safety of the shelter to manipulate the headlamp so that it represented an aircraft moving over rough ground.

Later, two ingenious devices were introduced to improve the deception. Landing aircraft were simulated by means of a carriage, fitted with a headlamp, which ran on a wire the length of the landing-strip. When enemy aircraft were within sight of

4

the runway the lighted headlamp was propelled along it by a cordite cartridge at the speed of a landing aircraft. The cartridge burned out after 650 yards and the headlamp came to a slow and realistic stop after another 350 yards. The second device was again a headlamp suspended on a wire, which followed a zigzag course across the dummy landing-strip. The lamp was pulled along the wire by an electric motor and gave the illusion that the aircraft which had just landed was now taxiing.[9]

The dummies were a mixed blessing. They protected RAF stations by transferring the risks elsewhere, which was unpopular with the civilians at the receiving end. In Scotland, for example, a dummy six miles from its parent drew so many attacks that the farm labourers in the area asked to be billeted in a nearby town.

At first the Q sites had a good deal of success. By the end of 1941 there were about 100 of them and they had received more than 350 attacks. Their effectiveness diminished, however. In the second half of 1941 attacks on them became infrequent; and in the last quarter there was only 1. Despite this the fact remains that from June to October 1940 they absorbed twice as many attacks as the aerodromes they were protecting. They therefore made some contribution to winning the Battle of Britain. Indeed, they were technically so successful that a mobile version sent to the RAF in North Africa was actually used for operational purposes.[10]

Colonel Turner, who had great faith in his dummy landing-strips, was a hard taskmaster. He constantly bombarded station commanders with his criticisms. They did not study instructions or try to understand how the fake lighting-systems could best be used. Some feared the dummies would lead enemy aircraft to the genuine aerodromes and were therefore reluctant to light them. Operators sometimes tried to attract the enemy by switching the lights on and off, which would immediately arouse suspicion. Or they would forget to dim the lights as enemy aircraft approached, which is what would have

happened on a real aerodrome. Turner believed that careless-
ness had given away many decoys. The value of a night dummy
depended on how often and how intelligently it was used.[11]

The construction of day dummy aerodromes, which had
been deferred in September 1939, was started during the
'phoney war'. The first became operational early in 1940, and
by November 1940 there were 60 in use. They presented more
problems than the night version. They had to be far enough
from the parent to prevent enemy reconnaissance aircraft from
photographing parent and dummy together, and it was often
difficult to find suitable grassland in the right place. Real
hedges had to be trimmed to look like the artificial hedges used
to camouflage real aerodromes – brushwood tied with wire and
pegged to the ground – a nice example of the use of truth to
convey a false idea. Ideally, the day dummies would have had
imitation hangars, but these were thought too costly.[12] As far as
possible, they were maintained like genuine aerodromes – for
example, bomb craters were filled.[13]

For nearly a year the Luftwaffe failed to identify most of the
'K sites', as the day dummies were known; but in December
1940 a map taken from a shot-down German plane showed that
many of them had by then been spotted. Only 3 were still
marked as genuine aerodromes. How the Germans got hold of
this information was a mystery. The sites might have been
photographed from the air and seen to be fakes; more probably
an RAF pilot with a map showing the dummies had been
brought down over enemy territory. Turner himself believed
that enemy agents were responsible. He pointed out that to
publish the whereabouts of proposed sites to interested parties
(for example, the War Agricultural Committees, so that they
might lodge objections) was crazy. 'The only further publication the Germans would like, I think, is the exact latitude and
longitude and a description from the BBC.'[14]

The day dummies were less successful than the night. By the
middle of 1940 there had been 13 attacks on them, but the
aerodromes which they protected had suffered twice that

number. One of the problems was that newer satellites were beginning to resemble fully-fledged RAF stations, which made convincing imitations impossibly expensive. It was also becoming more difficult to spare the men to run the dummies, although the standard complement of 24 (compared with the 2 needed to operate a night dummy) had been reduced. In any case, daylight attacks were now less frequent. The balance of air power was changing in the Allies' favour as new factories came into operation and the production of aircraft steadily increased. It was therefore decided to build no more day dummies, and by January 1942 all but three had been abandoned, the last one closing in May. Like the night dummies, however, they had played their small part during the critical days of the Battle of Britain.[15]

If the day dummies were to look real they had to have their dummy aircraft. In September 1939 the Air Ministry arranged for the production of prototypes – the Hurricane fighter and the Battle and Whitley bombers – to supplement the display of obsolete or unserviceable genuine aircraft. The dummies had the same shape as the aircraft they represented, but only rudimentary outlines of engines, undercarriages, and airscrews. Of course, they had to be indistinguishable from the real thing when seen from the air. In particular, the trestles on which they stood – it was too costly to give them wheels – must cast no shadow which might be spotted by the stereoscopic reconnaissance camera.[16]

The quotations received from aircraft firms were so high – as much as £2,000 for a dummy which it was thought should cost no more than £50 – that the Air Ministry decided to call in the film industry 'who have great experience of deceptions of all kinds'. By the end of 1939 nearly 400 dummy aircraft – Hurricanes, Battles, Whitleys, Blenheims, and Wellingtons – were in production, for more than half of which Gaumont British and Sound City Films were responsible.[17]

All three Commands refused dummy aircraft for their operational stations in the belief that they would be more trouble than they were worth. Bomber Command, perhaps with tongue in cheek, pointed out a flaw in the Air Ministry's instruction that dummy aerodromes should be equipped with 10 dummy aircraft – this might lead the enemy to conclude that every aerodrome with 10 aircraft must be a fake, although 'this may be rating the German intelligence too high'. Colonel Turner replied that the point had not escaped him, and that it was open to stations to meet it by not using the whole of their ration of 10 dummies.[18]

When it was decided to abandon K sites in 1942, more than 400 dummy aircraft became redundant. Dummies continued to be produced, but from then on they were only used for strategic deception – to suggest the build-up of forces for a major assault – rather than as bait for the protection of real aircraft. It was impracticable, however, to produce imitations of the larger aircraft coming into service. They would have had to be made from scarce wood and steel to withstand strong winds, and it would have been difficult to move them about the aerodrome, which was essential if it was to appear real.[19]

The Air Ministry was naturally very anxious that the aircraft factories on which they depended should suffer as little as possible from air attack, and wanted to embark on an ambitious programme of dummy factory building.[20] In the event only four factories were built, since the protection they afforded was not worth their great cost. They did, however, have some successes. In August 1940 the dummy at Coven, which was intended to protect the Boulton & Paul aircraft factory at Wolverhampton, was attacked by three waves of bombers, while the parent factory was left unmolested; and in the same month the dummy at Leamington Hastings, protecting the Vickers Armstrong works at Baginton, near Coventry, was attacked.[21]

A logical extension of the principle of the dummy aerodrome was the fake fire in open country which enemy airmen would attack while they left important targets unscathed. These fires – code name 'QF' – were built first to protect aerodromes, where they were operated in conjunction with the fake lighting. They had to be lit at just the right moment – after the first wave of bombers had attacked and before the second wave arrived, so that the latter would be left with the impression that the fires had been started by their predecessors, and proceed to waste their bombs on them. The first QF was installed in August 1940. By November there were 30, but with the weakening of the enemy air threat the numbers were gradually reduced until in August 1944 only 8 remained.[22]

The devastating attack on Coventry on 14 November 1940 – codenamed Operation *Moonlight Sonata* by the Germans – led to the protection of all principal towns by deceptive fires. The first, hasty improvisations, in which the film industry again played a part, were at Coventry, Birmingham, Bristol, Sheffield, Derby, and Crewe. These were all important industrial centres, but it was the morale of the workers rather than the plant and buildings that the new fires were designed to protect. The effect of the Coventry raid had been alarming and the Government had had difficulty in keeping workers in the factories. By the end of the year 18 towns had the benefit of artificial fires and 68 were eventually given this form of protection.[23] Although the main objective was to keep up civilian morale, the needs of industry were not forgotten. The fires were so sited that no important factory lay between them and the town and thus became an accidental target.[24]

The fake fires, originally called 'Crashdecks', but renamed 'Special Fires', or 'Starfish', were quickly developed into sophisticated arrangements of combustible material which simulated several different sorts of fire. The most usual arrangement was to have two groups of 120 metal baskets carrying the material to be burned, one group being a reserve for the following night. The baskets were linked in smaller groups to make it possible to fire a 'short Starfish' of say 16 or 32 baskets. The full Starfish was divided into three sections, each of which burned for an hour, so that the whole fire would last for three hours. There were several variants: 'cribs', large baskets filled with wood; 'repeaters', coal fires sprayed automatically at

9

intervals with paraffin to give them renewed vigour; and oil fires, drums filled with creosote and surrounded by a pool of the same material.[25]

It proved difficult to perfect the oil fires. It was plaintively observed that all technical experience had hitherto been concentrated on measures to avoid them.[26]

The success of the Starfish depended very much on weather and the nature of the enemy attack. It was pointless to fire them in bright moonlight, or when there was a clear sky, since enemy bombers would then have little difficulty in recognizing them as decoys. The ideal conditions were when cloud came between the bombers and their objective, but if there was some ground mist it might be worthwhile firing the Starfish even when the sky was clear. The order to fire was given by No. 80 (Signals) Wing, which was supposed to know how enemy attacks were developing. However, because of poor communication, both human and telephonic, liaison with the local control, which might be in the hands of either the RAF station, Balloon Command, the Chief Constable, or the Civil Defence Committee, was often unsatisfactory.[27]

This could lead to failure to make the best use of the decoys. When, on 8–9 May 1941, a heavy raid on Hull 'set the whole place on fire', the Wing plotting table showed no enemy aircraft at all in the Hull area, and the Wing only learned of the attack accidentally, after a second-hand report from Sheffield. Although the town had been on fire for an hour, the local controller had not thought of telephoning for instructions. By the time the Wing learned of the attack, communication with the Starfish had been cut and an admirable opportunity of deflecting the attack on the city had been lost.

On the same night No. 80 Wing, knowing that large numbers of enemy aircraft had been diverted from a raid on Derby, guessed that their alternative destination might be Nottingham. When they got in touch with the local controller they found that they had guessed correctly. Huge fires were already burning in the middle of the city. They immediately ordered one of the Nottingham Starfish to be lit, but again it was too late to do any good.[28]

Most of the fake fires failed to attract bombs, but there were some successes. Each bomb dropped on a Starfish represented a small victory, and helped improve civilian morale. Bristol benefited as much as any city. It was estimated that 40 per cent of an attack on Bristol early in 1941 had been diverted to the decoy fires. On another occasion a Bristol decoy collected 210 bombs; and on the night of 15–16 March 1941 100 high explosive bombs and a huge number of incendiaries landed on the decoys in a six-hour raid. In March 67 bombs hit the Cardiff decoy, while only 5 fell on the city.[29] On the night of 17–18 April the Starfish guarding Portsmouth received 170 bombs and 26 parachute mines, 90 per cent of the total attack.[30]

The number of Starfish sites increased to 235 in 1943, but with the change in the balance of air power, many were then closed and their operators transferred to decoys overseas.[31]

Many towns, important factories, and key installations were protected by elaborate fake lighting schemes simulating marshalling-yards, furnaces, chimney flares, skylights not blacked out, light escaping from doors carelessly left open, tramcar flashes, railway signals, locomotive glows, and so on. Two schemes were tried out in May 1940, one near Sheffield, and the other near Chesterfield. The former simulated a row of furnaces at two-thirds actual size, two lengths of roadway in an industrial estate, and four marshalling-yards covering several square miles. The Chesterfield decoy represented a marshalling-yard and part of an industrial estate.[32]

The Air Ministry had taken the lead in the early deception work, until in the middle of 1940 Colonel Turner's Department became responsible for overall deception policy. Before this takeover the Admiralty had made one or two essays into the deception field, with notable lack of success. During the 'phoney war' of 1940 there was great pressure, particularly from the Prime Minister, to do something – almost anything – against an enemy who seemed to be all-conquering. Since a meaningful naval operation was out of the question, minds turned to sleight of hand. One Admiralty contribution was the construction of dummy warships.

The original plan was to build flotillas of dummy destroyers, using the hulls of coastal steamers. These would be employed as decoys to bring enemy aircraft to battle, which would then be ambushed by British aircraft. Alternatively, it was hoped that enemy reconnaissance planes would spot the dummies at anchor in British ports. This would mislead the German fleet into thinking it was safe to emerge from their well-defended harbours, and they would then be surprised by genuine Royal Navy ships which had been lying in wait for them at sea. It is clear evidence of the desperate straits in which Whitehall Departments found themselves that the Admiralty and the Treasury should have allowed such an enterprise to make any progress. It must have been difficult to take seriously even the cover plan designed to mask the purpose of the operation. The dummies were deemed to be 'cinema ships' for a propaganda film.

The Ministry of Shipping argued that not a single ton of shipping could be spared for make-believe operations, and succeeded in reducing the fake fleet, first to six, and then to four. One of the four dummies could not wait to play her part, as the Admiralty file notes regretfully. She attracted a German bomb and was burned out, while still a coastal steamer. The others, the *Hodder* (which evacuated the militiamen of Jersey in June 1940 just before the Germans occupied the Channel Islands), the *Holdfast*, and the *Emerald*, were duly converted to paper, string, and canvas destroyers.[33]

The idea that these three might be used to decoy the German navy into a losing battle was now seen to be too ambitious. The alternative that they should become bait for enemy bombers had little to commend it now that the Battle of Britain was in full swing and large numbers of the Luftwaffe were regularly visiting Britain uninvited. On 15 August the Air Staff formally told the Lords Commissioners of the Admiralty that in view of recent developments they regarded the provision of decoys as unnecessary – a nice understatement.[34]

The fake destroyers were offered to The Nore, Dover, and Portsmouth Commands; but there were no takers. Dover Command agreed that the enemy might be fooled into thinking that a destroyer flotilla was again based there, but considered that the deception would do more harm than good. The dummies were so fragile that they would have to be moored alongside their jetties and the bombs they attracted would damage the jetty installations. Their presence would crowd real ships closer together, so that they presented an easier target. 'Therefore I venture to suggest that the enemy's expenditure of bombs would be far from wasted.' Further, the Germans would be encouraged to step up their long-range shelling of Dover.[35]

Portsmouth Command conceded that dummy battleships might bring on an air battle and also divert attacks from important targets; but it was asking for trouble to invite German dive-bombers into an area which they had not yet favoured. 'Our immunity so far has been of great value and I would be averse to anything being done to jeopardise it.' It was added, however, perhaps out of politeness to those who had dreamed up the cinema ships, that sooner or later in a war almost every device had to be used. The dummies might come in handy in the future.[36] The point made by the Air Staff was echoed: there was no longer any need to lure enemy aircraft into battle. It was decided to lay up the dummies until further notice.[37]

The increased activity over Britain in the summer of 1940 may be the reason why another early Admiralty deception plan, even more extraordinary than the 'cinema ships', was never implemented. Operation *Ruthless* was to be carried out by the RAF at the behest of the Admiralty, who in 1940 were desperately anxious to examine certain special equipment carried on German air-sea rescue boats. The idea was that a Heinkel 111 which had landed undamaged in Scotland should be flown by a British crew wearing German uniform, and simulate a crash landing, with smoke pouring dramatically from flares attached to its engines, near a German rescue boat in the Channel. They would take to their rubber dinghy and, when safely on board the rescue boat, would shoot the German crew and head for Dover with their prize. The planners accepted that the boarding party, besides running the risk of plunging straight to the bottom of the Channel in their Heinkel, were liable to be shot as *francs tireurs* if things went wrong, and so provided them with a cover story no less flimsy than the operation itself. They were 'a group of young hotheads' who found the war too tame and had stolen the aircraft for a lark. They were not provided with a satisfactory explanation as to how they found themselves in German uniform.

The plan – worked out to the uttermost detail – was sent to the Air Ministry by Fighter Command on 26 October 1940; but it is the last document on the file. There is no indication that the operation was ever cancelled. However, it must have been because the Heinkel earmarked for the plan joined Flight 1426 (the Enemy Aircraft Circus, a group of captured enemy aircraft), and survived until the end of 1943. Then, while giving a demonstration at an American base in England, it landed down-wind, narrowly missed a head-on collision with the Junkers 88 which a few moments earlier had been following it, and crashed.[38]

The Admiralty continued to try and use deception to bring about an air battle on terms advantageous to the RAF. In August 1941, three destroyers bombarded Dieppe in an attempt at provoking enemy fighters to attack, but the weather was unsuitable for fighter operations. The destroyers withdrew without putting on the second part of their performance; this was to simulate the mining of one of their number with a depth charge, and then take in tow the supposedly-crippled vessel, which was intended as an enticing target. It was argued that the

Navy, like a good conjuror, should not repeat the trick, but in fact they did. A naval force comprising two destroyers, six motor-gunboats, and eight smaller craft trailed its coat up and down the Channel, but waited in vain for enemy aircraft. The Luftwaffe would no longer commit its bombers to daylight attacks in the area covered by RAF fighter patrols.

In July 1940, the Joint Intelligence Committee (JIC) produced a paper entitled 'Action designed to Disconcert the Enemy in relation to the Invasion of the United Kingdom', which led the propaganda department to collaborate with the Services in putting out rumours which they hoped would deter Hitler from invading Britain. The Secretary to the Cabinet, Sir Edward Bridges, thought that the British were not very good at this sort of thing; and added that the sudden spread of rumours, some of them fantastic, was unlikely to help: '... it might be better just to let it be known that we have had nice time to get ready now, thank you, and we are ready any day that suits Brother Boche!'[39] Nevertheless, rumours calculated to deter German invasion plans were passed to agents on the continent for dissemination. The following is a selection of those put out in 1940:

Britain has a new machine-gun, recently tried out in France. In one day, 12 dive bombers were brought down: the next day 2 more before breakfast. After that the Germans had had enough.

Overhead telegraph wires include a high tension wire as an anti-parachutist measure.

The Home Guard are being armed with machine-guns.

Troop-carrying planes landing on British aerodromes will meet an unpleasant surprise. Beneath the runways are powerful mines ·filled with a new explosive called 'Aclamite'.

Troops that reach the beaches will be attacked by mines, operated by secret rays.

Two hundred German parachutists were shot in a town in western Germany for refusing to volunteer for the parachute invasion of Britain.

Britain has an immense number of armoured vehicles capable of charging down transport-planes on the ground.

The Post Office have closed a number of pillar-boxes in country districts at crossroads. They disguise mines to blow up the crossroads by remote control.

These imaginative figments may have influenced the German decision not to go ahead with the invasion, codenamed *Sealion*. On the whole it seems unlikely.

In August 1940, the Director of Plans at the Admiralty suggested spreading the rumour that a British force was about to forestall *Sealion* by invading Norway. This led the Inter-Services Security Board (ISSB), which at this time was concerned with deception, to contemplate a full-scale feint operation in which barges, other craft, and possibly dummy ships would be assembled at an east coast port in Scotland. But they dropped the idea. No deception could succeed if the enemy did not think it plausible. The Germans knew that it was too late in the year for a real enterprise against Norway. They were equally well aware that every man in Britain was needed to repel the threatened invasion of southern England. Even if something like the Zeebrugge raid of the First World War was simulated, the chances were that the Germans would attack the ships before they left Scotland. The JIC agreed that the German High Command would not be taken in. They also observed that another condition of a successful deception exercise was that details about it should be leaked to the enemy. If the British public became aware that an expedition had been mounted, but had never left port, it would be very bad for morale. The earlier ill-fated invasion of Norway (May 1940) and the more recent failure at Dakar (September 1940) were still fresh in people's minds. So the first feint invasion remained no more than a bright idea.[40]

Churchill took a special interest in camouflage. Soon after he took office, he dictated a characteristic minute about using smoke to protect factories. This idea had been rejected two years earlier for reasons which did not convince him. He thought that if a large area were made misty, factories would not be identified and hits would be regulated by pure chance. If areas without factories were also made misty, enemy aircraft might be induced to attack them. 'This day should be set up a committee to review again the whole question of smokescreens ...' It was to report in three days – a tall order.[40]

The committee decided that smoke was good camouflage; but the only way to produce it was to waive the smoke abatement regulations in industrial areas (which Churchill himself had suggested) or to use smoke generators burning oil. They went to great trouble to test the Prime Minister's suggestion that smoke-producing briquettes should be burned 'in cottage fires'. Every householder in Luton and Burslem (near Stoke-on-Trent) was given pitch and sawdust briquettes and asked to light them at a given time. On the chosen night the moon was hidden, so the experiment failed. Further trials were held at Burslem, Blackburn, Halifax, and Oxford, but they were marred by gales and enemy action. Yet another trial was held at Widnes on the River Mersey, and it too was ruined by enemy action. So the Churchill sawdust and pitch defence against the Luftwaffe never went into production.[42]

When smokescreens were tried out at Ministry of Supply factories, they sometimes combined with local fog to produce an oily mixture obnoxious to the work force. People living nearby threatened to leave the district. The effect on anti-aircraft gun crews and searchlight operators was even more devastating. They sneezed and coughed, and after an hour or two they developed severe headaches. However, smokescreens continued to be used, and proved effective in military operations, especially in attacks on beaches.[43]

After the Germans had captured Crete, Churchill asked: 'How do we stand on the strategic and tactical camouflaging of defences against enemy attacks on airfields?' He suggested that for every real gun there should be two or three dummies. The best camouflage was a confusing variety of gun positions in which no one could tell the real from the sham. In late 1941,

Churchill asked the War Office expert on camouflage to listen to his nephews, John and Peregrine Churchill, on the subject. 'The first . . . executes camouflage, the second is concerned with its technical aspects. The first is an artist, the second an engineer.'[44]

A special study of camouflage was made in 1941. It was found that money and labour had been wasted because the importance of concealment had not been taken into account when new buildings had been planned, and it was now difficult to give these buildings the protection they needed. Camouflage should be henceforth catered for much earlier in the planning stage. There were still 1,400 vital points waiting for camouflage in the civilian programme alone, and the number was increasing all the time.[45] It was decided that camouflage against day raids was still necessary, and that it should be improved by using either steel wool or 'B.G.'* (which simulated grass) instead of paint. The study also decided to abandon the attempt to hide non-tidal water, even though it was an obvious landmark for enemy aircraft. It had been established in 1936 that coal dust sprinkled on still-water killed the reflection at first, but was soon blown to the edge and made lakes even more conspicuous.[46]

Finally, the camouflaged pill-boxes which sprang up all over Britain must be mentioned. These would have been manned by the Home Forces and the Home Guard to oppose the invaders in the streets and in the fields, and were intended to show the strength of the nation's will to resist. They were camouflaged in a variety of disguises that were often ingenious and sometimes hilarious – florists' shops, petrol stations, newsagents, summer-houses, ice-cream kiosks at the seaside, haystacks. What success they would have had will, happily, never be known.

---

* The code letters 'B.G.' were chosen after numerous experiments to find a suitable material had all turned out to be 'N.B.G.' Eventually calcium alginate, a seaweed extract, was found to be 'B.G.'

2 DECEPTION IN THE DESERT

The first phase of the War ended with the Battle of Britain in September 1940, a British victory less overwhelming than was believed at the time, but nevertheless decisive. It led to a stalemate: the Germans were unable to add Britain to their earlier conquests, but the Allies did not yet have the strength to attempt an invasion of the continent. In Britain, defensive deception – camouflage, fake airfields, artificial fires, and dummy lighting, designed to protect civilians and the armed forces from enemy attack – had played its part; but deception in support of offensive plans was not yet possible. The necessary spare resources in men and materials did not become available until 1942.

It was in the Middle East, where British forces were meeting the enemy face to face, that offensive deception was first used successfully. General Wavell, the Commander-in-Chief, was himself a great believer in its usefulness. At the end of 1940 he established 'A' Force under the command of Brigadier Dudley Clarke, a unit whose main purpose was to devise deception plans and to execute them on the battlefield.[1] It was a small organization – three years after its formation it had only 41 officers, 76 N.C.O.s, and three units of company strength, specially trained in the operation of visual deception devices. It did, however, employ numerous agents in the territories where it operated – the Mediterranean, Iraq, Persia, and much of Africa. The Force had a small mobile headquarters, operating through an 'Advanced HQ West' for the allied Commander-in-Chief, a 'Tactical HQ West' for 15th Army Group, and an

'Advanced HQ East' for Iran, Iraq, and East Africa. There was also a 'Tactical HQ East' to serve with any commander operating independently in the Middle East.

Dudley Clarke received his instructions directly from the Chiefs of Staff, since he had to be in no doubt about global deception policy; but he carried out the orders of the individual commanders in the area, ensuring that their plans were reconciled with each other and with the overall policy. Rumours spread, say, in Iraq might have implications for a forthcoming action in the western desert; and it was essential that the whole deception policy in the region should be controlled by the same hand.

A separate branch of 'A' Force was concerned with the recovery of prisoners of war and stragglers, largely through Arab agents who were paid *per capita* for the men they brought back to the British lines. RAF crews and members of both the Special Air Service and Long Range Desert Group carried 'blood chits' which were encashable by the Arabs who helped them in this way.

Dudley Clarke's men used a wide variety of fake equipment, and manufactured much of it themselves.* Between September and December 1941, for example, they produced large numbers of dummy tanks, fighting vehicles, lorries, and 'sunshields' – special covers for tanks which were in the form of dummy lorries. At the time they were also engaged in testing new devices, including track simulators and track eliminators, which, as their names suggest, were used respectively to make artificial tracks in the desert (to give the impression that a convoy had gone in a certain direction) and to wipe out genuine tracks (to conceal the fact that a genuine convoy had been on the move).[3]

Experience gained in Britain in the earlier years of the War was not entirely relevant to conditions in the Middle East. This was particularly true as far as camouflage was concerned. The

* On 5 July 1942 'A' Force Depot was redesignated 74th Armoured Brigade (Dummy Tanks), which continued in existence as 24th Brigade (23 August 1943), 87th (26 May 1944), and again 24th (14 July 1944).

nets used to hide guns and vehicles in the varied countryside of
Britain were naturally much too dark for the desert. The overhead artillery net, a standard issue to the Eighth Army, was
worse than useless. It made the guns it was supposed to conceal
even more conspicuous from the air. Middle East Forces therefore had to develop much of their own equipment. When the
design, say, of a dummy tank, was found to be suitable for
desert conditions, its manufacture was farmed out to individual
commands and formations. The difficulty of bringing supplies
from Britain encouraged the fullest possible use of local
materials, especially fabrics for making dummy tents and
vehicles.

Again, given the nature of the terrain and the bright sunlight
of the desert, buildings could be simulated by painting shadows
on the ground, although a series of aerial photographs would
reveal that the shadows remained motionless all day. Nevertheless, these 'buildings' made it more difficult for enemy bombers
to locate their target; and even the RAF found it confusing to
land on a runway covered with two-dimensional houses. Slit
trenches were simulated in the same way.

Camouflage enterprises carried out in 1942 included the
manufacture of paint substitutes – 'Camcolour' and
'Camemulsion' – at a cement works. These materials, which
cost much less than commercial paints, were used to camouflage Beirut harbour, to tone down the Haifa refinery, and for
colouring runways. The camouflage units landscaped all the
aerodrome areas in Syria to match them with the surrounding
terrain; helped the RAF by providing dummy German tanks
for dive-bombing practice; and arranged for the production of
thousands of 'easily transportable dummy personnel'.[4]

Improvisation was always necessary. In January 1943 Allied
headquarters told formations how to tone down the highly-
conspicuous yellow tents which had been issued. They were to
make charcoal from scrap wood, crush it, mix it with water, and
then swab it on to the tents with an empty sandbag. 'Snow
paint' was developed for vehicles in the Italian campaign – a

mixture of chalk, lime, salt, and gum arabic, which was issued in powder form and had to be mixed with water.[5]

At about the same time, General Eisenhower expressed great dissatisfaction with the state of camouflage discipline. It was no excuse that nets and paint were not readily available. Existing cover could be better used. Tents could be darkened with mud and oil. Concealment and dispersion standards would have to be improved.[6]

In November 1941 General Auchinleck launched Operation *Crusader* to push the Germans and Italians back from the Egyptian frontier.

Before the general advance into Libya began, concentrations of troops were organized at Jarabub and Siwa, far south of the planned line of attack. It was hoped that the Germans would observe them and deduce that an armoured division was about to move against them in that area. If they did, it would keep large forces away from the main battle zone.

Siwa was converted into a fake forward base, and manned by two simulated armoured brigades. This process, which started with slight activity representing the arrival of advance parties, the building of poorly-camouflaged stores and ammunition dumps, and the manufacture of wheel-tracks in the desert, was spread over two weeks, and carefully synchronized with preparations for the genuine attack in the north. The fake camps were meticulously prepared. Cookhouses were erected, latrines dug, and slit trenches provided on the scale which the imaginary forces would have required. As the days passed, these activities were stepped up and when Siwa had been made to look fully operational, the advance party went on to Jarabub, forty miles away, to carry out a similar transformation. As the day of the attack approached, everything possible was done to make the fake concentrations appear genuine. False radio signals were transmitted, and there was as much real movement of false troops and false movement of real troops as possible.

After the success of Operation *Crusader,* the inquest on the deception was pleasantly self-critical. As a rule, the success of deceptive activities was overestimated, especially by those directly responsible for them. It had been impossible to give the two chosen areas enough life to make them convincing, partly because some of the genuine troops which had been supposed to move through them did not turn up; and partly because there were too few vehicles to match the size of the formations simulated. There had been too few real trucks to carry the materials needed to make fake tents and vehicles; and, less excusable, the lack of operational direction meant that the synchronization of the deceptive plan with the genuine operation had been imperfect. The verdict was that a deception could not succeed unless it was planned with the same degree of thoroughness as a genuine operation – a lesson which had to be learned again before the critical deceptions of 1944 were launched.

But the enemy *had* been misled by the fake concentrations. Captured German intelligence documents showed that the strength of the garrisons at Siwa and Jarabub had been estimated by the Germans at one infantry brigade, two to three armoured car units, and the Egyptian Camel Corps. This estimate was far less, it is true, than the whole armoured division which had been intended, but better than nothing. (The deception experts could take no credit for the presence of the Camel Corps since they had not attempted to simulate a single camel.) There remained the question which is seldom answered satisfactorily in these situations – did the enemy alter his dispositions by a single man or gun as a result of his forced miscalculations, and if he did, did it have any effect on the outcome of the battle?

The deceptionists were also called in to protect the railhead at Capuzzo, which would play an important part in the Eighth Army's advance, and had to be kept intact at all costs. It was too big to camouflage, especially in the open desert, so it was proposed to build a fake extension to the railway. There would be a dummy railhead at Misheifa, ten miles ahead of the genuine article, designed to simulate a marshalling-yard for the delivery of tanks. This ploy had the added advantage that when enemy reconnaissance planes saw the direction the fake extension was taking they would draw the wrong conclusions about the ultimate destination of the railway, and perhaps even about the British long-term strategy.

At first there were not enough rails for the ten miles of line that the plan required. As an alternative, miniature trenches were scored in the ground in the hope that when their shadows were seen from the air they would look like railway lines; but this was not really satisfactory. Even if the simulation had been convincing, there was always the danger that the line would be swept away by a sandstorm. Eventually enough real rails were found and hauled into position by tractors. A fake train was built, but shortage of suitable materials meant that it had to be half-size; so the gauge of the line was reduced to match the scale of the rolling-stock.

The lines were laid day by day at the normal rate, so that enemy aircraft would report progress as they saw it; and when the railhead was completed the immobile dummy engine and wagons were positioned under cover of darkness. During the early stages of *Crusader* the fake was bombed on eight separate occasions and collected over a hundred bombs, although not a single bomb landed on the genuine railhead. Later a map found in a German aircraft brought down near Misheifa showed the dummy as the real terminus of the Desert Railway.

Deception was used more directly to facilitate an attack during the investment of Bardia in December 1941. It was planned to launch a genuine attack on the town from the south-west, while a simulated infantry battalion and a squadron of tanks made a feint attack from the north. On the days leading up to the attack real tanks made numerous trips into the area where the feint was to be mounted. By night dummy tanks and armoured vehicles were moved into the same area and hidden in a wadi. Night patrols did their best to make their presence felt, guiding lanes of petrol-cans were laid towards the town's defences where they could be seen by the enemy, and the surrounding barbed wire was several times destroyed by Bangalore torpedoes.

The night before the attack there was increased activity by the real tanks, which then withdrew. The dummy tanks and vehicles were moved into positions where they could just be seen by the garrison. When daylight came the enemy subjected the dummies to mortar and artillery fire for about two hours before spotting that they were fakes. Meanwhile the genuine attack was in progress in the south. In fact it failed, but the deceptionists believed that if their ploy had gone undetected for another two hours the real attack would have had a good chance of success.

There was little opportunity for the British to practise deception when the Axis forces returned to the offensive in June 1942, capturing Tobruk and pushing the remnants of the Eighth Army back to the Egyptian frontier. An army on the run has only enough time to implement the most elementary measures. Nevertheless, while Rommel's forces were preparing to make their final assault on Egypt, the deception staff were again called in.

Rommel planned to attack the British line well to the south of El Alamein, aiming to storm the strategically vital Alam Halfa Ridge. Unfortunately there was no scope at short notice for deception in the region of the chosen battleground; and the best that the deception staff could do was to try to convey the impression that the positions defending Alexandria and Cairo were much more strongly held than was the case. If Rommel did succeed in breaking through at Alam Halfa, he might thereby be induced to pause and regroup before advancing to the Nile delta. Even a few hours' respite would be invaluable to the defending forces at such a critical time.

Part of the deceptive plan – code-named *Sentinel* – was to fill the lightly-defended stretches of country between the existing strongpoints with dummy 25-pounder guns and their associated gear. All the fake equipment needed was available in dumps further east, but in the event there was no time to bring it forward. Other elements in the plan were more successful, or were at least given a chance to succeed. They included the fictitious strengthening of the defences in front of Cairo by two divisions, simulated by the arrival of a large number of vehicles. This was backed up by the leaking of information which supported the fiction. Enemy air reconnaissance would suggest that these divisions were well-placed to oppose a German attempt to cross the Nile at Cairo, and that they could move forward to support the main concentrations of the Eighth Army. A third fictitious division was created near Alexandria.

There was also a scheme to mask the movement of the Eighth Army Headquarters. When the real staff moved out, their tents and vehicles were replaced with dummies. Each group was closely imitated, and the movement of men and vehicles in the dummy Headquarters was simulated at the level which would have been necessary had the Headquarters still been a going concern.

It is unlikely that these last-minute measures seriously affected the plans of the Axis High Command, or that if Rommel's forces had broken through at Alam Halfa their progress would have been slowed by the threat of 30,000 non-existent Allied troops. The victory of Alam Halfa – no less crucial than the victory at El Alamein – was won not by deception, but by Montgomery's brilliant generalship and by the fighting qualities of the British and Commonwealth forces under him.

Nevertheless, it was becoming accepted that deception in all its forms could be a useful weapon. The period between the successful defence of Alam Halfa and the Eighth Army's attack at El Alamein (which Montgomery considered essential to rebuild his forces) was used to evolve elaborate deceptive measures, on a scale previously unequalled in military history. The overall deceptive plan was given the code-name *Bertram*, made up of subsidiary plans code-named *Diamond, Brian,*

Munassib, Martello, Murrayfield, and *Meltingpot.* Their purpose
was to conceal as long as possible the intention to take the
offensive; and when this could no longer be done, to mislead the
enemy about the time and place of the attack.[7]

The first task was to conceal the huge build-up of supplies in
the northern sector, from which the offensive was to be
launched: 2,000 tons of fuel, 600 tons of food, and over 400 tons
of engineers' stores near El Alamein itself; and 3,000 tons of
ammunition and 600 tons of ordnance stores near Imayid,
twenty miles to the rear. The problem was solved by disguising
the stores as something more innocuous and then inviting
attention to them, much as a conjuror gets his audience to look
at a fake prop; but the trick had to be done on an empty stage,
for the desert sites were open and featureless, without trees
under which stores could be hidden. The boxes of food were
built into stacks shaped like lorries, which were then covered
with the type of netting normally used to conceal vehicles.
Small tents were erected nearby, also filled with boxes of food,
the implication being that they were there to house the drivers
of the fake transport. A few genuine lorries were driven around
the site from time to time to give a hint of life.

One of the incidental difficulties was that stores stacked in
this way invited theft. The danger was mitigated by putting
those things which were in greatest demand locally – tinned
milk and sugar – in the middle of the concentration, where they
could more easily be guarded. The outlying 'vehicles' were
composed of bully beef and biscuits, which were not popular
with the Arabs. The dump, built in four nights by a party of 80
Australian infantrymen, consisted of about 40 dummy vehicles,
each with its accompanying tent.

A genuine ammunition dump at Imayid, already known to
the enemy, was extended, in the hope that the enlargement
would not be spotted. The additional stacks were covered with
hessian; and sand, in plentiful supply locally, was shovelled
against the sides to soften the shadows and make the extension
invisible from the air, except at very close range.

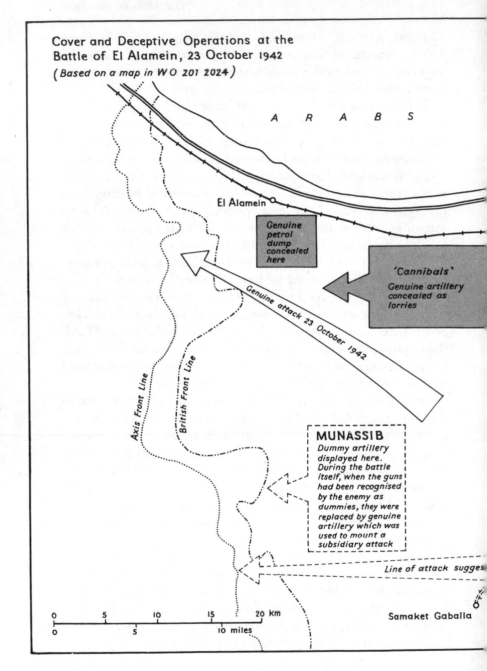

Cover and Deceptive Operations at the
Battle of El Alamein, 23 October 1942
(Based on a map in WO 201 2024)

A R A B S

El Alamein

Genuine
petrol
dump
concealed
here

'Cannibals'

Genuine artillery
concealed as
lorries

Genuine attack 23 October 1942

Axis Front Line

British Front Line

MUNASSIB
*Dummy artillery
displayed here.
During the battle
itself, when the guns
had been recognised
by the enemy as
dummies, they were
replaced by genuine
artillery which was
used to mount a
subsidiary attack*

Line of attack sugges

Samaket Gaballa

| 0 | 5 | 10 | 15 | 20 km |
| 0 | | 5 | | 10 miles |

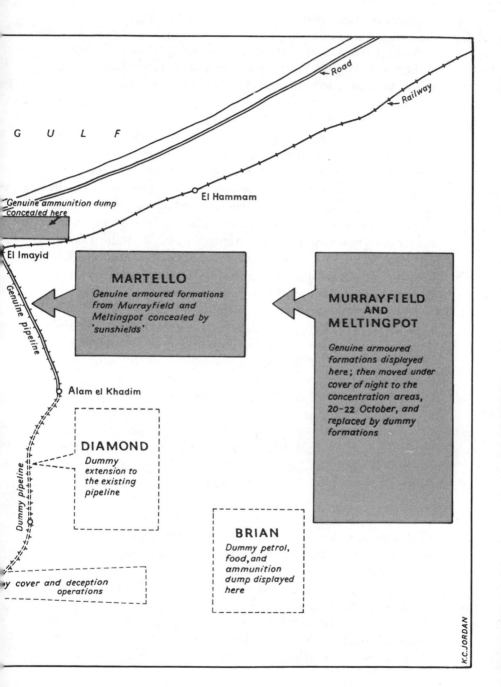

G U L F

Road

Railway

Genuine ammunition dump concealed here

El Hammam

El Imayid

Genuine pipeline

MARTELLO

Genuine armoured formations from Murrayfield and Meltingpot concealed by 'sunshields'

MURRAYFIELD AND MELTINGPOT

Genuine armoured formations displayed here; then moved under cover of night to the concentration areas, 20-22 October, and replaced by dummy formations

Alam el Khadim

DIAMOND

Dummy extension to the existing pipeline

Dummy pipeline

y cover and deception operations

BRIAN

Dummy petrol, food, and ammunition dump displayed here

K.C.JORDAN

29

An important element in the overall deception scheme was to make the enemy conclude that the attack would come in the south. One ploy to convey this idea was the construction of a dummy pipeline, ostensibly to carry water to the troops being concentrated in the south. The pipeline (code-name *Diamond*) stretched twenty miles, from the real water supply at Alam El Khadim to a point four miles east of Samaket Gaballa. The trench to carry the supposed pipe was excavated in the usual way. A five-mile length of dummy railway-line (made from empty petrol cans strung together) was laid in the trench to simulate the pipe – such is the versatility of the deceptionist. Before each five-mile stretch of trench was filled in, the dummy pipe was taken out under cover of darkness, to be used again in the next stretch. Dummy pump-houses and fake reservoirs were constructed along the way.

Brian was also intended to imply an attack in the south. Dummy supply-dumps, the exact counterpart of the genuine dumps hidden in the north, were established a few miles from the southern end of the fake pipeline. Associated with these dumps were three small administrative camps to house the personnel supposedly controlling them. Transport was scarce, and it was decided to reduce demands on it by making do with two-dimensional dummy ammunition stacks, simulated from dark green steel wool and dark garnished nets. Even these needed 70 three-ton loads, and the round trip from the main camouflage store to the dummy dumps took each vehicle two days.

Plan *Munassib* was a neat piece of double bluff. A week before the battle was due to start, gunpits were dug and dummy guns were erected at the eastern end of the Munassib depression (south of the sector from which the main attack was to come), in numbers which represented three and a half field regiments. These were left without movement for a week to convince the Germans that they were dummies. Then one night real guns were substituted. When the battle started in the north, the Germans in the south were attacked by guns which they had assumed to be dummies. This elaborate deception was intended to confirm in the enemy's mind that the main threat lay from the south.

Martello and *Murrayfield* were complementary plans, and were probably the most important component parts of *Bertram*. Between them they made it possible to spirit the tanks of Xth Corps invisibly to the forward areas.

Martello aimed to mask the movement of Xth Corps. By 6 October, three weeks before the attack was due to start, about 4,000 real vehicles, 450 dummies, and more than 600 sun-shields were concentrated in an assembly area near El Imayid. This was to accustom the enemy to seeing a mass of transport, equal to that of Xth Corps.

On the nights of 21 and 22 October, the genuine tank force moved forward to the assembly area under cover of darkness and hid under the sunshields, where they were invisible from the air. Similar sleight of hand was used to move forward the guns needed to support the advance. These were concealed by the so-called 'cannibal' method, which consisted of hiding a 25-pounder gun and its limber under a dummy lorry, so that the wheels of gun and limber appeared to be part of the vehicle. All that had to be done to make the gun ready for action was to pull it and the limber from their hiding-place – 360 guns were concealed in this way. The whole force of tanks and guns were in place ready to attack on 23 October; but so far as the Germans were concerned not a single tank, vehicle, or gun had moved.

Nothing was left to chance. It was not enough to hide the tanks and guns. The fact that they had moved from the rear-ward area also had to be concealed. This was done through Plan *Murrayfield*. 1st Armoured Division and 24th Armoured Brigade (Dummy Tanks) moved forward from Wadi Natrun to El Imayid in two stages. The first move was carried out openly by day as a training exercise to a staging area south of Burg-el-Arab. Then at night the vehicles moved off to their forward positions under *Martello* and were immediately replaced. 1,500

31

vehicles from 2nd New Zealand Division, 1,370 dummy 3-tonners and 15-cwt. trucks, 64 dummy guns, and 300 dummy tanks occupied the exact spaces which the formations had just left. Although thousands of vehicles and tanks had been moved, it would appear to enemy reconnaissance that not a single one had changed its position.

Under Plan *Meltingpot*, the 10th Armoured Division moved by day from Wadi Natrun to a staging area far to the south. Then at night the Division moved back secretly to the main assembly area in the north, leaving behind a mixture of real and dummy equipment to convince the Germans that they were still in the south.

It was necessary to back up those movements which the enemy was supposed to observe with false radio messages. The appropriate signals were drafted well in advance. Although the sum total of the messages would be full of meaning for the enemy monitoring service, they are quite incomprehensible to the layman. For example, here is a fragment of the script prepared for the Xth Corps to use in talking to the 10th Armoured Division:

Xth Corps: Hullo, XYZ, Bring big brother to set. Over.
10th Armd. Div.: Wait. (Interval). Hullo, Z. Big nine here. Over.
Xth Corps: Hullo, George. Is your other brother near you? Over.
10th Armd. Div.: Yes. He is near to me and to the wheatcake. Over.
Xth Corps: Good. That's all I wanted to know.

This was a radio telephone conversation, but the same technique was used for wireless telegraph:

Mock rear Xth Corps to Mock rear 1st Armoured Division:
Pressbox Nailfile Bugbite to Hilltop small Bugbite to clear Quickstep Crabapple Clearer Handover Universities Blackswans not completed to Welterweight Nailfile then brittle. Antonio 2205 2217.

It was not the content of these messages that mattered, although they had to have enough in common with genuine messages to arouse no suspicions. The purpose of the fake scripts was to establish in the enemy's mind that identifiable formations were many miles from their true location.[8]

The success of the Eighth Army's deception and cover plans surprised even their authors. When allowance had been made for the fact that the German Intelligence services were poor, it seemed remarkable that such a vast deception should have succeeded on such a limited front, which in many respects resembled 'the highly-organized, heavily-concentrated, and continuously observed battle-front areas of 1914–18'. Captured enemy documents and statements by prisoners-of-war provided concrete evidence of the extent to which the German Command had been fooled. They had no idea that the Xth Armoured Corps was assembling in the northern sector. The commander of the Panzerarmee Afrika, General von Thoma, who was taken prisoner in the battle, said that German reconnaissance had failed to observe any increase in the number of heavy vehicles in the north – the only visible increase had been in the south. This was supported by statements from captured Italians, and by an enemy map, which placed three British armoured divisions in areas where fake concentrations of motor-transport had been deliberately displayed.

Von Thoma confessed that he had been certain the attack would come from Munassib in the south; and as a result two Axis armoured divisions had been retained in the southern sector four days after the genuine attack had been launched in the north. Further, the Eighth Army was able to put into the field one whole armoured division more than the Germans thought possible.[9] The deceptive measures at El Alamein had the effect of shifting the balance of forces in favour of the British; and in doing so there can be no doubt that they contributed significantly to the Eighth Army's famous victory.

3 THE NORTH AFRICAN LANDINGS

The military situation was transformed by the Japanese attack on the American fleet in Pearl Harbor on 7 December 1941. The United States moved from a position of benevolent neutrality towards the Allies to one of active hostility towards Japan and her Axis partners in the West. At the Washington conference ('Arcadia'), which began on 22 December 1941, the Americans agreed that Germany must be regarded as their main enemy for the time being, and that they would concentrate their efforts in the European theatre. The ring round Germany would be closed. The Allies would seize the North African coast, held by the Germans and Vichy France, thus opening the Mediterranean to Allied convoys and saving them from having to sail round the Cape to reach the Middle East. In November 1942 the Anglo-American invasion of North Africa (Operation *Torch*) was launched.

By this time deception techniques and policy had made considerable strides. Colonel Turner's Department had improved the means of visual deception. The Inter-Services Security Board's responsibility for deception policy, which had never amounted to very much, had been transferred at the beginning of 1941 to a small Deception Staff within the Joint Planning Staff. This was run by Colonel Oliver Stanley, a former Secretary of State for War, who considered that opportunities for deception must be awaited, not made.[1] Little was attempted for the four months while he was in charge; and he came in for criticism from General Wavell, who advocated a policy of bold and imaginative deception.[2] The War Cabinet

Office admitted that there was room for improvement, and Stanley was replaced by Colonel John Bevan, a stockbroker who had served with distinction in the First World War. Bevan at once provided the drive that had been missing. The Deception Staff was enlarged, and for security reasons given the name of the London Controlling Section (LCS).[3]

When Bevan succeeded Stanley, he was surprised to find that there were no precedents to guide him. It seemed that he was expected to devise deceptive plans out of his own head, without much help from any of the existing government agencies. However, he did receive crucial help from two sources. The first was the growing number of double agents controlled in Britain by MI5; these could be used to pass on information to German Intelligence. The second was the Ultra code-breakers at Bletchley, whose activities revealed much about German strategic thinking, and helped suggest which deceptive crumbs the enemy High Command would be most likely to swallow.

On 1 August 1942, Bevan submitted plans to pin down German forces in northern France, and to simulate a threat to Norway; which with luck would keep the enemy in doubt about the destination of the forces being concentrated in Scotland for Operation *Torch*.[4] He first suggested that the fictitious operation to contain German forces in northern France should be given the code name *Passover*, in the hope that the name itself would suggest a cross-channel expedition against the Pas de Calais. He wanted the Norwegian deceptive operation to be called *Solo*, on the ground that the name might lead a German intelligence officer who was good at anagrams to deduce that the *Torch* forces were bound for Oslo. This reveals how inexperienced he was in the new art – after all, he had been Controlling Officer for only a few weeks. Normally an operational code name should have contained no hint about the enterprise it covered. If the Germans assumed that the Allies were playing to this rule, *Solo* and *Passover* would at once exclude Norway and the Pas de Calais as probable objectives.

35

The Germans would look elsewhere for the true destination of the *Torch* forces – unless, of course, they thought that the suggested code names were a double bluff. Fortunately, it was discovered that *Passover* was a code name reserved for the United States forces, and Bevan was forced to surrender it. It was replaced, first by *Steppingstone*, and finally by *Overthrow* – a comparatively unsuggestive name, whether taken in the military or cricketing context. *Solo*, however, remained unchanged.

There were a number of ancillary plans: *Kennecott*, to allay the suspicions of the Vichy Government; *Pender*, to cover the arrival in Gibraltar of General Eisenhower and Admiral Cunningham, the *Torch* commanders; *Quickfire*, to deceive the enemy about the destination of troops arriving from the United States; and finally *Sweater*, to deceive those troops about their mission. There was also the *Cavendish* exercise, in which the forces and shipping earmarked for *Overthrow* would carry out genuine training during the ten days leading up to the notional cross-Channel assault.

OVERTHROW

Bevan chose to model his fictitious operation against northern France on the two abandoned cross-channel expeditions planned for 1943. Immediate problems presented themselves, however. To coincide with the North African landings, *Overthrow* had to reach a climax late in October. This rendered the deception implausible right from the start, since it was accepted that a successful attack across the Channel could not take place after 1 October, because of the weather. As it turned out, an even later date had to be accepted, since *Torch* was postponed until the beginning of November.

This setback led the Chiefs of Staff to consider whether it was worthwhile squandering valuable resources to support an already shaky deception. Would the organization of assembly areas, the movement of troops, aircraft, and anti-aircraft guns to south-east England, the building of hides to conceal non-

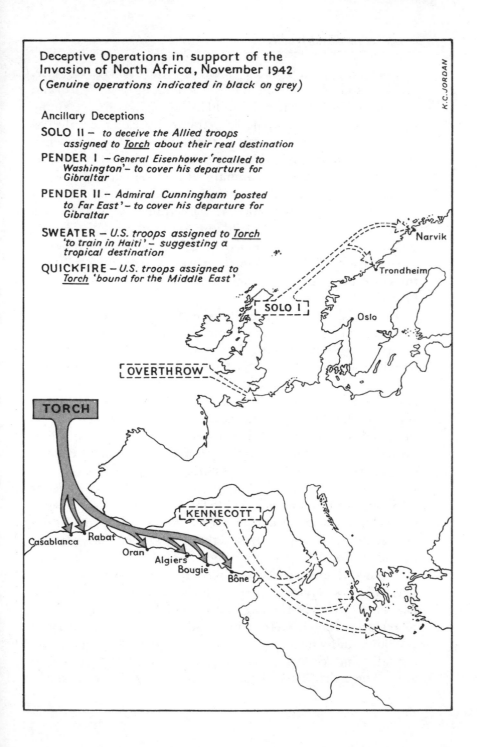

Deceptive Operations in support of the
Invasion of North Africa, November 1942
(*Genuine operations indicated in black on grey*)

K.C.JORDAN

Ancillary Deceptions

SOLO II – *to deceive the Allied troops
assigned to* Torch *about their real destination*

PENDER I – *General Eisenhower 'recalled to
Washington'– to cover his departure for
Gibraltar*

PENDER II – *Admiral Cunningham 'posted
to Far East'– to cover his departure for
Gibraltar*

SWEATER – *U.S. troops assigned to* Torch
'to train in Haiti' – suggesting a
tropical destination*

QUICKFIRE – *U.S. troops assigned to
Torch 'bound for the Middle East'*

SOLO I

OVERTHROW

TORCH

KENNECOTT

Narvik

Trondheim

Oslo

Casablanca Rabat

Oran

Algiers

Bougie

Bône

existent landing-craft, and all the rest of the *Cavendish* exercise, pay a reasonable dividend in terms of helping *Torch*? Petrol and tyres would be wasted, men would be taken away from training for three weeks, there would be extra pressure on the railways. The concentration of aircraft in the south-east at a time when the metropolitan air force had already been weakened by the demands of *Torch* would impair the overall defence of the United Kingdom. Finally, the aerial bombardment of centres of communication in France and Belgium, essential to give *Overthrow* full credibility, would antagonize the Vichy Government, just when it was hoped to secure their connivance in the invasion of French North Africa. The Chiefs of Staff therefore decided to cut their losses and abandon much of *Cavendish*.[5]

The decision to dispense almost entirely with visual display undermined *Overthrow* right from the start, but the London Controlling Section, facing their first real challenge, struggled on with the rest of their plans. Coastal shipping was held up in the Channel ports to suggest that convoys were forming there. A few hides were constructed along the South Coast to hint at concealed landing craft. Pierheads were camouflaged for the same purpose. Decoy lighting installations were built, as if to protect the ports from which the presumed invasion fleet would sail. There was aerial reconnaissance over the areas in France where the expedition was supposed to land. A circular letter went out to all Commands asking for the names of officers who were familiar with the northern French coast; large quantities of French dictionaries were bought; and French currency was provided. The Admiralty was asked to find pilots familiar with the French Channel ports. The departure point of British Overseas Airways service to Portugal was moved from Poole in Dorset to Foynes in Ireland – a step which would suggest that secret preparations were being made on the South Coast of England, and which enemy agents in neutral Portugal could not fail to notice. A ban was imposed on travel to the coastal areas where the *Overthrow* forces were supposed to be assembling. Messages 'to indicate a threat to northern France were prepared and passed through various channels to the enemy'.[6] It was unlikely, however, that any of these measures would carry much conviction, given the absence of extensive visible preparations in south-east England.

The only other thing that the LCS could do was to invent rumours to lend colour to their fiction. They were designed initially to deceive the British public, in the hope that they would in due course reach the ears of the enemy. Apart from anything else, the dissemination of these rumours was necessary to explain away activities in connection with the genuine *Torch* expedition which could not be hidden. The latter were bound to arouse comment, and security measures could not entirely eliminate the danger that gossip would reach the enemy. Therefore MI5 were asked to start rumours, especially at the ports, to give a false impression of the destination and the timing of the expedition. Here are some examples:

I was lunching with a member of the Thames Yacht Club on Friday who told me, after a second glass of port, that all available small craft are to be assembled again along the Kent coast: just as they did at Dunkirk.

My brother, who is a wine merchant in Ashford, is having the devil of a job to supply the demands of the RAF messes in that part of Kent. The number of officers has almost doubled in the past five weeks.

I was talking to one of our Law Lords the other night, and he was telling me that immediately we have established a second front in France a Commission of Judges is to be sent over for the purpose of trying any Gestapo men and other Germans we may capture, who are accused of atrocities. I gather the Commission has already been appointed which looks as though there's a good hope of a second front being opened this autumn after all.

The reason why Penguin books have gone off the market recently is because the firm which prints them has been given a rush order for a million Anglo-French phrase books.

A chap who I know is in the Royal Army Service Corps was telling me the other day that they are receiving training now in driving their vehicles on the right-hand side of the road, so that looks as though we are soon going back to the Continent all right.[7]

The *Overthrow* papers illustrate one of the problems which confront the student of strategic deception. The number of people who were allowed to know that any given plan was a deception was limited. A much larger number were innocently involved in carrying it out. It is sometimes difficult to tell who was in the know and who was not. For example, in September 1942 GHQ Home Forces asked the Political Warfare Executive (PWE) to define policy in regard to dealings with the French so that the troops taking part in *Overthrow* might be correctly briefed. What should their attitude be towards quislings? What arms would be issued to Frenchmen who wanted to fight alongside the Allies? Would they be put into uniform? PWE replied in a lengthy memorandum, which took the questions at their face value. It is impossible to decide if either the author of the Home Forces paper or the member of PWE who replied to him was consciously playing the deceptive game, or whether they were both under the impression that *Overthrow* was a genuine operation.[8]

SOLO ONE
Solo One was designed to make the enemy believe that the concentration of shipping in the United Kingdom for Operation *Torch* was in fact to be used in an expedition against Norway. It was known that the Germans were worried about Norway; and both the time of year and the ports used by the *Torch* shipping made Norway a plausible target. It was therefore agreed to try and deceive the enemy into believing that the *Torch* forces were being assembled for an attack on the Norwegian ports of Narvik and Trondheim.[9]

The planning for *Solo One* was carried out in four fortnightly periods. In the first, the forces ostensibly carmarked for Norway were nominated and their commanders appointed. Intensive intelligence studies of the target areas were organized, use being made of papier mâché models and aerial photographs. A call went out for instructors in mountain warfare.

In the second fortnight the printing of specimen forms – dealing with billeting, requisitioning, and kindred matters – was put in hand. An order was placed for 20,000 shoulder flashes printed with the word *Norge*, for issue to Norwegian resistance groups. Officers with a knowledge of Norwegian or Swedish were summoned, and a course in mountain warfare for junior officers was started. It was at this point that the assembly of shipping for *Torch* began.

In the third stage there were exercises in combined operations against rocky coastlines. Members of the Norwegian forces in Britain began to appear in the concentration areas in Scotland. Enquiries were put out for the supply of Norwegian currency. There was intensified aerial reconnaissance of Norway.

Finally, two weeks before the notional departure of the fictitious expedition, arctic kits were delivered to regimental quartermasters' stores, there were lectures on the dangers of frost-bite, company commanders were issued with maps of Norway, and final embarkation exercises were held.[10]

Other measures included the simulated arrival of fighter bombers and Coastal Command aircraft in the Scottish assembly areas, by means of fake wireless telegraph activity; discreet inquiries by officers in London and Edinburgh shops for arctic clothing and footwear; and the placing by the Ministry of Supply of a very large order for anti-freeze. When the notional expedition was due to depart, fourteen United States merchant vessels which had been standing by to join a Russian convoy made a dummy run as far north as the Orkneys, so as to suggest that they too were bound for Norway.[11]

Just like *Overthrow*, *Solo One* was backed up with suitable rumours.

My dad is a quartermaster sergeant in the Royal Scots, and when he was home last week I overheard him tell Mum that a lot of arctic clothing had recently arrived at his stores.

My fiancée is a nurse up in Scotland, and when she was last on leave she showed me the new panties with which they have been issued. They are thick pure wool and would cost £3 a set if you had to buy them. I hope to goodness they're not going to send her to Iceland.

Have you seen the new zip-up windproof jackets they are issuing now? They are as light as a feather and keep one warm as toast. My brother in the Glasgow Highlanders showed me one that had just been handed out to him before he was returned to his Depot on account of varicose veins.

My brother in the King's Own Scottish Borderers had rotten luck last week. They were practising mountain climbing in Scotland. He slipped off a ledge and it was only by the grace of God that he didn't kill himself. As it was, he fell 25 feet and only broke his arm.[12]

It was assumed that enemy air reconnaissance was bound to spot the departure of the convoys bound for North Africa; and it must then very quickly become obvious to the enemy that their destination was not Norway. Bevan planned to meet this difficulty by substituting either Dakar or the Azores as the fictitious destination of the expedition, once Norway had been ruled out by the enemy.

A threat to the Azores would upset the Spaniards and the Portuguese; a threat to Dakar would alert the Vichy forces in North Africa, and weaken still further the chances of the Vichy Government conniving at an Allied invasion of their North African territory.[13] Both might lead to increased U-boat and Luftwaffe activity in the Atlantic. The Chiefs of Staff decided to reject Bevan's proposal.[14]

The Germans were at this time claiming in their propaganda that the Allies did intend to attack Dakar, partly to see what reaction it produced from the Allied propagandists, and partly to impair the Allies' relations with Vichy. It was therefore on the cards that if Allied rumours began to confirm Dakar as the objective of the *Torch* convoys, the Germans would immediately rule it out and look elsewhere for the true objective. It was clear that the Prime Minister had failed to grasp this point when, after seeing a record of a conversation between a German agent in Madrid and his contact in Berlin, he asked: 'What are we doing? Surely all kinds of troop movements are possible to emphasize the idea of Dakar!' Bevan, no doubt surprised that the Prime Minister should thus advocate the line which he himself had earlier proposed, explained that Dakar had been deliberately left out of the cover plans. The world at large, inspired by German rumours, was now tipping it as the objective. 'Any action on our part to confirm Dakar might therefore be playing into the enemy's hands.' This was put in a draft minute for the Chief of the Imperial General Staff (General Sir Alan Brooke) to send to the Prime Minister; but Brooke scrapped the whole draft, and replied by simply listing all the current troop movements in Africa, adding that they would continue to focus attention on Dakar. The Prime Minister was thus deliberately left with the mistaken impression that Dakar *was* to be included in the cover plan.[15]

In an account of the Allied intelligence services as seen by the German High Command, General Kurt von Tippelskirch cites the Allies' North African cover plans to make the point that cover and deception material put out by an adversary can make it easier to guess his real intentions. According to Tippelskirch, 'reports of an impending action against Dakar were played into the hands of German intelligence agents to such an extent and through so many ways that an attempt at deception could be inferred with certainty, with the aim of disguising a major operation at some other place'.[16] Despite the Allies' doing all that they could to soft-pedal Dakar, the Germans were under the impression that they were playing it up. Speculation in the world press and guesswork by German agents not under Allied control had produced the effect the Allies were seeking to avoid – which just goes to show that the perfect deception plant is very difficult to cultivate.

SOLO TWO
Solo Two was designed to mislead the troops bound for North Africa about their destination, and through their careless talk,

to mislead the enemy. They would be allowed, indeed encouraged, to understand that they were bound for the Middle East via the Cape. The size and composition of the expeditionary force was compatible with this idea; and the objective fitted in with known Anglo-American strategy.

The LCS provided a series of announcements which hinted at a tropical destination. For example, it was announced to the troops that tropical kits and mosquito nets would not be issued until they were on board ship. Cholera injections would be available on the journey. Men were forbidden to buy unwashed fruit at the ports of call, and when they went ashore after sundown they were ordered to wear jackets to ward off mosquitoes. There were lectures about the dangers of lice, malaria, and dysentery. Army cooks were given instruction in the preparation of rice, as they were told it was possible that the troops would have to live off the country when they reached their destination.[17]

Thus half the rumours put out in connection with Operation *Torch* hinted at a tropical destination: the other half suggested arctic Norway. An inspired enemy intelligence officer might have arrived at the climatic mean between the two.

KENNECOTT

Many of the preparations for *Torch* had to be carried out in Gibraltar. For example, 240 fighter aircraft were delivered there in crates for local assembly; and 12 tank landing-craft had to be overhauled. It was absurdly easy for enemy agents to observe what was going on from across the border in Spain, so as far as possible these activities had to be explained away.

This was at first done by spreading the story that the preparations related to Malta. It was said that the island was now to be supplied from Gibraltar, because of increasing difficulties in bringing supplies from the east. The troops assembling in Gibraltar were part of a force bound for Malta. For local consumption it was rumoured that a separate headquarters was being set up on the Rock to take transit matters off the shoulders of Fortress Headquarters. The Governor flew to Malta ostensibly to discuss all these arrangements with his opposite number there. Maps of Malta were sent out for the use of British and American pilots arriving in Gibraltar. Admiralty signals traffic indicated that the landing-craft assembling in the harbour were intended for operations outside the Mediterranean.[18]

The whole of this fiction ceased to be credible when it became apparent that the build-up in Gibraltar was in preparation for offensive operations, and when most of the *Torch* convoys making their way south through the Atlantic turned east and passed through the Straits of Gibraltar. After that the substitute fiction was that the Allies were about to attack Sicily and establish a bridgehead in the south of Italy. This was put across principally by 'A' Force, which supplemented the threat against Italy with threats against Crete and Greece, from which British forces had been ignominiously thrown out in 1941.[19]

PENDER

Pender I and *II* were part of the Gibraltar cover. The former indicated that General Eisenhower had been recalled to Washington for important conferences; and therefore could not possibly be in Gibraltar. The latter suggested that Admiral Cunningham, in command of the naval element in *Torch*, had been appointed Commander-in-Chief of the Far Eastern Fleet. He was *en route* for Lagos, whence he would fly to take up his new appointment. Cunningham himself helped to spread this rumour, as did the Governor of Gibraltar.[20]

QUICKFIRE and SWEATER

Quickfire was a deceptive plan to mislead the enemy about the true destination of the United States forces bound for North Africa. General Eisenhower suggested pretending that the troops were destined for Australia. The United States Chiefs of Staff, however, preferred that they should appear to be going to the Middle East. A full-scale plan was circulated on 19

September 1942, providing for the fictitious assembly of British and United States Air Forces in the Middle East, movement of the United States Atlantic Fleet to the eastern Mediterranean via the Red Sea, and formation of an expeditionary force to capture the Dodecanese Islands.[21]

Sweater was a cover plan for the deceptive *Quickfire*. It explained away the preparations for a campaign in a hot country, and deceived the troops themselves about their true destination. They were led to believe that they were bound for the Caribbean, to train for tropical warfare. Even the officers who implemented the plan were not let into the secret.

On 29 September the United States Chiefs of Staff suggested that the Secretary of State should approach the Government of Haiti about using their territorial waters for amphibious training over the following months. The Secretary of State instructed the United States Minister in Haiti to approach the Haitian President without delay. If the President agreed to a reconnaissance to choose beaches and camp-sites, a team of seven officers would be sent at once. The plan for the exercises would, of course, be put to the President before it was implemented. The greatest care would be taken not to interfere with ordinary life, and compensation paid for any damage. The Minister was to stress that absolute secrecy was essential – a line usually taken by the deceptive planners when they wanted to encourage leakage.[22]

The Haitian President was happy to accede to the American request. The seven-man team went off to make their survey, ignorant of the fact that their mission was part of an elaborate hoax.[23] On 16 October, the State Department suggested that the Haitian government might care to send a representative to Washington – all expenses paid by the United States – to join in planning the exercises, and to suggest how Haitian forces might participate, if they wanted to. An earnest official in the State Department who was not in the know held up this telegram, and suggested that it would be better to discuss the matter with the Haitian Military Attaché in Washington, not realizing that the intention was to create the greatest possible interest in Haiti, so that German agents there would become aware of what was going on. He was instructed to send the telegram immediately, and given no reason as to why his sensible suggestion was rejected. The telegram concluded: 'You [the American Minister] will probably wish again to stress the extreme secrecy of all phases of this matter.'[24]

On 9 November – two days after the landings in North Africa – the seven-man team reported that the area proposed for the training exercises was unsuitable, and recommended that the project should be abandoned. This was no doubt the correct decision, but the Chiefs of Staff preferred to run down Plan *Sweater* less abruptly. They regarded the training exercises as being deferred, rather than abandoned. The Minister in Haiti was instructed to tell the President that in view of the United States' other military commitments the exercises had been postponed. The change of plan was not communicated to the Haitian government until 15 November, to play down any suspicion that *Sweater* had been linked with *Torch*.[25]

What did this series of eight related plans accomplish? Did they contribute substantially to the undoubted success of the Allied landings in North Africa?

As usual, the evidence is sketchy. It seems that the threat to Norway did have some effect. The Narvik–Trondheim area – which is precisely where the Allied expedition was supposed to land – was declared a protected zone. It was understood at the end of September that the Germans were expecting an attack by ten divisions. In October they made a second protected zone along the Norwegian–Swedish border.

They probably did not take the cross-channel threat seriously. It was hamstrung from the outset by the decision to cancel the genuine troop and aircraft movements originally planned for Exercise *Cavendish*. On 3 October, four German agents in

Lisbon sent a joint report saying 'that an action of considerable size appeared to be in preparation in Great Britain'. They supported this with much circumstantial evidence, but none of it connected with *Overthrow*; and they concluded that a cross-channel operation was not contemplated.[26]

The arrival of Eisenhower and Cunningham in Gibraltar was apparently concealed from the enemy. The German press reported that Eisenhower had gone to Washington, and hazarded a guess that his next assignment would be to gain a foothold on the west coast of Africa. Even this evidence may be suspect, however. The line taken by the German press may have been no more than kite-flying to see what reaction, if any, there was to their reports in the Allied press.

Why, then, was the invasion of North Africa so successful? How were the convoys able to travel great distances through the Atlantic and the Mediterranean unmolested? The answer seems to be that the success of *Torch* was due more to good security and lax German intelligence, rather than to the wiles of the deceptionists. The enemy carried out no aerial reconnaissance of the ports in Britain where the *Torch* shipping was concentrating. Although they spotted the unusually large convoys approaching the Straits of Gibraltar, the Luftwaffe made no attacks until the ships had actually entered the harbour at Algiers. They had assumed that the force was making for Malta – and convoys bound for Malta were always attacked for the first time east of Algiers. During the fortnight leading up to 8 November, the Germans sent only one reconnaissance flight over Gibraltar, and made no attempt to bomb the great concentration of ships and aircraft there. But it does seem that the activities of the deceptionists did at least succeed in spreading confusion about Allied intentions: intercepted enemy reports suggested that the Germans had been unable to make up their minds as to whether the next Allied move would be to attack Sicily, Tripoli, or Crete, or to relieve Malta.[27]

Sir John Masterman, himself the controller of the MI5 double agents, has given this view of the success of *Torch:*

'Nevertheless it must be admitted that the success was not primarily a triumph for deception, and still less for the double agent system. The real triumph of *Torch* from our angle was *not* that the cover plans were successfully planted on the Germans, but that the plan was not disclosed or guessed. In other words it was a triumph for security.'[28]

4 THE INVASION OF SICILY

It was decided at the Casablanca conference in January 1943 that the Allies' next objective must be the capture of Sicily – a huge undertaking, involving 160,000 men and 3,000 ships and landing-craft, code-named Operation *Husky*.

This was an enterprise which the British had almost attempted during the previous year, in the hope of capitalizing on General Auchinleck's success in North Africa. Then the Prime Minister and Chiefs of Staff had been strongly in favour of it. Operational plans were evolved, and supported by cover and deception plans. The latter were an expedition to Murmansk, to divert the enemy's attention from the Mediterranean; and a cover plan which would explain away the large numbers of British aircraft massing in North Africa for the attack on Sicily by suggesting that they were on their way to help the Russians on their southern front.[1]

It was realized only at the eleventh hour that the available resources in 1942 were totally inadequate. A War Office memorandum, prepared a day or two after the decision to go ahead with the invasion had been taken, said: 'It would be a profound mistake, even a fatal one, to expend our meagre resources prematurely and in the wrong place. It is to be hoped that we shall be able to control our impatience and that we shall not make a false move merely for the sake of making a move of some kind.' Happily this advice was accepted and the project was dropped – after the Prime Minister had rather unfairly blamed the Chiefs of Staff for their lack of judgement, for he had been just as much in favour of invading Sicily as they.[2]

A year later things were different. Britain was no longer alone. The combined might of the Allies made an invasion of Sicily much more feasible. The Americans, however, were at first unenthusiastic. General Eisenhower would have preferred to occupy Sardinia, and in this he had the support of the British Joint Planning Staff who argued that the odds were so heavily against a successful invasion of Sicily that the operation should not be attempted – a strange assessment in the light of their enthusiasm for the project a year earlier.[3] However, Churchill wanted Sicily, so Sicily it was.

The British Chiefs of Staff were by now fully convinced of the value of deception; but they felt that their American opposite numbers still had a good deal to learn about the art. They feared that because of this deception might not be allowed to play its full part in the attack on Sicily. General Alexander was therefore asked to send a small team from 'A' Force headquarters in Cairo to form the nucleus of a deception planning staff in Eisenhower's headquarters at Algiers.[4]

The broad outline of *Barclay*, the deception plan supporting the invasion of Sicily, was agreed between London and Washington, but the detailed arrangements were worked out by 'A' Force. The first programme was pretended assaults by the fictitious British Twelfth Army on western Crete (26 May); on the Peloponnese (28 May); on the islands of Pantelleria and Lampedusa (2 June); and by American troops under Patton on Sardinia and Corsica (4 June); and on France (6 June). These were the dates on which the pretended attacks were supposed to be carried out: of course, threats were to be gradually built up in the preceding weeks. On 15 May, however, it would be decided to 'postpone' all these supposed operations; and news of this would be allowed to filter through to the enemy around the end of May. Two months later the 'postponed' threats would be revived. They would now be timed to culminate in the same sequence as before, with the same interval between them as had originally been planned. The first – the threatened attack on Crete – would reach its climax 12 days after the invasion of Sicily had begun, and the last – on France – 11 days after that.[5]

This phoney 'postponement' was built into the various deceptive plans supporting the invasion of Sicily because there was a limit to the lifetime of a threatened assault. A genuine operation might need, say, eight weeks from the decision to carry it out to the day on which the assault troops actually made their move. An attempt to spin out a simulated operation of the same magnitude for longer than these eight weeks was unlikely to succeed; but the 'natural' lifetime of a threat could be prolonged by allowing the enemy to think that for certain plausible reasons it had been postponed.

However, Dudley Clarke, the commander of 'A' Force, decided on reflection that a 'postponement' of two months was too long. In that period the effect of earlier threatening measures would probably have begun to wear off. The solution was to have two 'postponements', first to late June, and then to late July. It was reckoned that this was more likely to keep up the tension and prevent the enemy from moving troops away from the threatened regions. It was also decided, very wisely, that to mount so many threats in the Mediterranean would stretch the Germans' credulity too far. Moreover, the fact that Sicily was almost the only objective not threatened might lead them to guess the truth. To prevent this the simulated threats to north and west France, Pantelleria, and Lampedusa were abandoned.[6]

The surviving threats – that the next major Allied operation would be against either Corsica, Sardinia, the south of France, or Greece – were planted by 'A' Force on the German intelligence service through agents and double agents within the triangle contained by Gibraltar, Teheran, and Cape Town. (This shows how vast 'A' Force's parish had become.) The London Controlling Section organized complementary leakage outside that area. Their most brilliant deceptive ploy was what Bevan described as 'the crucial *Mincemeat* letter' – the fake document which was delivered along with other papers to the

Germans by means of a corpse floated ashore from a submarine on to a Spanish beach. The letter suggested that Sicily was the cover objective for an assault on Greece – the exact reverse of what was really intended.[7]

If the Germans swallowed what was being presented to them they would be expecting an Allied attack against Greece a fortnight after the invasion of Sicily had begun; and attacks on Corsica, Sardinia, and the south of France a week after that. With luck they would be focussing their attention well away from the genuine assault area when the Allied expeditionary forces set sail for Sicily.

'A' Force were instrumental in preventing one move which would have undermined these plans – the transfer of 15th Army Group Headquarters to Malta, the Allied territory nearest to Sicily. They pointed out that the Germans' radio monitoring service would quickly discover that a new major headquarters had been set up there. In particular, the radio link with Washington would be detected. When Lord Gort, Governor of Malta, left his residence to make way for General Eisenhower, there would be widespread comment. It would be impossible to prevent careless talk about the new headquarters among merchant seamen plying between Malta and North Africa, or among the crews of communications aircraft which flew to and from Malta daily, whose indiscretions were notorious. When the Germans found that Eisenhower had chosen Malta for his headquarters it would be virtually impossible to maintain the fiction that the Allies intended to invade Greece.[8]

'A' Force, whose opinion carried a lot of weight, begged that the invasion of Sicily should be controlled from a headquarters other than Malta. As an alternative they suggested Bizerta, or Algiers, either of which would support the deceptive plans. If Malta *had* to be chosen the fact must be disguised as much as possible. Eisenhower's move there should be deferred until the last moment, radio signals traffic kept at a low level, personnel attached to the headquarters kept to the absolute minimum. On no account should senior officers fly flags on their cars, and the Commander-in-Chief should be seen as little as possible.[9]

In the event Eisenhower remained in Algiers. A dummy headquarters was established at Oran, far to the west of the pending operation. It started transmitting on 27 June, and maintained traffic between North Africa and London at the approximate level which the genuine headquarters would have required – about 1,500 groups each way daily. The messages were given added realism by the inclusion of the average number of priority signals and repeats for clarification. The operational station at La Marsa, near Carthage, took over when the invasion began, on 10 July 1943.[10]

The deceptionists were seldom given their head in the implementation of cover and deception plans. As a rule it was impossible to do everything that the perfect deceptive plan called for without conflicting in some way with the genuine operational plan; and inevitably the latter was given priority. It was sometimes arguable that the priorities should be reversed, that some aspect of the genuine plan should be modified or eliminated to make way for a deceptive ploy; but the genuine planners would hardly agree to this without certain proof that the real operation would benefit. In the nature of things that proof could never be provided.

The deceptive plans for the invasion of Sicily suffered as much as any from this fact. For example, the deceptionists looked to the propagandists – the Political Warfare Executive (PWE) based in London – to reinforce the deception plans; but they were hampered by a lack of facilities.

The idea was to support the military threats by controlling the number and the nature of propaganda leaflets dropped from Allied aircraft. The number of leaflets calling on the German forces to surrender would be increased gradually as the presumed invasion approached. After the first 'postponement' of the fictitious assault the numbers would be reduced.

54

The leaflet showers would again be intensified as the next theoretical assault approached. These propaganda attacks would be in the south of France, Sardinia, Corsica, and the Peloponnese – the places which were *not* to be invaded. Sicily would be relatively starved of leaflets. This led a critic in the War Office to suggest that the propaganda attacks would draw attention to the genuine objective by placing it in a sort of leaflet vacuum. On the other hand, the enemy faced the possibility that in not dropping leaflets on Sicily the Allies were engaging in a double bluff.[11]

However, as it turned out, the propagandists could not be given the aircraft they needed to carry out their leaflet-dropping programmes. Aircraft based in Britain could not operate against ports in the south of France because of the short summer nights. The towns selected by PWE for leaflet treatment could most conveniently be attacked from North Africa, but all the aircraft there were needed to back up the genuine invasion. Only Paris presented no problem. This meant that the leaflet-dropping programme had to be reduced from the 5,000,000 needed to sustain the various threats and postponements to 800,000 dropped only over Paris, which left PWE with little opportunity of influencing German intelligence. The threat of an invasion in the south of France therefore had to be developed through radio propaganda rather than through leaflet-dropping.[12]

PWE had planned an extensive programme of genuine activities to back up their propaganda. They wanted aerial reconnaissance of beaches in southern France; preparatory attacks on transport in the region, in particular 'train-busting forays'; and aerial bombardment of selected strategic targets. The last would be timed for the eve of the invasion of Sicily. All this was considered to be the minimum package needed to make the Germans believe that the south of France was the genuine target. When Squadron Leader Dennis Wheatley (the best-selling novelist) put the programme to the Air Ministry, he admitted that it should be the responsibility of air forces based in North Africa, but they were no more able to spare aircraft for deceptive bombing than for dropping propaganda leaflets. He knew there were many calls on the RAF; but could they help?

They could not. PWE had already been told that the short nights ruled out operations from Britain against the south of France. Photographic reconnaissance would be at the expense of their existing programme. The only 'train-busting' aircraft available was the Mosquito, but the south of France was beyond its range. Lancasters could be provided for ordinary bombing, but the opposing fighter forces were so strong that unacceptable numbers would be shot down.[13] Thus both the numbers of leaflets dropped, and the number of genuine activities backing up the deceptive plan were much less than the planners had hoped.

This had one incidental advantage. When the propagandists implemented a deceptive plan they had to steer a difficult middle course between convincing the Germans that an Allied attack was imminent, and encouraging resistance groups to go into action in support of an attack that would never materialize, who would then find themselves exposed to the full weight of German reprisals. In any case, it was bad for morale if hopes of liberation were raised by 'the voice of London', only to be dashed; and it was also bad for the credibility of both the BBC and PWE's own radio stations, which broadcast to the whole of occupied Europe.

The Allied High Command was counting on resistance groups to make all-out attacks in support of the invasion of Europe, when in due course it was launched. At that point they must believe implicitly in the instructions issued from London, and carry them out to the letter. But in France PWE had already cried 'Wolf!' twice – at the time of the raid on Dieppe, and before the invasion of French North Africa – and there was a real danger that French resistance would cease to believe anything that London said. PWE's solution for the purposes of the Sicily deception plan was to remind the *maquis* that they would be told when to go into action. 'We shall give you our instructions as soon as it is a matter of calling upon you for your active help. In the meantime keep away from all preliminary operations.' It was hoped that this line would leave the Germans with the impression that something was in the wind, without encouraging the resistance groups to think that the ultimate D-Day had arrived.[14]

It was mooted that PWE should help the invasion of Sicily by broadcasting a phoney proclamation by the King of Italy. Bevan suggested a leaflet saying that Italy had asked for an armistice, but it was felt that this would discredit Allied propaganda. Eisenhower and Alexander, however, believed that a bogus proclamation would reduce Italian resistance during the landings in Sicily. A proclamation was drafted which included the passage:

Italian courage and endurance have been so fully demonstrated in countless actions fought out on foreign soil that no one can doubt that, if need be, we are prepared to die to a man in defence of the homeland. But now after thirty-eight months of the bitterest conflict ever waged in history, with the flower of our manhood either dead or prisoners, with our women and children hourly crushed beneath falling buildings or burned to death, with our great centres of industry being steadily blasted into ruins, abandoned by our German allies, who have failed to deliver even one-third of the war material promised to us, and with the ever-growing might of Britain and America arrayed for the final assault against us alone – the time has come to make an end.

In conclusion, the King was made to say that he had dismissed Mussolini, and was forming a broader-based government. History showed that the British and Americans had been magnanimous in victory; and he had therefore agreed to an armistice, so that their beloved country might be preserved from anarchy.

The United States Chiefs of Staff, their British colleagues, and the Prime Minister all agreed to this *ruse de guerre*. Then they had second thoughts and decided that the ploy would do more harm than good, by showing the world that the Allies were capable of descending to a level of propaganda worthy of the Axis powers. The false proclamation was never broadcast, and Mussolini was allowed to remain in office for a few weeks longer.[15]

British diplomatic missions also played their part in the deceptive plans, by putting across the idea that Italy was not to be the Allies' next target. The Minister in Switzerland was provided by the London Controlling Section with an indiscretion suitable for a high-level dinner party: 'Tunisia has, of course, cost the enemy dear in men, shipping, and planes, but it has taken a long time and our rather ambitious plans for the simultaneous invasion of the south of France and Greece may have to be modified.' Ergo, there was no question of invading Sicily – which would be repeated all over Berne.[16]

Sir Victor Mallet, the British Minister in Sweden who was later to play a big part in the *Graffham* diplomatic deception, was instructed to spread the idea that, since the Allies thought that Germany was not strong enough to keep Italy under control, there was no need for them to invade the country. He was also to foster the idea that the Allies believed bombing could win the War, by indiscreetly referring to secret graphs he had seen which revealed that the weight of Allied bombs dropped on Germany was now two thousand per cent higher than the weight of German bombs dropped on Britain.[17]

Both the planners of genuine operations and those concerned with deceptive plans had to contend with speculation in the press. The press could be used to foster deception; but equally it might seem to give away the Allies' true intentions. At the end of June many newspapers were suggesting that the Allies' next objective was Sicily. A Reuter's story from Washington said quite positively: 'Allied airborne troops will attack Sicily.'[18] The Chiefs of Staff considered providing selected editors with notes setting out the arguments for undertaking operations in parts of the Mediterranean other than Sicily; but before the notes could be circulated the press of its own volition began to forecast that Greece was the next target.[19]

It is difficult to decide how far deception contributed to the success of the Allied invasion of Sicily. At the beginning of May – ten weeks before the attack – Bevan's assessment was that the Germans believed Sicily to be the likely target, with Rhodes/Crete, Greece, Sardinia, and the south of France (in descending order of probability) as possible alternatives.[20] The formal inquest into the Allied operation recorded that the deception planners had successfully carried out 'the largest exercise in systematic deception yet attempted in the Mediterranean theatre'. 'A' Force reported that substantial German forces had been sent to the Balkans, and that reserves in Italy had been divided equally between Sardinia, Corsica, and Sicily. Captured German documents and the interrogation of prisoners revealed that the assault forces had achieved complete surprise. Up to the very last moment the Luftwaffe thought that Sardinia might be the objective. Tactical diversionary threats, including a feint by the navy, had kept substantial enemy forces many miles from the Sicily beachheads. The assault convoys themselves had contributed to the fiction that Greece was their intended target by converging in the general area of Malta, and then suddenly turning north to approach Sicily under cover of darkness.[21]

A mission from 21st Army Group (which was due to invade Normandy twelve months later) satisfied itself that strategical and tactical surprise had been achieved in spite of enormous difficulties, thanks to deceptive measures which had caught the enemy on the wrong foot, and had actually induced him to move reserves away from the assault areas. The Allied High Command knew from messages sent by the German commander Kesselring (which were decoded at Bletchley), that he was uncertain where and when the attack would come. 'It was only when the armada of ships coming up from Alexandria had been spotted by the Germans on July the ninth that Ultra informed us that the troops on Sicily and elsewhere were put on the alert.'[22]

However, factors other than deception contributed to the Allies' success. They had complete air superiority. The beach defences were very thin. Many of the mines had not been armed. The Italians put up feeble opposition. Further, the effect of the deceptive plans is called in question by two Italian intelligence reports. The first, of 24 June 1943, argued that Allied exercises near Oran meant that there would be a paratroop attack on Sicily. The second, of 1 July, narrowed the likely target of the Allied assault down to Sardinia or Sicily, and concluded that the weight of the evidence pointed to an attack on the latter.[23]

It seems, therefore, that if the Axis commanders had trusted their intelligence reports they would have been better prepared to meet the Allied invasion, although it may well be that their faith in these reports – which hindsight would have shown to be accurate – was undermined by 'A' Force.

The capture of Sicily provided a stepping-stone to the mainland of Italy. On 3 September 1943 – the fourth anniversary of Britain's Declaration of War on Germany and less than three weeks after the end of resistance in Sicily – men of the Eighth Army landed on the toe of Italy between Reggio Calabria and Villa San Giovanni. They did not have the benefit of elaborate deceptive plans, partly because there had been no time to draw them up, and partly because there had been negotiations with the Italians about an armistice, and it was hoped that the Italian Government would throw in the towel. It was also hoped that if the Italians pulled out of the War the Germans would withdraw from Italy. This proved to be a vain hope. The Allies had to face a long and bitter struggle against the senior Axis partner in Italy, which ended in stalemate more than a year later.

5 DECEPTIVE OPERATIONS, 1943

It was accepted by the Allies at the beginning of 1943 that there was no hope of opening the decisive second front that year, unless the Germans collapsed. The only way to keep up the pressure on the enemy – apart from the bomber offensive – was to make the fullest use of deceptive threats.

On 10 February 1943, the British Chiefs of Staff approved the deception policy for the rest of the year. They hoped for the early agreement of the United States Chiefs of Staff, 'otherwise we shall never get the pot boiling in time'; but this was not forthcoming until 3 April.[1] General Sir Frederick Morgan, Chief of Staff to the Supreme Allied Commander, was then directed to carry out a deception scheme lasting the whole summer, to keep alive in the Germans' minds the possibility of cross-channel operations from Britain. The deception was to climax in a feint attack, which would stimulate aerial battles with the Luftwaffe on terms favourable to the Allies.[2]

The overall deception plan, *Cockade*, had three component parts: *Starkey*, the amphibious feint across the Channel; *Tindall*, a purely fictitious operation to contain German forces in Norway; and *Wadham*, another purely fictitious operation which implied a large-scale American landing in Brittany.

A big army training exercise, *Harlequin*, would be run in conjunction with *Starkey*. Troops would assemble at south coast ports as if they were about to embark on a genuine cross-channel expedition. Aircraft and gliders would be moved into the south-east counties, accompanied by batteries of anti-aircraft guns. All this activity would be observed by German reconnaissance; and the enemy would conclude that a massive invasion of France was about to be attempted. At least, that was the theory.[3]

STARKEY

Like all deceptive operations, *Starkey*, commanded by Air Marshal Sir Trafford Leigh-Mallory, Commander-in-Chief, Fighter Command, and General Ira C. Eaker, Commanding General, United States Eighth Air Force, was a blend of truth and falsehood. The genuine troops earmarked for the operation included the Royal Marine Division, five commandos, a parachute brigade, an air-landing brigade, and Canadian units: these were supplemented by two fictitious corps, the VIIIth and the XIIth, representing 60,000 non-existent men. The naval force was originally planned to include two battleships, 12 'Hunt' class destroyers, 24 minesweepers, and 59 smaller ships; all the landing-craft that could be scraped together; and as much merchant shipping as could be spared from coastal convoys.[4] Aerial cover would be provided by 45 British and 15 American fighter squadrons. In addition, American bombers would carry out 3,000 day sorties, and a similar number would be flown by the RAF. The planners concluded that this was the minimum amount of aerial activity needed to convince the enemy that a genuine invasion was in prospect.[5]

Neither the Admiralty nor the Air Ministry, however, was prepared for deception at any price. The First Sea Lord, Admiral Sir Dudley Pound, argued that battleships should not be endangered in a fake operation. They could not knock out heavy coastal artillery, and might themselves be knocked out. The Germans would then claim a great victory, which it would be hard to explain away to the British people. Against this, Vice-Admiral Lord Louis Mountbatten, Chief of Combined Operations, argued that battleships were essential; and Morgan claimed that the Luftwaffe would not take the bait unless they saw battleships in the 'invasion force'. In the end the Chiefs of Staff decided that battleships were out.[6]

The air element in the plan was also whittled down. General Eaker said his directive was to destroy German industry, and he could not spare all the aircraft asked for. He agreed to only 300 bomber sorties; training missions by 'freshmen' squadrons, and operational missions prevented by bad weather from going to Germany.[7]

Bomber Command were even more reluctant to help. The Commander-in-Chief, Air Chief Marshal Sir Arthur Harris complained that the mock invasion would cause a 'fearful diversion' from the bomber offensive. If Fighter Command wanted to have a go at the Luftwaffe, they would be better advised to give Bomber Command some ponderable assistance in attacking Germany: '. . . what they do for us is infinitesimal'. The proposed deceptive operation was just the sort of thing an idle army doted on, and must be stopped. The Chief of Air Staff, Air Chief Marshal Sir Charles Portal, was equally critical. 'The so-called plan is nothing more than a list of actions designed to deceive the Germans. It is not a co-ordinated plan and contrary to Leigh-Mallory's opinion any item can be omitted without much effect on the others.'[8]

On 24 August Harris received a signal from the Air Ministry setting out the bombing effort which had been agreed for Operation *Starkey*. He exploded, and in reply sent three angry telegrams in quick succession. First, he objected to receiving peremptory orders to take part in a futile operation at the expense of a fatal reduction in his bombing programme. Leigh-Mallory was now assuming the right to call on Bomber Command aircraft at will. In his second telegram *Starkey* became 'at best a piece of harmless play-acting'. In the third he claimed that his Command was being turned into a maintenance unit, to supply aircraft to be employed as and when AOC-in-C, Fighter Command considered fit and appropriate.[9]

Harris had his way. The bomber offensive against Germany was left intact. Bomber Command's only contribution would be from the Operational Training Units, and those Wellington squadrons which could not undertake operations over

Germany. Morgan, who had already lost battleships, claimed feebly that the loss of the heavy bombers would not weaken the cross-channel feint, although they had been deemed to be essential in the first plan.[10]

To increase the credibility of the deceptive operation, Morgan proposed that the troops should be told that they were taking part in a genuine invasion of the continent. He feared that unless this were done it would become common knowledge that *Starkey* was a fake, and German intelligence would pick up the fact. Then, when the convoys turned back from the French coast, it would be explained to the troops that the expedition had been called off because the German coastal defences were still too powerful. Had this line been followed it must have had a serious effect on the morale of the troops. In the first place, they would have asked why the High Command had not satisfied itself about the strength of the coastal defences before the invasion convoys sailed; and in the second place, memories of the curious episode would linger in the minds of the assault forces when in due course the genuine invasion took place. Men would wonder if the High Command had got it wrong once again. The Chiefs of Staff saw the point, and Morgan's proposal was turned down.

However, having rescued Morgan from the frying-pan, they proceeded themselves to jump into the fire. They arrived at the incredible decision that when the fake invasion had run its course it should be announced to the world that it had been a fake. The dummy landing-craft and other deceptive devices used in the operation would be shown to the press so that they could report with conviction that *Starkey* was not a failed invasion.[11] Happily, the Controlling Officer spotted the blunder before it was too late. He pointed out that if the press were shown the deceptive devices the chances of using them with success in 1944 would be seriously jeopardized. Further, any official announcement that the operation had been a deception would reveal to the Germans that their agents in Britain had been manipulated by the Allies. It would no longer be possible to use these agents. The point was quickly taken. The Chiefs of Staff admitted that to announce the expedition as a deceptive operation might have 'certain unsatisfactory results'. They decided that instead a group of accredited British, Dominion, and American journalists would be told after the event that *Starkey* had been a full-dress rehearsal for the invasion of the Continent – nothing more and nothing less.[12]

The Political Warfare Executive were again called in to use the resistance groups to put across the idea that the threatened invasion was genuine, but without committing them to a major complementary effort.[13] The danger that an operation to deceive the enemy would also deceive the resistance groups, which had become apparent at the time of the invasion of Sicily, now manifested itself in a more acute form. When PWE first studied the problem, they came to the conclusion that the proposed operation would bring hopes of immediate liberation to the whole of Europe; and that when these hopes were not realized, morale would fall disastrously. This was an inconvenient conclusion, for it strengthened the case against *Starkey*. However, the propagandists were trained to make black white, if necessary. They put forward the alternative proposition that since the peoples of the occupied countries had no wish to see their homelands devastated they would be delighted when the threatened invasion did not materialize.

PWE and the Special Operations Executive (SOE) decided to scatter enough hints of underground activity to make German intelligence in France believe that preparations were being made to receive a genuine invasion; but not so many that the resistance movement would come to the same conclusion and go into action prematurely – a difficult balance. PWE circulated to the resistance forces simple instructions in the use of certain small arms, hoping that the Germans would conclude that consignments of these weapons were being dropped by parachute. The BBC broadcast talks for the benefit of patriotic civilians; for example, 'Resistance and security', 'Enemy troops dispositions and plans', and 'Recognizing Allied troops'. As

Starkey approached there would be a flurry of meaningless code messages in the BBC's French, Belgian, Dutch, and Norwegian services, ostensibly directed at the resistance movements. In Britain, the BBC would become an 'unconscious agent of deception' by being allowed to react naturally to inspired leaks about the impending invasion 'in a normal and uninformed way'. The last upset Morgan, who wrote: 'Now, where are we? You will see PWE suggests leading the BBC up the garden path ... Now, for pity's sake, tell me who tells who what and when, and what he expects them to believe anyway.'

In the event, it was decided to water down this programme in case it led to serious trouble for the resistance.[14] At the end of August, by which time it was hoped that the Germans would be convinced *Starkey* was genuine, the resistance groups would be told through secret channels that the 'invasion' was no more than a rehearsal. It was intended to put across the same idea in a broadcast round about the same time, but it was realized that this would rob the operation of its climax. There was instead a more subtle announcement:

Be careful of German provocation. We have learned that the Germans are circulating inspired rumours that we are concentrating armies on our coasts with intentions of invading the continent. Take no notice, as these provocations are intended to create among you mani-festations and disorders which the Germans will use as an excuse for repressive measures against you. Be disciplined, use discretion, and maintain order, for when the time arrives for action you will be advised in advance.

This warning begged the question of whether *Starkey* was a fake or a rehearsal, and left it open to the Germans to decide that a genuine operation was being planned.[15]

Colonel Turner of the Air Ministry was given general oversight of the physical deception arrangements in support of *Starkey*; but the resources that were put at his disposal were totally inadequate. There were so few real or dummy craft available that there was no point in setting up fake lighting to simulate the movement of a military force which the visible craft could not possibly carry. He had therefore decided to provide only lighting schemes to attract enemy bombers away from troop concentrations, and to abandon the simulated movement by night of large vehicle convoys. The schemes which he did provide included 14 coastal and 21 inland sites affording protection to Southampton, Portsmouth, Dover, and Newhaven. The coastal decoys simulated embarkation lighting, except that a whole simulated port was provided for Southampton in Pennington Marshes beyond Lymington, and another for Newhaven at Cuckmere Haven, west of Seaford. The inland lighting represented camps, dumps, and small motor transport convoys.[16]

There was so much lighting – permitted and illegal – along the South Coast that the intensity of the fake schemes had to be kept unnaturally high in the hope that it would catch the enemy's eye. Decoys on the coast were lit sparingly lest the Luftwaffe note them for future reference – they would be needed for the invasion proper. Inland, where there were more alternative sites available for use in 1944, they could be lit for longer periods. In the areas where the *Harlequin* troops concentrated before embarking on the 'invasion' convoys, the existing decoy lighting schemes were switched off so that they would not attract attacks on the nearby transit camps. Decoy fires protecting Winchester and Canterbury were, however, allowed to remain operational.[17]

Colonel Turner's Department was also responsible for the display of dummy gliders and dummy aircraft. Between 4 and 20 August nearly 400 dummy gliders were taken from store and erected at those aerodromes on the South Coast which would have been used for a genuine invasion of France. There were also 128 dummy Spitfires and 64 dummy Hurricanes, which the station commanders were instructed to move from time to time to give them some semblance of life.[18]

The first active contribution to the build-up of the invasion threat was made by small Combined Operations teams in July and August. Fourteen raids (code name *Forfar*) on the French Channel coast had been planned: their aim was to suggest to the enemy that information was being sought in preparation for an invasion. The men taking part were told that the objective of the raids was to capture a prisoner – it was too risky to tell them what the real purpose was. If they were captured they might be made to disclose that *Starkey* was only a feint, which would waste months of planning. Further, the men might not have relished the thought that they were risking their lives simply to create an impression in the mind of the enemy. In fact the raids were singularly unsuccessful, and might seem to have set a pattern for the *Starkey* deception as a whole.

Of the fourteen planned, only eight were carried out. Of these, *Forfar Easy* spent ninety minutes ashore but failed to make contact with the enemy. Their only trophy was a sample of barbed wire. *Forfar Beer* met an enemy trawler on patrol, and returned to Newhaven without landing. They made two later attempts. On the first occasion they landed, but were immediately driven off by a severe storm. On the second, they found the cliffs too difficult to scale. *Forfar How* failed to land because the surf was too strong. *Forfar Dog* scaled the cliffs but could not get through the wire at the top. They too had to be content with bringing back a sample of wire. At the beginning of August, *Forfar Love*, two two-man canoes which had been dropped near Dunkirk by motor gunboat, found so much activity on shore that they paddled for home. The men were picked up by a Walrus flying-boat which, with the help of two passing Spitfires, proceeded to sink the canoes. This led to a row with Dover Command, whose rescue craft spent hours searching for the canoes, unaware that the RAF had sunk them.[19] Thus, unless the Germans happened to notice that two small pieces of their wire had been purloined, the Combined Operations contribution to *Starkey* went for nothing.

The planners had estimated that 450 landing-craft of all

types would be required to convince the Germans that *Starkey* was a genuine invasion attempt and not just another Dieppe raid, but only 360 craft were available. The deficiency had to be made good with dummies. They could not cross the Channel, but if they were seen at their anchorages by German reconnaissance planes beforehand it might be assumed when the cross-channel convoys set sail that they were among them. 75 dummy Landing Craft (Tank) – known as 'Bigbobs' – and 100 dummy Landing Craft (Assault) – 'Wetbobs' – supplemented the genuine fleet. This made a respectable total, roughly three times the size of the fleet used in the Dieppe raid. The Bigbobs were 160 feet long and 30 feet wide, made from steel tubing and canvas. They had wheels so that they could be pushed to their moorings, and in the water they were supported by floats. The smaller Wetbob was made of rubber, and was inflatable. Twenty Wetbobs could be carried in a 3-ton truck, rolled up like carpets.[20]

The landing-craft fleet was spread along the south coast from Falmouth to Rye, an artistic blend in which the craft in the west were dummies and those in the east mainly genuine. Since the dummies could not move, their progress along the coast to the concentration areas in the east had to be simulated. A few were displayed at Falmouth and Dartmouth, where they were launched by United States troops. Then a day or two later others appeared at Poole, and later still at Beaulieu and Chichester. It was hoped that this would create the illusion that those seen first at Falmouth and Dartmouth had moved eastwards by night, and been replaced in the ports from which they had sailed by newly-launched craft. This was the best that could be done to give life to the dummy fleet; but it was feared at the time that it would be difficult to deceive the Germans, who themselves made use of dummy craft.[21]

The illusion that the landing-craft were on the move was heightened by the use of radio signalling, which the Germans always monitored. A certain call-sign would be used, first at Falmouth by one of the Bigbobs there, and then, as that particular craft was ostensibly moving along the coast, the call-sign would keep in step with it. It was difficult to find the right equipment for this job, but eventually the Canadian Army provided wireless telegraph trucks, which travelled eastwards from Falmouth, transmitting prefabricated messages from whichever anchorage the Bigbob was supposed to have reached.

Radio deception was also used to simulate the assault training of an amphibious force of divisional strength in the Solent area. Three headquarters stations on board ship were simulated, only one of which was actually on a ship (HMS *Albrighton*), the others being at HMS *Vectis*, the shore station at Cowes, and at Fort Southwick, headquarters of the Commander-in-Chief, Portsmouth. The Army also carried out five fictitious radio exercises in the Southampton area: *Bicycle* (a brigade exercise on 13 August); *Tricycle* (a divisional exercise on 16 August); *Icicle* (brigade, 21 August); *Sidecar* (brigade, 27 August); and *Tandem* (division, 4 September).[22]

A detailed programme was drawn up for the purposes of 'Special Means' – the leakage through agents in enemy territory and double agents under the control of MI5 of selected facts and fictions in support of Operation *Starkey*. These leakages were mainly intended to make the Germans aware of developments which could not be observed by reconnaissance aircraft. For example, it was leaked that troops were assembling for the invasion attempt, that the coastal area between Southampton and Gravesend had been declared a restricted zone from 15 August, that the non-existent Sixth Army was standing by to move to the embarkation ports, and that merchant ships were being loaded for a cross-channel expedition. As it might have seemed suspicious if the agents reported only those things which could not be seen from the air, they were also required to report some aspects of the invasion preparations which could have been observed by aerial reconnaissance.

These included the build-up of dummy landing-craft – which would of course be reported as genuine – and the numerous camps which appeared in the concentration areas. A genuine agent would have had little difficulty in observing these things, and German intelligence would expect them to be reported.

However, the double agents were not asked to report the display of dummy gliders and dummy aircraft, nor the movement of anti-aircraft guns into the south east. They were certainly not to say anything about the *Forfar* raids, which were supposed to advertise themselves – although they signally failed to do so.[23]

General Morgan regularly reported progress to the Chiefs of Staff. On 20 July, he was still hoping that *Starkey* would succeed in its main aim of bringing on a major air battle, in spite of the fact that battleships were not to be employed, and that the air forces had been drastically reduced. On 3 August, the operation was proceeding according to plan 'as nearly as possible' – a slight weakening of confidence. Later in August the enemy increased his aerial reconnaissance over the south of England – an encouraging sign. Presumably he was interested in the growing concentrations of ships and landing-craft. Morgan thought the operation was proceeding satisfactorily – 'in the main'. Perhaps the Chiefs of Staff now detected a note of uncertainty, for they asked him to provide a formal appreciation by 2 September – only a week before the mock invasion was due to sail.[24]

Morgan submitted his report on 2 September and elaborated it when he met the Chiefs of Staff next day. Operations in general and air operations in particular had suffered from the weather. Minesweeping, which had been delayed, had provoked no more than a little desultory fire from coastal batteries. In his opinion the overall enemy reaction was not enough to justify laying on the final phase of the 'invasion'. The Chiefs of Staff could not make up their minds one way or the other; but next day they reached the conclusion that *Starkey* would go ahead. They comforted themselves with the thought that if the operation was seen to have failed it could be passed off as a diversion in the interests of Operation *Avalanche*, the assault on Salerno which was due about the same time.[25]

The Prime Minister, who was in Washington, was told of the decision. Earlier he had asked whether there should not be a larger mass of shipping in the supposed invasion fleet; but the Ministry of Transport had replied that the consequent reduction in shipments of coal to south-east England could not be afforded. Churchill sent a one-line telegram: 'Good luck to *Starkey*!' The Russians were also told about the operation, and they were warned that German propaganda would claim that the second front had been frustrated.[26]

Starkey was supposed to commence on 8 September, but the continuing bad weather caused a postponement for 24 hours. By this time the air forces had been in action for more than three weeks; and for a time it looked as if the objective of reducing the strength of the Luftwaffe might be attained. In attacks on French airfields 45 German fighters were destroyed for the loss of 23 Allied planes. After 25 August marshalling-yards, ammunition dumps, camps, barracks, beach defences between Boulogne and Le Touquet, and roads and railways were attacked; but the weather seriously interfered with the programme. Of the 42 aerial operations planned, 14 were abandoned and only 15 were carried out in full.

On 9 September, the convoys assembled off Dungeness and made for the coast of France under an umbrella of 72 fighters. Medium bombers attacked French coastal batteries and airfields. Ideally, all seven batteries in the area would have been bombed, but the available aircraft could deal with only two of them, on which they dropped 650 tons of high explosive. The beach defences were also less heavily bombed than had been planned because ground mist at their bases prevented some aircraft from making a second sortie.[27]

The convoys – two naval, and 19 merchant ships (one of the

original 20 had engine trouble) – proceeded solemnly towards Boulogne until they were within 10 miles of the coast. They waited expectantly. Nothing happened. The coastal batteries remained silent, not because they had been knocked out. Not a single enemy vessel ventured out to meet the fleet. Not a single enemy aircraft appeared over the Channel. The expedition turned for home at 9 a.m. and disappeared into a smokescreen laid by the naval vessels and low-flying aircraft. *Starkey* had accomplished nothing.[28]

The inquest concluded that at no time had the enemy been deceived into thinking that a major landing was intended. The evidence that the operation might have had some influence was very thin. A few minor repositionings of R-boats and E-boats were seen as possible reactions to the threat, but this was clutching at straws. Fifty bombers had been transferred from Italy to Belgium – but they had probably nothing to do with *Starkey*. Enemy reconnaissance from the sea had increased.

On the other hand there was abundant evidence that the Germans were unmoved by the threat. They carried out six aerial reconnaissances in the week ended 19 August; but thereafter there was only one in the *Starkey* area. The transfer of divisions from the north of France to the south and to Italy continued throughout July and August. No fewer than twelve left between 23 June and the climax of *Starkey*; and only one or two came in. Calais and Caen were left with virtually no reserves. Berlin radio referred to evidence of 'concentrations of major airborne and other special formations in south-east England, as well as the presence in English harbours of numerous small shipping units'. So there was no doubt the preparations had been observed, even if the double agents had not been believed. The great aerial battle, which was the main objective, never took place. Bomber Harris must have given a wry smile. The futile play-acting which he had criticized had failed to capture the attention of its audience across the Channel.[29]

The official verdict was that the Germans had appreciated

the true nature of the operation. They had taken the minimum precautions to oppose a possible raid, but they had deliberately refused to play the Allied game by sending the Luftwaffe into the air.[30]

Alternative communiqués had been drafted at the beginning of September so that something could be issued to the press as soon as the result of the operation was known. The first was a news flash: 'With reference to reports of activity/gun-fire/air battles off the south coast this morning the German radio is making sensational claims which in no way correspond to the facts. A joint Service communiqué will be issued later in the day.' The later announcement was to conclude: 'The enemy launched E-boat and air attacks as a result of which he suffered considerable casualties.'[31]

Alas, this proved to be too optimistic. The actual communiqué simply said that a full-scale rehearsal of pre-invasion activities had taken place ... assault troops had not been embarked but some of the landing-craft had been exercised in the Channel with naval and air protection. Valuable lessons had been learned.[32]

TINDALL

Tindall, the second element in *Cockade*, was a deceptive operation against Stavanger, to pin down German forces in Norway. The enemy troops occupying the country were the minimum needed to hold it. Each area of strategic importance had been made self-supporting, so that if any one region was threatened there was a good chance that the occupying army would be contained, and perhaps have to be reinforced.

Stavanger, on the south-east coast of Norway, had been the key to the German invasion in 1940, and was the obvious place to go for. It was within range of airborne attack from Scotland; and it had airfields which could be used to build up an invasion force. There were large numbers of troops in Scotland which could be notionally allocated to *Tindall*. There were always substantial naval forces in northern waters; and the Germans knew that there were enough aircraft of all types in Britain to carry out a large-scale airborne operation. Therefore an assault on Stavanger had no difficulty in passing the plausibility test.[33]

The Controlling Officer thought that the Germans would be more worried by the possibility of an attack on Trondheim or Narvik in the north, but these had to be ruled out as targets for the deception operation because they were beyond the range of air cover. Further, to threaten them would attract the Germans' attention to an area which might conceivably become the scene of genuine operations later in the year. This danger was always at the back of the deception planners' minds. Much harm could be done if a deceptive operation brought enemy forces to a sector which might later become a genuine objective.[34]

While a threat to Stavanger on its own was entirely plausible, it was feared that the Germans would consider that *Tindall* and *Starkey* taken together were beyond the Allied resources available in Britain and therefore believe in neither. For this reason it was decided to divide *Tindall* into three stages, the first of which would be planned to reach a climax on 12 September. Round about 25 August, however, the operation would be dismounted – to give the impression that the resources assembled for *Tindall* were needed to reinforce *Starkey*, and had been suddenly transferred to the south of England. Then, after *Starkey* had run its course, the threat against Norway would be remounted and timed to culminate in mid-November.

The plan was approved by General Morgan on 30 June 1943. The programme of deception was to start with photographic reconnaissance of key points in the Bergen–Oslo–Kristiansand–Stavanger area between 15 July and 25 August, a necessary preliminary to a genuine invasion. A real operation on the scale to be simulated would call for eight fighter squadrons and a torpedo bomber squadron, rather more than was immediately available in Scotland; but this was deemed unimportant, since evidence of the fighter aircraft need not be presented until just before the operation commenced.

However, it was necessary to display dummy bombers well in advance. By 15–20 August, forty dummy Blenheims and Bostons were to be on show at Peterhead, and ten at each of Fraserburgh and Fordoun airfields. They would represent half the aircraft in five light bomber squadrons, the other half being notionally concealed in hangars and dispersal areas. The transport and assembly of these dummies was of course to be hidden from enemy reconnaissance, otherwise the cat would be out of the bag.[35]

To foster the idea in the enemy's mind that the invasion would be airborne, large numbers of gliders were displayed on twenty-three airfields running from Tain and Inverness to Perth and Errol. On each of the twenty there would be 11 or 12 genuine Horsa gliders, and another 20 notionally hidden in hangars and hides; and on each of the other three there would be 6 of the larger Hamilcar gliders, with another 13 notionally concealed. On some airfields, where it could be conveniently arranged, a few aircraft for towing gliders would be displayed. This implied a total of nearly 260 real gliders, and about 440 supposedly hidden near the airfields.[36]

The plan required works in progress on the selected airfields to be visibly accelerated. Runways from which the gliders would in theory take off would be lengthened – or so it would be made to seem to enemy air reconnaissance – by means of camouflage and fake construction activity. New gunpits would be dug and dummy guns installed to represent an increase of fifty per cent over the existing defences. Refuelling vehicles would be ostentatiously displayed. At Peterhead, Fraserburgh, and Fordoun, where the dummy bombers were to be set up, tents would be erected on a scale implying a fifty per cent increase in the capacity of the stations; and at the airfields with gliders, tentage to accommodate two airlanding brigades would be provided. Some of the tents would be occupied by station personnel to give signs of life.[37]

That *Tindall* was a deceptive plan had to be concealed as far as possible from those concerned with its implementation. The cover story for their benefit was that some of the ever-increasing numbers of United States troops coming to Britain might have to be accommodated in the Salisbury Plain area. This would in turn mean moving certain training establishments from there to Scotland. It might also be necessary to transfer dummy aircraft from airfields in the south to make room for the real aircraft coming in with the Americans. Pending final decisions about these matters, it would be necessary to carry out glider tests at Scottish airfields to establish that it was feasible to move the training establishments. Runways would have to be extended in anticipation of the transfer of airborne training to Scotland. It was hoped that all this would provide those concerned with a satisfactory explanation of the *Tindall* activities.

In fact the subordinate deception was a signal failure. The troops had no doubt that the idea of moving airborne training to Scotland was a bluff and said so freely. This upset the War Office, who wondered what chance there was of deceiving the Germans if they could not deceive their own rank and file.[38]

Unlike *Starkey*, which had the benefit of many genuine troops, *Tindall's* forces were almost entirely notional – the handful of sceptics who had to give life to the camps, the signals men who organized the radio deception, and the RAF crews who carried out aerial reconnaissance over Norway were the only real elements. There was, however, no limit to the number of troops conjured up for the purposes of the supposed operation: a dummy headquarters, three divisions, two airlanding brigades, three parachute brigades, and five commandos.[39]

It soon became apparent that the plan was too ambitious. A large contribution was called for from Colonel Turner, who was told on 15 July that he must start erecting hides for 210 gliders in distant Scotland the very next day. He pointed out that it would take 22,000 man-weeks to do the job, that if grouped together the hides would occupy a rectangle a mile long by half a mile wide, and that they would absorb 5,000 tons of steel, as well as large quantities of other scarce materials. Fifteen trains would be required to take the materials to Scotland, and fleets of lorries to carry them from the railway stations to the airfields. In short, he was faced with the impossible.

However, he said that his problems were nothing compared with those of the RAF, who faced even greater difficulties in getting the gliders to Scotland. The lack of co-ordination, and the failure to understand the deception problem, were alarming. He begged that the matter be taken up on a high level. 'I submit that it is useless for Chairborne Contrivers to prepare schemes on subjects of which they have no personal knowledge (e.g. gliders, deception) without consulting those who know something about them ... I submit that no operational scheme can be successful unless the equipment and time is available to carry it out ... I submit that to attain success in deception one must have, first, a co-ordinating committee of experts ... I submit that deception is best obtained by a slow and natural build-up of a scheme. This means it must start a long way ahead of the actual date of the operation.'[40]

There was no denying the wisdom of this, although it was to be some time before it was to be generally accepted by Allied commanders. However, it was too late to rescue *Tindall*. Once again the minimum scheme considered necessary to put across the deceptive plan was cut down to match the available resources.

The first step was to reduce the number of airfields to be 'activated' from twenty-three to eighteen. Then the total complement of nearly 260 real gliders was reduced to a mere 36 because the movement to Scotland of so large a number would interfere with airborne training.[41] There would be no more than 2 Horsas on each of the eighteen airfields – in fact the final total was only 32. The rest of the plan – the dummy aircraft, and anti-aircraft guns, the additional tentage, and the radio deception remained intact.[42]

Although the gliders were supposed to be positioned between 15 July and 25 August, none had arrived by 28 July. On 2 August, 2 arrived at Perth, and it was the end of the month before all were in position. When they were towed from England to their destinations in Scotland the routes were planned to take them over populated areas so that they would be seen by as many people as possible. It was hoped that careless talk, which the public were as a rule encouraged to avoid, would lead to rumours about the movements which might reach Berlin.[43]

Hardly had the gliders arrived and been put on show when they had to be removed and hidden under the second stage of *Tindall*. By 2 September, all had disappeared. The dummy aircraft at Peterhead, Fraserburgh, and Fordoun were also hidden away. The second stage of the deception relied mainly on radio, but it was no more successful than the other stages. There was no time to work out a convincing scheme to train the radio operators, or to provide them with the necessary elaborate scripts.[44]

The third and final stage of *Tindall* began on 21 September when the token forces in the dummy camps were brought back to life. The pretence was that the resources which had been employed in Operation *Starkey* were being brought back to Scotland to be used in the invasion of Norway. The gliders – the total complement had now increased to 70 – were dragged from their hiding-places on 7 October, along with the dummy anti-aircraft guns. Vehicles, real and simulated, were put in position. Cookhouses were built and activated by means of smoke generators.

When the men implementing the illusion entered into the spirit of the thing the effect was very convincing. When they did not, perhaps because they thought they were wasting their time, it was not. One of the best camps was at Edzell, where

Much ingenuity and imagination had been used in erecting the camp. Apart from the spacious layout ... the cookhouses etc. had been enlarged. The troops were occupying different tents every night so that the tracks had been made naturally. Slit trenches had also been dug. Dummy men had been placed to resemble troops getting into aircraft. Every member of the platoon had seen the camp from the air at least once with the result that the platoon was very keen to improve the appearance of the camp.

One of the worst was at Montrose.

This camp was disappointing. There was little sign of activity. Whitewash and straw had been used to make paths but it was obvious that they did not in many cases lead into the entrances to tents and marquees. This gave an artificial appearance to the camp. The cookhouses were inconspicuous and there was no smoke. A number of dummy men had been placed seated at tables in the middle of the camp and it was difficult to understand the meaning of this layout ...[45]

Perhaps the platoon in question were in the habit of playing cards on duty and sought to provide the enemy with a faithful representation of their normal activities.

In his report on Operation *Tindall*, General Sir Andrew Thorne, General Officer Commanding-in-Chief, Scottish Command, said that it had completely failed to interest the enemy. There had been no increase in enemy air reconnaissance over Scotland, which suggested that the vast array of deceptive devices scattered over the country from Tain to Perth had gone unnoticed. There had been no reports that the Germans suspected that anything out of the ordinary was taking place. Even the·RAF's photographic reconnaissance of the 'invasion area' in Norway, which was intended to put the enemy on his guard, had been carried out too late to be of any use.

The main deception had related to the presumed arrival and departure of aircraft in north and east Scotland, backed up by ground and air testing of transmitters, for which real aircraft had been used; and the radio simulation of an army of two corps, which included an airborne force and two special service brigades. But there had not been enough time to work out credible schemes, based on an analysis of actual radio traffic over a period. Nor had there been enough time to familiarize the operators with their unusual tasks. The sudden change which had been necessary in this sensitive sphere would almost certainly have led the enemy monitoring service to suspect that something fictitious was being cooked up for them. It would have helped if glider training had been carried out at some of the airfields, but there had been no towing aircraft to spare for this. The only flights were those made when the gliders were delivered to the airfields.

Thorne shared Turner's view that the time available between the issue of the order for the operation and its execution was far too short. Everything had to be rushed. There was no opportunity for adequate planning, briefing of personnel, or for the collection of stores. The camps had not become realistic until near the end of the operation. The absence of any reconnaissance parties from Airborne Division, which might have convinced those involved in implementing the plan that it really was intended to transfer airborne training to Scotland, had seriously prejudiced the cover plan. 'Judging by the lack of enemy recce which this operation was designed to achieve, it would appear that the operation was a failure.'[46]

WADHAM
The purpose of *Wadham* was to convince the enemy that a large combined seaborne and airborne assault was being prepared to capture the Brittany peninsula in the early autumn of 1943, the object being to compel him to keep in France troops which might otherwise be sent to the Russian front. There would be a notional threat, based partly in Britain and partly in the United States, to capture Brest. The troops supposedly taking part would be mainly American, so the plan was put under the command of General Jacob L. Devers, Commanding General, European Theater of Operations, United States Army (ETOUSA).

Wadham was very largely fictitious, in the sense that the troops nominally associated with it were not required to do anything very special other than to get on with their normal training. They included the genuine 5th and 29th United States

81

Divisions, which were already in Britain, the United States 3rd Armoured and 101st Airborne Divisions, which were still in America, and the wholly imaginary 46th United States Infantry Division. 400 United States gliders in Britain and 400 United States troop-carriers in North Africa were also associated with the threat. In fact, the real formations notionally involved could not be fully trained or equipped in time for *Wadham*, but it was hoped that the enemy would not spot this discrepancy. A genuine training exercise, *Jantzen*, would be passed off as part of the *Wadham* preparations. The Controlling Officer would let it be known through the double agents that the troops coming from the United States were in fact fully assault trained.[47]

There was one point in favour of the scheme. Brest, St. Nazaire, and Lorient were all U-boat bases, and therefore targets which could properly be attacked by the combined bomber offensive. Bomber Harris could not claim that attacks on them were mere play-acting. In addition, dummy aircraft – Mustangs and Thunderbolts, representing the latest types from the United States – would be displayed on those airfields in south-west England best placed to launch an attack on Brest. They would simulate the assembly of an appreciable fighter force to escort and cover the convoys when they arrived from the United States. There would be a sprinkling of real aircraft to lend colour to the display of dummies.

The threat of paratroop and airborne attack would be indicated by the display of as many United States gliders as could be found at the time; and parachute training of American troops already in Britain would be intensified. There would be a combined operations training exercise in the Appledore area, a logical jumping-off point for the west coast of France.

The naval force presented no problem. There were always plenty of ships available for a notional expedition. All that had to be done was to compile a list of those needed – taking care, of course, to ensure that they were in home waters and not in the Far East or the Antipodes. However, there were no landing-craft available: *Starkey* had taken them all. This did not matter much since *Wadham* was set for 30 September – three weeks after *Starkey* was due to be completed – and it would not be necessary to position any landing-craft for *Wadham* until about two weeks before the operation was due to commence. For the time being *Wadham* could make do with dummies; and by 6 August 75 Bigbobs were in place. A week later it was leaked to the Germans that *Wadham* would be launched only if *Starkey* was a success. It was hoped that this knowledge would induce them to make an even greater effort against *Starkey* in the belief that they were killing two birds with one stone.

The motions of planning were gone through in Britain and the United States; and the Germans were told what was in the wind through a series of carefully organized leaks. These included the news that the training of American forces on the east coast of the United States and in the west of England had been stepped up; and the announcement of the name of the force commander who was visiting England to inspect American troops in the west country.

The film industry, which had helped with deception in the early days of the War, was again called in. This time it was asked to carry out one of the most ingenious and perhaps the least effective of the ploys – the making of a film called 'Invasion preparations at fever heat'. It showed United States troops undergoing amphibious training at an English base. Because of the need for speed in producing the film, two directors and six cameramen were borrowed from the United States Office of War Information. They were sent to Bude in Cornwall to make a four-minute newsreel item which would be released in Lisbon and the United States in the hope that it would reach German intelligence.

The film, which was to be completed by 15 August, had to convey the idea that the assault training of the American troops was much further advanced than it really was. This was to be done partly by including internal evidence which would suggest that it had been shot much earlier in the year – perhaps a shot of the commander's office with a calendar in the background showing a date in June, or the blending in of shots of trees not yet in leaf.[48]

Apart from the display of aircraft and gliders and dummies, intensive air reconnaissance, and the bombing of the submarine pens on the west coast of France, the main positive step to make the enemy believe that *Wadham* was genuine was a commando raid, operation *Pound*. Ten men in two motor-gunboats were to land and take a prisoner on the Island of Ushant. This was supposed to leave the Germans with the impression that their purpose was to gather intelligence about the strength of the defences in the region. *Pound* was little more successful than the *Forfar* raids in support of *Starkey*. The raiders came back empty-handed. They had made their presence felt by exchanging fire with a German strongpoint, but it was hardly enough to induce the enemy to believe that a vast combined operation was on the point of descending on Brittany.[49]

In fact, *Wadham* was so weak as to be laughable. On 9 September, the day the *Starkey* convoys made their move, Morgan sent a message to General Devers asking him to dismount *Wadham* forthwith, although the deception had been supposed to continue to the end of the month.[50] It was freely admitted that *Wadham* had failed. The enemy did not think that a large-scale operation against Brittany was being mounted, and he had not hesitated to move troops from the area. He had been fully convinced by aerial reconnaissance 'and doubtless by other sources' that the invasion of Europe was not yet due.[51]

6 THE OVERALL DECEPTION PLAN, 1944

The deception planners cannot have faced 1944, the year in which the long-awaited invasion of Europe was at last to be attempted, with much confidence. Many of their plans in the previous year had been a total failure. If the new plans made no greater impact than *Starkey*, *Tindall*, and *Wadham* had done, the prospects for Operation *Overlord* (the code-name for the Allied invasion of France) were bleak. Nevertheless, the planners set about preparing for 1944 with undiminished enthusiasm.

Their new schemes would be on an unprecedented scale. They aimed first to give the Germans the impression that major Allied attacks against the occupied countries and satellites might come almost anywhere. Then, when it became obvious, as sooner or later it must do, that preparations were being made in Britain for a cross-channel invasion, the plan was to persuade the enemy that the main assault would be against the Pas de Calais or the Belgian coast. With luck, this would cover up the fact that the Normandy beaches were the true objective. It would also be suggested that the attack would come much later than was planned, so that if the enemy guessed the true objective he might still be caught unawares. It was hoped that the widely-scattered threats would compel the Germans to dispose much of their strength in north Italy, south Germany, southeast Europe and Scandinavia, leaving northern and southern France relatively weakly defended.[1]

The Controlling Officer sketched out his first thoughts for the *Overlord* strategic deception plans in July 1943, nearly a year before D-Day. The lesson that these matters must not be rushed had finally been learned. He believed that it might be possible to achieve tactical surprise in the invasion; but he had no hope of strategic surprise. However, since part of the large naval forces involved in the cross-channel assault would assemble initially in Scottish ports, Norway would for a time remain in the enemy's mind as a possible target. Only after these ships had sailed southwards would it become apparent that France was the ultimate destination.

Bevan hoped that Operation *Starkey*, which in the middle of 1943 was still in the preparatory stage, would be regarded by the Germans as a genuine invasion attempt which the Allies had called off at the last moment because the defences in northern France were impregnable. If the Germans did believe this, they might also believe that the Allies would not risk a cross-channel invasion in 1944, when the defences would be even stronger. A more likely alternative would be the invasion of the Balkans.

On 14 July, Bevan sent his plan to General Morgan, still acting as Chief of Staff to the as yet unappointed Supreme Commander at the Supreme Headquarters, Allied Expeditionary Force (SHAEF), and in that capacity responsible for pressing on with all planning for the invasion of Europe, genuine and deceptive. He told Morgan that as soon as *Cockade* had run its course, the Chiefs of Staff would instruct him to finalize cover and deception plans for 1944, and that he wanted to get on with the job without delay. The essence of his proposals, on which he would be grateful for comments, was that threats should be mounted against all areas held by the Germans except northern France and Belgium.[2]

Morgan did not like the plan. It was the same mixture as before. In the past the enemy had been threatened with knock-out blows from several directions at once, but there had been only one single genuine assault. 'I believe that even he must be getting to know this gambit pretty well by now'; and he would certainly know it much better by the time *Cockade* was finished. He told Bevan in rather a pompous letter that he too had had a first thought – of some magnitude. The time had come to strike a new note. The Controlling Officer was proposing to follow the old line, intended to cover up Allied weakness. Now, however, the Allies had tremendous power within their grasp. Why not say so? The one thing the German feared was overwhelming force. After all:

the cause of the whole of this present bother is that the German set out to dominate the world by force. The whole of his psychology is based upon the relentless use of irresistible force. It follows that the one thing he must dread is the use of irresistible force against himself. As I have said, we are within an ace of being able to exert in actuality an irresistible power against him. Let us then for goodness sake start telling him so, and go on telling him so ... I believe that even before the blow falls we may get the Boche into such a state of jitters that it will be all over bar the shouting ... If we can put the wind up him to an adequate extent beforehand, the battle will be as good as won before it is joined ... Now, would you please have a thought on these lines?[3]

This revealed a remarkable failure to understand the theory of deception on the part of a key figure in the planning of the key operation in the whole of the War. It also revealed a failure to appreciate the German will to resist even when the War was manifestly lost – a factor which seriously worried Eisenhower towards the end of 1944 and led him to ask the Chiefs of Staff to devise deceptive or psychological plans to break the enemy's will to resist, which sheer military force was failing to do.[4]

Bevan tactfully agreed with everything Morgan said, but pointed out that his proposition was one for the Political Warfare Executive, not the deception staff. It was up to the propagandists to strike terror into the soul of the Germans, to make enemy troops and civilians believe that the Allied forces were twice as strong as they really were, so well-equipped and trained that it would be futile for the Wehrmacht to resist. They should stress the Allies' colossal resources, and the fact that they were steadily building up assault forces which in size, composition, and efficiency were unparalleled in history. He had recently said precisely this to General Dallas Brooks,

87

second-in-command of the Political Warfare Executive. If the propagandists' line was not believed, no harm.

It would be quite a different matter, however, if the deception staff tried to put across the same line. *Their* secret channels led straight to the German High Command. He thought it possible that the Germans might be fooled into believing that the Allies' strength was about 20 to 30 per cent greater than it really was; but to claim any higher figure would simply discredit them. The right deception policy for *Overlord* was to show the maximum plausible strength, and no more.[5]

Morgan's alternative plan was no doubt as foolish as Bevan suggested; but his criticism of the proposed overall deception measures seems on the face of it to be well-founded. If the Germans were to be threatened everywhere except in the one area where the attack was coming they might be expected with their long experience of Allied deception to arrive at the truth – unless they thought that the Allies were engaging in a double bluff, the deceptionist's nightmare or salvation. The real point is that while there was no hope of hiding the cross-channel invasion preparations until D-Day, there was a chance of convincing the Germans that some other part of *Festung Europa* would be attacked so that they would be inhibited from moving their scarce reserves to France.

Bevan stuck to his first thoughts, and incorporated them in his preliminary version of the overall plan (code-name *Jael*), which provided for a two-stage deception. The first would run until the moment when the enemy guessed that the main assault in 1944 must be across the Channel. In this period the objective would be to induce the Germans to make faulty dispositions. The second stage would run from that point until *Overlord* D-Day. Bevan thought that several things, quite apart from deceptive threats, would lead to faulty dispositions. The German armed forces were now fully stretched. The political and economic situations in Germany and the occupied countries were deteriorating, and might call for the maintenance of stronger garrisons. The attitude of the satellites was becoming more favourable to the Allies and might force the enemy to use additional troops to keep them under control. The Controlling Officer freely admitted that there were weaknesses in his proposals, in particular the fact that the *Overlord* preparations must be spotted from the air. He feared that the announcement of a new Supreme Commander would indicate that the centre of gravity of the Allies' strategy was shifting from the Mediterranean to north-west Europe. The continued bombing offensive against Germany would encourage the enemy to keep strong Luftwaffe forces at bases from which they would also threaten *Overlord*. Statements in the press and on the radio by prominent speakers were likely to hint at operations from the United Kingdom.[6] The War Office was even more pessimistic. It would be quite impossible to conceal the preparations on the South Coast of England. 'Any hope which there may ever have been on this point has been completely dispelled by the amount which has already been said from various platforms on this subject.' It remained only to deceive the enemy as to the exact time and place of the invasion.[7]

Bevan's draft Plan *Jael* was circulated on 8 October 1943. The final version was agreed with Morgan, who had deferred to the Controlling Officer's greater expertise, on 23 October. Bevan had assumed that the Allies would be strong enough to simulate threats against a number of places simultaneously 'on the coasts of Europe anywhere from north Norway to Gibraltar, and from Gibraltar to the Dardanelles'. The final plan was less fulsome. The Allies would simply have enough forces to threaten major operations from both the United Kingdom and the Mediterranean.[8]

While Morgan was unsuccessfully trying to teach Bevan his business, his own SHAEF planners were busy working out a tactical deception plan for the Normandy invasion, which would be fitted into the overall strategic plan. The plan, christened *Torrent*, was amateurish. It was seen at first as no more than a diversionary operation (on the lines of the ill-fated

Starkey), which would lead the Germans to think that the main assault would come somewhere to the east of the Pas de Calais; and it seems to have been tackled by Morgan's staff with rather less skill than the London Controlling Section would have deployed.

The head of SHAEF's Naval Branch confessed that when they started to plan *Torrent* he was not quite clear what was involved in a cover and deception plan. He proposed that the Allied troops should be told that there was to be a big combined operation in 1944. If practicable, it would take place in north-west Europe, 'otherwise you will all be sent to operate overseas as was done with the forces who trained in England during the winter and spring of 1942 to 1943. The foregoing is all perfectly true, and it does not help the enemy in the slightest degree.' It might have been added with perfect truth that it would not help the Allies in the slightest degree either. 'Furthermore, what we tell our own men must not only be true as far as it goes, but must seem to them to be true as well.'[9] Yet in earlier deceptive operations, for example *Solo*, it had been taken for granted that the deception of the troops could be an integral part of the total deceptive ploy.

When Dudley Clarke, the commander of 'A' Force, who was in London at this time, was asked by SHAEF to comment on *Torrent*, he was very critical. The plan did no more than say that the objective was to deceive the enemy, without disclosing how this was to be done. 'What you really want to achieve is, of course, to make him dispose his forces in such a way in which they can do least harm to your operations.' It would have made more sense to start by writing down precisely what they wanted the Germans to *do*. Another great weakness was that the plan legislated for the period after D-Day of *Overlord*. No one knew what the military situation would be then. Tactical deception should be evolved nearer the time, in the light of prevailing circumstances.[10]

Nevertheless, Morgan told the Chiefs of Staff on 8 November that *Torrent* had been completed and that it would be issued as an appendix to the genuine *Overlord* plan. He added that he assumed that they would not want to be troubled with it as it was no more than a detailed part of the Controlling Officer's Plan *Jael*, which they already had under consideration.[11] This alarmed Bevan, who had been watching Morgan's performance with a critical eye, and who had almost certainly discussed it with his professional brother, Dudley Clarke.

He at once fired his own paper at the Chiefs of Staff. He claimed that it would be unwise to approve Plan *Jael* until it was known what decisions had been taken at Churchill's meetings with Roosevelt at Cairo which ended in January 1944. Secondly, when in due course a tactical cover plan for Operation *Overlord* was prepared, there could be no question of simply adding it to the genuine plans as an appendix. In view of its importance in its own right it must be put to the Chiefs of Staff for their approval. Thirdly, he objected to Morgan's plan, as Dudley Clarke had done, on the ground that it tried to legislate for the period after D-Day. No one had the slightest idea what the position would be then, and what measures would be called for. The Chiefs of Staff agreed with all this.[12]

Morgan had to accept that *Torrent*, into which a vast amount of his planners' effort had gone, and which now became simply 'the *Overlord* cover plan',[13] would be shelved until after the Cairo meetings. Nevertheless, he asked permission to circulate the plan provisionally so that those concerned with its implementation would have time to study roughly what was required of them. This was important, because there were some measures that would be effective only if they were put in hand right away. They included occasional periods of radio silence, so that the enemy would not be able to tell which silence period was actually masking *Overlord*; the preparation of dummy camps and deceptive lighting to simulate a gradual build-up of forces in the area between Yarmouth and the Thames estuary; and a balancing concealment in the west and south-west of England, where the genuine assault forces would be mainly concentrated.[14] These things could be done without prejudice to the overall plan, and the sooner they were put in hand the better. Morgan's proposal was approved by the Chiefs of Staff on 29 November.[15]

The final touches were put to Plan *Jael* at the end of the second Cairo conference; and on 27 December the Chiefs of Staff instructed that it should be sent to Washington for the approval of the United States Chiefs of Staff.[16] They duly approved it on 18 January 1944 – with the rider that they considered it to be so ambitious that the Germans might regard it as implausible. It was their view, however, that a maximum success might be forthcoming if a considerable degree of reserve characterized its execution. Happily, their secretary translated this gobbledygook into English: 'We feel, in brief, that it could easily be overplayed.'[17]

On 25 January the Combined Chiefs of Staff affixed their somewhat academic seal of approval to Plan *Jael* – academic because it was unlikely that they, the House of Lords, would undo anything that had the blessing of the two Lower Houses – the British and United States Chiefs of Staff. Six months from the time of the Controlling Officer's first thoughts, it was at last possible for the various commanders to set about doing what was required of them in the field of deception.[18]

The new plan broadly followed the line of Bevan's original proposals. The Germans were having to keep most of their troops on the Russian front; but they had good reason to believe that the Allies would undertake a major operation in western Europe in 1944. The preparations for *Overlord*, and to a lesser degree for *Anvil* (later *Dragoon* – the Allied invasion of the south of France) would be on such a vast scale that they could not be concealed. So the aim of the plan would be simply to persuade the enemy to dispose his forces where they would cause the least trouble, both to *Overlord* and *Anvil* and on the Russian front. Secondly, tactical cover to conceal the time and place of *Overlord* and *Anvil* would have to be provided for as long as possible.

Real and feint attacks and bombing raids would keep enemy troops pinned down in northern Italy and southern Germany.

Considerable forces could be retained in the Balkans, which the enemy would hold at all costs, by persuading him that Allied troops and landing-craft were concentrating in the eastern Mediterranean. It would help if Turkey joined the Allies, but the German fear of Allied infiltration into Turkey might be enough to do the trick. Ideally, the Russians would play their part by staging an amphibious threat to the Bulgarian and Romanian Black Sea coasts; and by simulating an attack on north Norway. The German position in Norway might be further undermined if they could be convinced that the Swedes were at last co-operating with the Allies. The Allied Commander-in-Chief (General Wilson) could be left to carry out his own tactical cover plan since the build-up for *Anvil* would be less obvious than that for *Overlord*, if only because it would take place further from enemy territory. General Wilson's plans would of course have to fit in with all the other deception plans.

Many fictions would be necessary. The idea must be put across that the bomber offensive was so effective that the Allies had given priority to the reinforcement of the long-range American bomber force at the expense of ground troops. This meant that no large-scale cross-channel operation could be attempted until the late summer of 1944. Bevan's original idea that the Allies dare not attempt to invade northern France was dropped. It would cease to be credible as the concentrations of troops and landing-craft on the South Coast of England became more and more evident. Instead convincing reasons would be spread around to support the idea that the invasion could not take place until late in the year. The formidable character of the coastal defences in northern France meant that extra time would be needed to prepare the invasion forces. Shortage of men had forced the British army to resort to cannibalization – to bring weak divisions up to strength by incorporating in them units from other weak divisions which were then disbanded. The number of United States divisions arriving in Britain was smaller than was supposed, and many of them had not completed their training. There was a shortage of

93

invasion craft because of the large numbers needed in the Pacific theatre. Therefore the main Allied effort in the spring must appear to be directed against the Balkans.[19]

These fictions would be made to appear as facts, or almost, by the use of all the tools of deception developed in the course of the War, including the movement and pretended movement of troops, camouflage, dummy aircraft and landing-craft, deceptive lighting, and the rest. Genuine diplomatic approaches to neutral governments would make the enemy think that these governments were now going to side with the Allies. The Political Warfare Executive would tailor its propaganda to support the general deception policy. The London Controlling Section and its opposite number in the United States, the Joint Security Control, would implement the plans through rumours and by the leakage of information to agents.[20]

The LCS was very quickly off the mark. On 9 January 1944, a fortnight before the Combined Chiefs of Staff had approved Plan *Bodyguard*, as *Jael* had been rechristened, it discussed with the JSC ways and means of propagating the main themes.[21] The idea that the strategic bombing offensive on its own could bring about a total collapse in Germany, and that the Allies had therefore given their bomber forces priority would be fostered by Allied diplomats and Service Attachés in Lisbon, Madrid, Berne, and Stockholm.

At their cocktail and dinner parties they would say, perhaps not to go beyond these four walls, that strategic bombing was succeeding beyond all expectations, and that there was no doubt that it could win the war. The bombing offensive was kept in the mind of the German High Command by a message sent to them through a secret agent controlled by the Allies on 10 February 1944: 'Have information that some of the production difficulties and engine troubles of the B-29 have been overcome and production is still increasing but is still behind schedule.' Other double agents were used to follow this up by hinting that the Allies had pinned their faith on the heavy bombers. They also passed information about work on new aerodromes for long-range bombers, and about the arrival in Britain of reinforcements from the United States. It was leaked – and this was the truth – that runway tests had been made at Caribbean ferry airports in preparation for the despatch of bombers to Britain. All this was backed up by the London Controlling Section, which provided confirmatory 'chicken food' in neutral capitals through non-diplomatic channels.

The idea that the Allies dare not attack France until the late summer of 1944 – after the Russians had launched their summer offensive – was supported by judicious indiscretions from British diplomats in neutral countries. The LCS, as part of their service, supplied suitable readymade indiscretions to the diplomats concerned. For example:

It is certain that in view of the hazardous nature of amphibious and airborne assaults, we shall not open the second front until we are absolutely ready and have overwhelming superiority. We cannot risk failure.

I am told that at the Teheran Conference the Russians were shown details of German coastal defences in north west Europe and fully appreciated that an enormous effort would be required to overcome them. General Montgomery's appointment has been a cold douche to the optimists who were expecting the immediate opening of the second front, as his invariable rule of the deliberate building up of overwhelming force before making a move is well known.

The theme that the British army was handicapped by shortage of men was put over by passing low-grade security documents to enemy agents. This was stage-managed in Washington. The shortage of landing-craft was highlighted by arranged questions in the House of Commons which the Government refused to answer. The American and Canadian press were used to start a 'squeal' about the shortage. A strike by 3,000 workers at the General Motors diesel engine factory in Detroit gave the JSC a fact on which to base rumours that strikes in the United States were curtailing the output of landing-craft for Europe which would probably affect the date of future operations.

95

The JSC provided one particular agent with a carefully worked out programme of 'intelligence' which started with a report that he was having difficulty in getting hold of factual information about landing-craft production. Then on 20 March he said that pressure was being exerted to clear bottlenecks. On 1 April he reported that Eisenhower had made a strong protest about the number of craft being sent to the Pacific at the expense of the European theatre. On 20 April the agent found it possible to transmit some production figures which were anything but encouraging – from the Allies' point of view.[22]

This, then, was the overall plan to fool the Germans about the most critical operation of the whole war. It was broken down into subordinate plans of which the principal were: *Fortitude North*, to contain enemy forces in Scandinavia; *Fortitude South*, a threat against the Pas de Calais; *Zeppelin*, covering the eastern Mediterranean; *Ironside*, *Vendetta*, and *Ferdinand* covering the western Mediterranean.

There were three non-military deception schemes: Plan *Graffham*, a diplomatic deception in support of *Fortitude North;* *Royal Flush*, a second diplomatic deception to exploit the expected change in the attitude of neutrals to the Allied cause after the successful invasion of the continent; and *Copperhead*, the notional journey of General Montgomery to Algiers.

The purpose of *Copperhead* was to lower enemy vigilance in north-west Europe immediately before the invasion was launched. It was known that a German agent armed with field glasses watched the arrival of all aircraft at Gibraltar from a vantage point just inside the Spanish border; and that he sent immediate and detailed reports to Berlin. The story was therefore invented that a meeting had been arranged between Montgomery, Wilson, and the American General Patch, to co-ordinate operations against the south of France as a prelude to *Overlord*. An actor who resembled Montgomery was received off

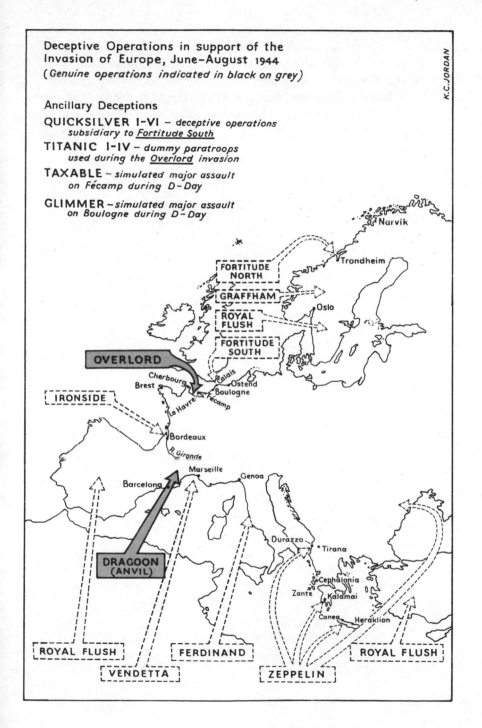

Deceptive Operations in support of the
Invasion of Europe, June–August 1944
(*Genuine operations indicated in black on grey*)

K.C. JORDAN

Ancillary Deceptions

QUICKSILVER I-VI – *deceptive operations
   subsidiary to Fortitude South*
TITANIC I-IV – *dummy paratroops
   used during the Overlord invasion*
TAXABLE – *simulated major assault
   on Fécamp during D-Day*

GLIMMER – *simulated major assault
   on Boulogne during D-Day*

Narvik

Trondheim

FORTITUDE
NORTH

GRAFFHAM

Oslo

ROYAL
FLUSH

FORTITUDE
SOUTH

OVERLORD

Calais
Cherbourg   Ostend
Brest   Boulogne
        Le Havre Fécamp

IRONSIDE

Bordeaux

R. Gironde

Marseille

Genoa

Barcelona

Durazzo
          Tirana

DRAGOON
(ANVIL)

Cephalonia
Zante   Kalamai

Canea   Heraklion

ROYAL FLUSH   FERDINAND   ROYAL FLUSH

VENDETTA   ZEPPELIN

an aircraft at Gibraltar, together with a Staff Officer and ADC, by the Governor, who took the party off to breakfast. After breakfast the fictitious Montgomery returned to the airfield and departed for Algiers, whence he was smuggled back to England.[23]

7 THE THREAT TO SCANDINAVIA

The threat to Scandinavia in 1944 (code-named *Fortitude North*),* was intended, like the other elements in Plan *Bodyguard*, to restrict the Germans' reinforcement of the Normandy assault area by inducing them to retain forces in other theatres, and to lower their vigilance in France generally. More important, it was designed to make them think that the invasion of France which they knew was coming was planned for much later than was actually the case.

So long as the Germans continued to occupy Norway, they were able to enforce the neutrality of Sweden. Equally, if the Allies succeeded in establishing themselves in Norway, they would be well placed to bring pressure to bear on the Swedes to show greater favour to the Allied cause, even if they did not actually join it. The Swedish Government might, for example, be induced to allow the Allies to establish air bases in Sweden, which would alter the balance of air power in the region. There were therefore good strategic reasons for invading Norway, and in spite of the fact that none of the earlier threats to Norway had materialized, there seemed to be every chance that the Germans would guess that this latest simulated attack was the real thing.

The timing of the threat was all-important. The sooner it could be established, the more likely it was to persuade the Germans to keep troops in Scandinavia which might otherwise

* It was originally code-named Plan *Mespot*, but the name was changed because Churchill did not like it. (WO 106 4165, 82B.)

99

have been moved to France. But because of the weather it would be implausible to mount an attack on south Norway before the beginning of April, or on north Norway before the beginning of May. Further, the deception plan would need to allow at least three months to drive the Germans out of Norway and to complete the occupation. But the genuine *Overlord* D-Day was planned for the beginning of June, only two months after the earliest plausible date for an attack on Norway. So, if the pretence that the Allies intended to attack Norway before the cross-Channel invasion was to be fully credible, the Germans must be led to believe that the genuine *Overlord* D-Day was planned for much later than the beginning of June. This could be done by encouraging them to think that the Allies would not launch a cross-Channel expedition until after the Russian summer offensive had begun. This meant early May on the southern Russian front, and late May on the northern. To allow even more time, it would be hinted that the Allies would wait until six weeks after the onset of the Russian attack, when as many German reserves as possible had been sent to the east, before making their move across the Channel.

This time-table put the notional D-Day for the cross-Channel attack forward to the middle of July, which allowed more time to carry out the supposed preparations for the invasion of Norway, although still less than was theoretically desirable.[1] If the Germans were taken in by *Fortitude North*, they might lay their plans for the defence of France on the assumption that the Allied cross-Channel attack would come six weeks later than was actually intended. They might even refrain from moving reserves from the Russian front to France in the weeks leading up to *Overlord* in spite of visible preparations on the South Coast of England.

The background story to convince the enemy that *Fortitude North* was a genuine operation was that the Allies had been holding substantial fully-trained forces in Scotland ready to move at short notice into any part of north-west Europe in the event of German withdrawal or collapse. Since there had been no sign of the hoped-for collapse, these troops would now be used to mount an operation against the Stavanger area in Norway. The operation was supposed to commence on '*Overlord* minus 30' – confirming the fiction that the invasion of France was really scheduled for some time late in July.

A month before this fictitious D-Day, British, American, and Russian troops, supported by Anglo-American naval forces, would invade north Norway to open road and rail communications with Sweden. A series of land and amphibious operations would take the Allies on to Oslo. The occupation force would be built up to six divisions, some trained for mountain warfare. When the invaders were firmly established in Norway, they would acquire air bases in Sweden either by negotiation or by force, and then go on to attack the Germans in occupied Denmark.

That was the scenario. Responsibility for executing the deception was delegated by General Eisenhower to the General Officer Commanding-in-Chief, Scottish Command, Sir Andrew Thorne, who in turn appointed Colonel R. M. Macleod to carry out the detailed stage-management. The main element in the plan was the use of fake radio signals to simulate the existence of 'the Fourth Army', which was supposedly being prepared in Scotland for a major amphibious expedition.[2]

The Fourth Army's first headquarters were in Edinburgh. Later it moved to Craigie House, Ayr. The Army itself was a blend of genuine and fictitious formations. There was the fictitious IInd British Corps, with its headquarters at Stirling, made up of the genuine 52nd and 55th British· Infantry Divisions at Dumfries, and the equally genuine 113rd British Independent Brigade at Kirkwall in the Orkney Islands; the fictitious VIIth British Corps, with headquarters at Trearne House, Beith, simulated by the genuine 52nd British Infantry Division and the 55th United States Infantry Division (the latter was supposedly in Iceland, although only one regiment was in fact there – the rest of the Division was still in the United

States); and the United States XVth Corps at Lurgan in Northern Ireland, which included the genuine 2nd, 5th, and 8th United States Infantry Divisions. Later, the non-existent 58th British Infantry Division, 'a battle-trained formation' based on Aberlour, was added to the order of battle as part of the IInd Corps;* and still later the fictitious 80th British Division made its appearance.[3]

The reader will probably find it a challenge to assimilate the blend of real and make-believe formations which went to make up the order of battle of the Fourth British Army. The German radio monitoring service faced the same difficulty; but the more complicated the order of battle the greater the challenge to the enemy intelligence experts, and the greater their satisfaction when they succeeded in piecing together the fragmentary reports which their listening posts provided.

Of course, it was not enough simply to create the main formations. The appropriate subordinate formations were equally important. For example, if there had been no sign of the Royal Army Medical Corps in the order of battle the German eavesdroppers would have certainly smelt a rat. Further, the greatest care had to be taken to ensure that the minor invented units did not actually exist. It would be fatal to the whole enterprise if a certain unit which was supposed to be part of the Fourth Army was identified by the Germans in Italy. The innumerable fictitious units created included the 303rd Anti-aircraft Regiment, 405th Road Construction Company (Royal Engineers), 55th Field Dressing Station, 87th Field Cash Office, VIIth Corps Postal Unit, and a Film and Photographic Section.[4]

Macleod's first task was to assemble enough men with the blend of experience and imagination needed to carry out the vast exchange of signals without which a genuine army could not exist. It proved difficult. When the headquarters of the

* The real IInd British Corps had been part of the British Expeditionary Force in France in 1940.

simulated army began to communicate with the outside world on 22 March, Macleod complained that he had not been able to get hold of the right people, which meant that the headquarters signals traffic was unconvincing. The position had not improved two days later when the component parts of the army began to talk to each other. The officer who had been assigned the job of organizing inter-formation signals relating to purely administrative business had not even put in an appearance. If the Germans heard nothing about the bread-and-butter aspects of running an army they would guess that it was a sham. To make matters worse, SHAEF had several times altered the plans, which meant that Macleod's limited staff wasted precious time rewriting their scripts. So great were the difficulties that Macleod proposed the deception be limited to a single corps. SHAEF did not agree. A whole army would be needed in a genuine assault on Scandinavia, so a whole army there must be.[5]

There were problems too with the genuine formations borrowed to give some substance to the fake army, which failed to grasp the significance of their role and the great importance which the Allied High Command attached to it. For example, the 55th British Division agreed to co-operate in the Fourth Army simulation only insofar as it did not interfere with its own training programme. Macleod had to appeal to the War Office to instruct the Division to give absolute priority to his requirements.[6]

The notional plan of campaign was that the VIIth Corps should invade north Norway, and the IInd and XVth Corps south Norway. The impression would be given that the assault forces were ready to sail from the Clyde at the beginning of May. The follow-up troops were supposed to leave from Invergordon, Rosyth, the Mersey, and Belfast. The 55th United States Division would be carried to Norway in ships brought from the United States. It was originally intended to base part of the imaginary army at Scapa Flow, which would have been a logical starting-point for the invasion of Norway, but this was ruled out because the Germans carried out routine reconnaissance of the Orkney and Shetland Islands. If they were to find out that the forces supposedly being prepared to attack Scandinavia were but a figment of radio deception, then the fat would be in the fire.[7] Perhaps this danger could have been met by organizing a visual display at Scapa Flow, but there were no ships or landing-craft to spare. In any case, the visual misdirection in Operation *Tindall* had been costly and ineffective. However, there was a small display of real and dummy aircraft at Peterhead, Fraserburgh, and Fordoun – about five squadrons in all, Bostons and Spitfires. To give them added realism dummy petrol-tankers and vehicles were parked on the dispersal areas, and empty petrol cans and other litter scattered around. The display attracted some attention from enemy reconnaissance and may have contributed a little to the overall success of the deception.[8]

Since the greater part of *Fortitude North* was to be implemented by false radio traffic, the usual mounting plan, which paid as much attention to detail as did a genuine operational plan, was considered to be unnecessary. Allied control of German agents was now so tight that there was little need to substantiate the existence of a fictitious division simulated by means of corroborative signs on the ground – vehicles bearing the divisional emblem and the rest. The danger of 'unauthorized' reports – from an agent *not* controlled by the Allies – could now be discounted.

The radio deceivers were assured of a captive audience, unlike those who mounted visual displays. The Germans could not afford not to listen to military radio traffic in Britain. Whether they believed what they heard was another matter.

If the notional outline plan for *Fortitude North* was simple, the arrangements to establish the fake radio links that supported it were not. The radio plan, which was given the code-name *Skye*, had to enable the simulated component parts of the Fourth

Army – scattered over Scotland, Northern Ireland, and Iceland – to communicate with each other on the scale which a genuine expedition would have required. The signals carried by the networks of 21st Army Group (at this time preparing for the genuine invasion of France) were studied so that the Fourth Army would know roughly what level of traffic they should aim at within Scotland. (Operation *Skye* was not required to establish links with Northern Ireland and Iceland, to establish the part supposedly played by the 55th United States Infantry Division. That was taken care of by SHAEF itself.)

The technique for transmitting simulated signals traffic was highly sophisticated. Normal practice was to send messages in high or medium-grade cipher, but there was always the danger that a message would be deciphered by the enemy. It followed that all messages, except those which were obviously being used for the purpose of training operators, should be plausible from the military point of view. If the German cryptanalysts came up with 'Little Jack Horner sat in a corner', or something of the sort, the whole of the *Skye* fiction would be blown. However, it would be going too far to try to keep up a series of logically-connected messages during the whole of such an extensive simulated operation. That would mean recruiting a vast staff to encipher and decipher every message passed. Nevertheless, it had to be arranged that all messages had at least a reasonable link with the type of activity being simulated, so that if the enemy did break the cipher the message would appear to be concerned with some activity related to a genuine operation. Questions asked on behalf of the 87th Field Cash Office must have something to do with pay and allowances, while those from the 55th Field Dressing Station must be related to the supply of drugs and medicines, or something of the sort. Pure nonsense was ruled out not only because the enemy might succeed in reading it, but also because it had been found in practice that it could lead to unintentional repetition, which the enemy experts would spot. While there was no need for individual exchanges to make sense in themselves, it had the advantage that it was 'somewhat less boring for the officers concerned'. Extracts from published matter were on no account to be used, as it was on the cards that the enemy had access to the original material, which would make it easier for him to break the cipher.[9]

It was necessary to explain away all the activities involved in *Skye*. For example, it took 8 officers and 24 radio-operators to simulate a divisional amphibious exercise, and a good many people would inevitably want to know what they were up to. So the story was put out that those involved in *Skye* were working on a series of large-scale training exercises in different parts of Scotland, which was plausible, as Macleod had in the past been concerned with genuine training exercises. The radio operators were specially warned about the need for security. They were told quite openly that they were taking part in an operation intended to deceive the enemy, and that the performance of each individual had a bearing on the success of *Skye* as a whole. The enemy listened to every message passed on the air and knew quite well that there was the possibility that he was being taken for a ride. Security therefore had to be perfect. A single careless mistake in operation, or careless talk with those who were not in on the secret, could give away the whole deception.[10]

Typical activities designed to deceive the enemy are illustrated by the programme of the 52nd Division. First, the Division maintained a five-day period of radio silence from 7 April. This was followed by an assault brigade signals exercise (12 April); an assault brigade amphibious exercise (15 April); radio silence (17 April); another two assault brigade amphibious exercises (20 and 24 April); radio silence (27 April–4 May); and finally a divisional amphibious exercise (10 May). On other dates normal transmissions would, of course, be kept going. If the Germans monitored this programme day by day, they would deduce that the 52nd Division was gradually being brought up to a peak of readiness for an assault – that is, if they did not guess that the whole programme was a hoax.[11] Similar activities were attributed to all the other many formations making up the Fourth Army; the whole required a gigantic volume of fictitious radio signalling.

There is evidence of this huge effort in a detailed record of the activities of the Fourth Army during its 'life' of just over a year – from 15 March 1944, when the first elements reported to Colonel Macleod in Edinburgh, to 31 March 1945, when all the radio transmitters finally closed down and the army was ordered to 'disband'. This 'War Diary' faithfully records the non-movements of the largely non-existent component parts of the fictitious army. For example: 'March 21 – detachment representing VIIth Corps moved to Dundee'; the innumerable exercises simulated by radio: 'April 12 – 55th Division exercise: five-day exercise'; the eventual movement of a large part of the army to England to support *Fortitude South*; the opening on 26 July of the radio link between it and the First United States Army Group (FUSAG), of which it had become a part; the establishment of a new headquarters at Hatfield Peverel on 5 September, and then in Kilnwick Percy Hall at Pocklington in Yorkshire on 14 October; and thereafter a further series of simulated exercises.[12]

The biggest single phoney exercise planned by the Fourth Army was *Cadboll*, a battle-training exercise supposedly involving the 55th and 58th Infantry Divisions, which was due to run from 3–7 June 1944. It was designed with the usual meticulous attention to detail. The signals units representing the two divisions were briefed to report to headquarters – and to the listening Germans – every supposed move. The plans covered many pages, but the following is a fragment of the 55th Division's pretended movements on 5 June:

0400 hours: Barrage comes down on Hagshaw Hill.
0500 hours: Attack on Hagshaw Hill goes in. 9th South Lancashires supported by 863rd Field Regiment. Hill held by 6th Highland Light Infantry.

0700 hours: Hagshaw Hill captured, but unable advance further. Consolidating. Intend reinforce 9th South Lancashires.

0900–1100 hours: 155th Brigade put in counter-attack on Hagshaw Hill, using 5th King's Own Scottish Borderers, supported by 80th Field Regiment. 164th Brigade driven off after bitter fighting. Heavy casualties. Brigade now reorganized on line of road running north and south through Douglas.

and so on until every hour of the four days was accounted for.[13]

Cadboll was typical of the many Fourth Army exercises carried out across the length and breadth of Scotland, unseen by the natives but closely watched by the enemy – except in one respect. It was doomed never to take place. The day before it was due to start, the IInd Corps, comprising the 55th and 58th Divisions, was suddenly ordered by SHAEF to come under the command of 21st Army Group, so that the threat against the Pas de Calais from the south-east of England would apparently be strengthened. The phoney divisions were to abandon all exercises and move to the Grantham area on 3 and 4 June, where they would remain until further notified by 21st Army Group, probably a week or so later. Then they would sever all connection with the Fourth Army.[14] The suddenness of this move upset Macleod, who had not been consulted. He at once pointed out to SHAEF that their precipitate action had made the forces under his command do things which were highly suspicious, indeed impossible. For example, the headquarters of the IInd Corps closed down at Stirling on 5 June and opened up again at Louth on the same day; but the two places were 350 miles apart and a genuine corps would have taken a week to complete the move. Therefore the advance elements should have had their marching orders on 29 May, and a warning order four or five days before that. The Fourth Army had been given no information about the pending move and there had been no chance to issue the orders. SHAEF had been foolish enough to whisk the IInd Corps from Scotland to England as if by magic – and the Germans would hardly be deceived by the trick. The move exposed further technical weaknesses of the same nature. The 55th Division appeared to have completed a move of 300 miles in a single day, because the same radio sets and operators (which could be identified by the enemy – operators were no less identifiable than fingerprints) were used to simulate it in both Dumfries and in Lincolnshire. The Germans might have spotted this discrepancy. Macleod was admirably restrained in his comments on SHAEF's action, which had put the whole of Operation *Skye* at risk. He said that the Fourth Army had been quite prepared to move anywhere at any time, but 'I think we might have been able to help more in making the picture as realistic as possible if we had known sooner what was going to happen.'[15]

This was a major flaw in the deceptive programme, but there were from time to time minor hitches which might also have given the game away. In a simulated 58th Division exercise in the mountains, for which signals had been pre-recorded on gramophone records during a genuine exercise at Catterick, there were tell-tale clicks every time a record was switched on and off; and the radio telephone conversations were marred by background noises which might have aroused the enemy's suspicions. Again, an exercise carried out by 52nd Division – *Carrot I* – was considered to be too good to be true. It would have been more convincing if a few deliberate mistakes had been inserted.[16]

Though *Fortitude North* depended very largely on radio deception, there were other elements. One of these was a visit by Sir Andrew Thorne to Northern Ireland to watch an exercise carried by the XVth United States Corps. His visit was not to be specially publicized – that might have seemed to be gilding the lily – but it was hoped that it would be observed and reported to the enemy.[17]

The Royal Navy tried to make a contribution. The Commander-in-Chief, Home Fleet, proposed that the deception should be supported by a series of raids in the Narvik area, simulating the sort of activity that would take place on the eve of a genuine assault. A reconnaissance was carried out on 26

April, but it made little impact because of bad weather. The weather also led to the abandonment of an operation to bombard Narvik. Aerial attacks on the battleship *Tirpitz*, bottled up in Norwegian waters, fitted in well with the *Fortitude* deception. Finally, the Admiralty co-operated with the Ministry of War Transport in arranging for spare shipping to assemble at Methil in the Firth of Forth, to suggest that a convoy was being put together. The average number of ships at Methil increased from 26 in the first week of April to 71 in the second week of May.[18]

The Navy, which would have been required to carry the assault forces to Norway if the operation had been genuine, also co-operated in the radio deception. Two separate naval forces were simulated in the Clyde – Force 'V' and Force 'W', which were supposed to transport the genuine 52nd and fake 58th Divisions respectively. The former went into radio action on 12 April in such a way as to suggest that it consisted of at least 38 ships. It was supposedly carrying out training for a long sea voyage, with an assault force destined for a fjord area. The latter consisted of 35 notional ships, with which it conducted embarkation and disembarkation exercises; for example, *Onion II*, a simulated landing near Gareloch or Ardrishaig. Force 'V' was also involved in a full-scale divisional exercise (*Leek II*) on 10 May, which purported to be in the Loch Fyne area. Uncoded radio messages left no doubt that a sea loch was involved.[19]

The first phase of *Fortitude North* was rounded off when General Eisenhower wrote to the Secretary of State for War saying that the threat to Norway which had been maintained by Scottish Command had greatly assisted the Normandy landings, and that he was most appreciative of the whole-hearted support which General Thorne and his staff had given SHAEF.[20]

The precipitate move of the non-existent IInd Corps from Scotland to East Anglia greatly diminished the Allied threat to

Scandinavia. The enemy discovered that the Fourth Army signals, which he had been picking up principally from Scotland, were now also coming from England. He was likely to conclude that for all practical purposes the northern threat had vanished; and that there was now nothing to stop him from moving troops from Norway and Denmark to the battle zone in France. A new deceptive plan, *Fortitude North II*, was devised to prevent this.

The planners went back to the original idea that troops were being held in readiness to fill any vacuum left by the collapse or withdrawal of the German occupation forces. The three *Rankin* plans had legislated for variations on this theme – rather optimistically, as it turned out, since the Germans showed no sign of collapsing anywhere; and for the purposes of the deceptive threat, it was now put out that since the Allied forces were firmly established in Normandy, there was no longer any need to risk an opposed invasion of Norway. For this reason the highly-trained Fourth Army and its associated air forces were supposed to have moved south, to take part in the assault on the Pas de Calais – still supposedly the Allies' main effort against Europe.

However, Eisenhower considered it necessary for political and for military reasons to occupy Norway as soon as there was any hint of a German withdrawal; and therefore something rather more powerful than the *Rankin* plan was devised. Sir Andrew Thorne was given three divisions and the appropriate number of landing-craft based in or near the Clyde, ready to carry out the occupation of Norway at short notice.[21]

Given the nature of the new pretended enterprise there was no longer any need for elaborate radio simulation of a major assault – for the purposes of the deception it was assumed that the arrival of the Allied forces in Norway would be virtually unopposed. The Admiralty did play its part, however, by simulating radio signals suggesting that naval forces capable of lifting three divisions were standing by; and the Air Ministry continued intensive reconnaissance of the Norwegian coast.

More important than both of these was the contribution made by the London Controlling Section, which used diplomatic channels and the double agents to put across the authorized version of *Fortitude North II*.[22]

It was one thing to persuade the enemy that the Fourth Army comprised many thousands of real men, and quite another to explain to troops and civilians what the handful of men simulating the army were doing. So in September 1944 the 28 officers and 334 other ranks who were the Fourth Army were designated 'No 12 Reserve Unit'. This gave them a name vague enough to mean anything, which could be used openly without arousing interest or suspicion. So far as the enemy were concerned, of course, No 12 Reserve Unit continued to *be* the Fourth Army.[23]

The fictitious army provided useful experience for the United States cover and deception staff. At first, the Americans concerned with *Fortitude North* were by their own admission sceptical about its value. It was only when they were allowed to know how the double agents were being used to put across deception plans, and when they realized that for some time the Germans had included fictitious formations in their estimates of the British order of battle, that they began to accept that there was more in deception than met the eye – when it was perhaps rather late in the day.[24]

There is no doubt that the threat to Scandinavia was taken seriously by the Germans and that it had an effect on their dispositions. At the beginning of March there were 18 divisions in Scandinavia, 12 in Norway, and 6 in Denmark. Before *Fortitude North* came into play the number of divisions in Denmark had been reduced to 5, but soon after the Fourth Army came on the air the German High Command decided that there was a real possibility of an invasion of Scandinavia.

Their forces were put in a state of readiness at the beginning of May, the effect of which was to halt the further depletion of their garrisons in Norway and Denmark, and thus to restrict the reinforcement of northern France from these countries. Then, in the middle of May, an additional first-class division was sent to Norway, and 4 of the garrison divisions there were upgraded to combat divisions – little more than a change of nomenclature of the German High Command. The most that could be spared for Denmark was a three-regiment division.[25]

According to the German High Command's assessment, the Allied forces in Scotland which had been threatening Scandinavia were weakened by the movement of formations to the south in the middle of May – a fortnight before the notional move actually took place. It was decided that the troops in Scotland would now be capable of only limited operations against Norway and Denmark – but the possibility of an attack remained.[26]

It therefore seems certain – at least as certain as it is possible to be in this realm of make-believe – that *Fortitude North* achieved its purpose and made a substantial contribution to the success of the Allied invasion of Europe.

8 RUSSIAN CHARADE

In December 1941, the first Controlling Officer, Colonel Stanley, had suggested using deception to help the Russians. The Allies had not as yet formulated a broad strategic plan to which worldwide deception could be related, so there was always the danger that local deception would cut across the eventual broad strategic plan. However, since no real operation was contemplated against south Norway, Stanley thought it would be safe enough to mount a deceptive threat against Narvik or Trondheim, in order to divert to Norway German forces which might otherwise be employed against the Russians. He was authorized to go ahead, so long as his activities did not extend north of Trondheim, as there was a possibility of a genuine British operation in that area.[1]

The following year, Stanley thought that the Russians might be encouraged to use deception to help themselves. He considered that in the Black Sea they had everything needed for a perfect deception plan, based on the idea of a seaborne operation against the Danube delta. If it came off, it might appreciably weaken the expected German offensive in the Ukraine that spring. Stanley also had in mind the simulated movement of British troops, and in particular air forces, to Iraq and Persia, the story being that they were en route for the Caucasus to relieve the Russians.[2]

The Foreign Office told the Chiefs of Staff that there was no guarantee the Russians would pay the slightest attention to these plans; but the Foreign Secretary might have a chance of mentioning them to Maisky, the Soviet Ambassador. There is

Pill-boxes disguised as:

an ice-cream kiosk on the beach at Felixstowe;

a haystack near the Folkestone–Ashford road;

a motor car.

A hangar big enough to house two aircraft, supposedly camouflaged as a gamekeeper's cottage.

An oil fire, fed by the storage tanks on the left. The purpose of these fires was to protect nearby airfields and factories. The fires would be lit during enemy bombing raids: the idea was that the Germans would then think they had scored a hit and continue to waste their bombs in the immediate area of the fires.

A 'satellite' airfield: thirty-eight aircraft are
effectively concealed in this picture. A and B mark
the positions of the camouflaged runways.

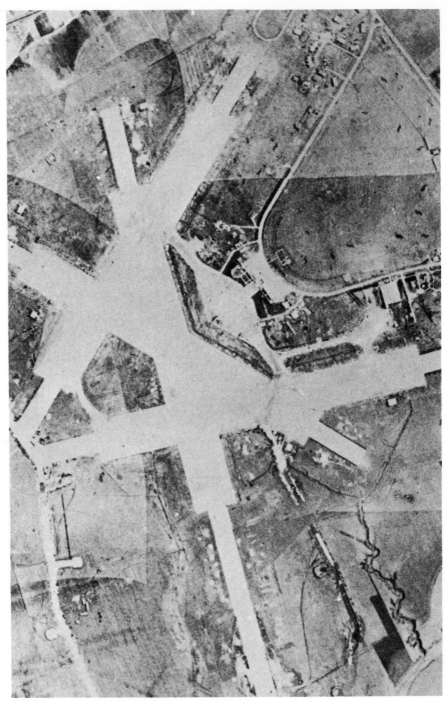

Aerial view of Lydda (Palestine)
airfield before camouflage.

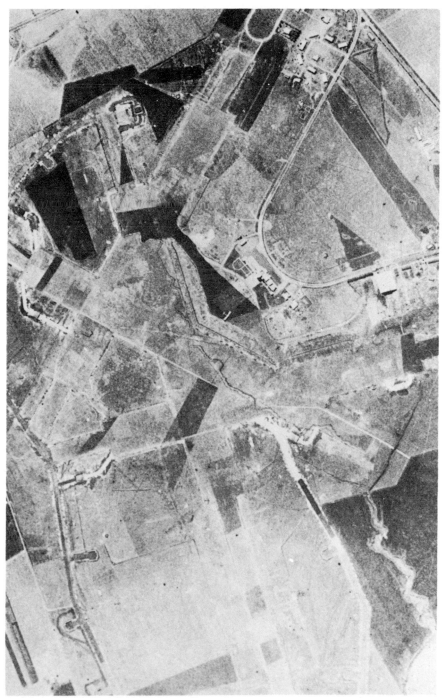

Aerial view of Lydda airfield after camouflage: The runways have been painted and the aprons ploughed to blend in with the surrounding countryside.

Dummy aircraft:

a very lifelike dummy Tomahawk fighter;

the kit from which the above was assembled;

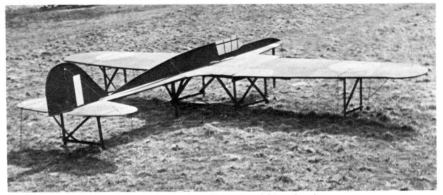

a flat dummy Spitfire. This appeared three-dimensional from the air.

Dummy airfield and camp at Forres in Scotland.
This was set up as part of Operation *Tindall*,
the deceptive threat against Norway in 1943.

A mobile dummy Sherman tank built on a metal framework over a Jeep.

Jeep and framework for dummy tank
without painted canvas 'body'.

Inflatable dummy 3-ton truck.

Dummy landing-craft (tank), or 'Bigbobs'. These full-size dummies
were 160 feet long, and could be erected and launched in six hours.

American inflatable dummy plane. Based on the United States Army co-operation aircraft, the dummy had a wing-span of 33 feet, and could be inflated in fourteen minutes.

American inflatable dummy armoured car. This model, which was 15 feet long, was inflated on its side and only then turned upright.

British dummy 25-pounder gun and limber. Made at Tobruk,
it was wooden and mounted on real wheels.

American inflatable dummy anti-tank gun. If this device
was not properly inflated the barrel tended to sag.

Dummy Crusader tank in the North African desert.
This model was used in the Capuzzo railhead deception.

Real Crusader tank hidden under a dummy lorry, or 'Sunshield'. These were used extensively to deceive the Germans about the build-up of tanks during the Battle of El Alamein.

Dummy truck, or 'Cannibal', used to conceal a gun and limber:

the gun without the covering;

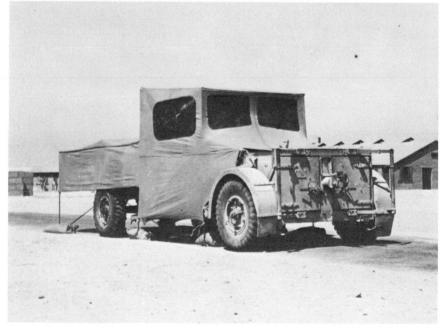

the covering in place. The wheels of the gun and limber were
arranged to look like the wheels of the phoney truck.

Half-size dummy train and railway lines used
in the Capuzzo railhead deception.

Dummy soldier at one of the fake pumping-stations on the *Diamond* dummy
pipeline. *Diamond* was one of the schemes used to deceive the Germans as to
the likely place of the British attack at the Battle of El Alamein.

Two examples of 'double deception':

a stores dump is arranged to look like a camouflaged lorry;

dummy lighters are partially hidden by camouflaged netting.
The Germans could not be expected to take dummies seriously unless they
were camouflaged like the genuine article.

no record that Eden did so; but in May 1943, the boot was on the other foot. Maisky suggested to Eden that the Allies could delay the German offensive in the East by organizing feint operations in a number of places. On this occasion the London Controlling Section told the Foreign Secretary that everything possible was already being done in the field of deception, and Eden left the matter there.[3]

Thus there was little in the earlier relationship with the Russians to suggest that there might one day be a fruitful partnership in a deceptive enterprise; but it was agreed at the Teheran conference that if *Bodyguard* was to have the best chance of success, the Russians, who were geographically well-situated to develop deceptive threats against both Norway and the Balkans, must be brought in.[4] After *Bodyguard* was approved, Bevan and his American colleague, Lt. Col. Baumer, prepared to go to Moscow, in order to explain the detailed proposals to the Russian general staff, to consider any modifications they might want to suggest, and to enlist their co-operation in implementing the plans.[5]

It was considered that the military mission in Moscow would be unable to provide the deception experts with all the introductions they would need; and the Embassy was instructed to take special steps to ensure that Bevan and Baumer were given access to the appropriate officers and officials. This may seem strange. It suggests that the military mission had not established the right contacts; or perhaps that deception was a second-class subject in the eyes of the Russians. In fact it took a long time for the visiting deceptionists to make any contact at all. On 3 February, four days after their arrival in Moscow, Bevan sent a telegram to London: 'I have not yet met the Russian representatives, but am living in hope.' There was a preliminary discussion on 7 February, and the first substantive meeting took place on 10 February, when the Russians expressed general agreement with the strategic objectives of *Bodyguard*.[6] The second, and indeed the only other formal meeting, was four days later. Discussion centered round three points: the notional timing for deceptive purposes of both the Russian summer offensive and the Allied invasion of Europe, Russian co-operation in the deceptive threat to Scandinavia, and the nature of the threat to the Balkans.

After the Cairo and Teheran conferences there had been worldwide speculation about the date of the final Russian and Allied offensives, and it had been generally assumed in the press that the two attacks would be launched simultaneously. *Bodyguard*, however, postulated different dates. It was to be pretended that the Russians would make their move at the end of June, and the Allies in the late summer. In both cases the real attack would come much earlier.

The Russians argued that press speculation had made different dates implausible. They therefore preferred early July for both notional assaults. This argument suggests that the Russians had not begun to understand deception as it was practised by their western Allies. There was no need to be influenced one way or the other by newspaper speculation. Rather it should be used as a smokescreen in deception planning. Bevan and Baumer, however, were so anxious to get their agreement that they recommended the proposed change, 'which would give the Russians much pleasure', be accepted without further discussion.[7]

The Allied Chiefs of Staff saw no objection to the change. They considered that it would fit in perfectly well with the tactical *Overlord* deception plan being worked out by SHAEF (*Torrent*), and with *Zeppelin*, the cover plan for the eastern Mediterranean, both of which were geared to a notional D-Day for *Overlord* of 15 July. Moreover, they were touched by the Russians' gratifying willingness to co-operate, and they instructed Bevan to agree simultaneous dates without further discussion.[8]

The proposals for a deceptive threat against Scandinavia presented little difficulty. The Russians said that the only plausible objective for them was Petsamo. Bevan believed they were genuinely afraid that the concentration of shipping needed to lend colour to a simulated assault on Petsamo would lead the Germans to bomb Murmansk; but they were nevertheless prepared to accept this part of *Bodyguard* as it stood.[9]

The main problem was how to deal with Bulgaria, which was at war with Britain and the United States, but not with Russia. The recent deterioration of Allied relations with Turkey made an Allied threat on Greece based on Turkish collaboration less plausible. However, the Joint Intelligence Staff considered that the threat of Russian action in or against Bulgaria would prevent the Germans from moving any of their forces out of the Balkans; and if Bulgaria abandoned the Germans' cause the enemy would probably have to send reinforcements to the area – which would of course help *Overlord*.

The Allies' Balkans threat envisaged a simulated amphibious operation against the Bulgarian or Romanian Black Sea coast. However, the Russians had no wish to threaten Bulgaria, arguing that such a move would not be plausible until they had recaptured the Crimea. On the other hand, they *were* prepared to mount a threat against the Romanian Coast. This upset Wingate, Bevan's deputy, and Dudley Clarke, who was in London at the time to co-ordinate the Mediterranean deception plans with those of SHAEF. Wingate pointed out to the Chiefs of Staff that the threat to Bulgaria was an integral part of the Mediterranean deception plan, and had been approved by Wilson, the Supreme Allied Commander in the Mediterranean. It was the corner-stone of Plan *Zeppelin*.[10]

The commander of 'A' Force elaborated his misgivings to Wingate, who passed them on to Bevan in a personal telegram. He said that a threat to the Romanian coast implied an opposed landing, which could never be plausible in the absence of landing-craft and the impossibility of providing fighter cover. On the other hand, an unopposed landing in Bulgaria was quite plausible. There would be no need for either landing-craft or fighter cover. The threat of a Russian attack on Bulgaria would support the story of Allied pressure on Turkey. Moreover, a successful threat to Bulgaria would lead to additional dispersal of German forces in the region, since genuine Russian pressure towards the river Dniester would tend to contain German troops in Romania.[11]

The notional date in Plan *Zeppelin* for the threat to Bulgaria was 20 May. Wingate considered that there was no need for the Russians to take overt action much before then; and if at that time they still felt that there were military objections to a threat against Bulgaria, there would be no difficulty in substituting Romania.[12]

But the Russians were adamant. They would not accept that the threat would ever be plausible, in spite of the arguments put forward by Dudley Clarke, who had more experience of deception than anyone else. Plan *Zeppelin* suggested leaking the story that Bulgaria had asked Russia for military aid, but the Russians vetoed this because they said it would undermine their anti-Bulgarian propaganda.

Bevan suspected that their real reason for preferring to threaten Romania was that they were hoping to get the Anglo-American bomber forces to intensify attacks on the Romanian oil-fields at Ploesti and Constantza.[13]

Eventually the Chiefs of Staff surrendered to Russian pressure and authorized Bevan to drop the threat against Bulgaria, warning him at the same time not to hold out any hopes about bombing the Romanian oil-fields.[14] If the Russians were not prepared to help there was no reason why the Allies should go out of their way to help *them*. However, the Foreign Office thought the Chiefs of Staff had been too hasty. Major-General Sir Hastings Ismay, Military Deputy Secretary to the War Cabinet, told Bevan that he was at liberty to continue to try and get the Russians to agree to threaten Bulgaria, even though the Chiefs of Staff did not feel strongly enough to risk a breakdown when so much had been achieved.[15] In fact, virtually nothing had been achieved.

The Foreign Secretary entered the fray at this point. He told Sir Archibald Clark Kerr, the Ambassador in Moscow, that the

Russians were refusing to co-operate in any deception plans for political reasons. The Allies attached great importance to the Bulgarian aspect of *Bodyguard*, and he was anxious that the Russians should be pressed further. He appreciated that the Russians were not at war with Bulgaria and that they had a special interest in that country; but the fact that Britain had a special position *vis à vis* Turkey had not prevented her from agreeing to use her position to try to meet Russia's wish that Turkey should enter the war. It was particularly disagreeable to find the Russians taking up an uncooperative attitude in a matter of such vital importance as the deception plan for *Overlord*. Britain would be placed in a false and humiliating position if she refrained from pressing the Russians to turn the heat on Bulgaria merely because it might run counter to their present propaganda. If the Controlling Officer wanted to pursue the matter, the Ambassador should make it quite clear to the Russians that their attitude was deprecated in London.[16]

The Russians did not help things by failing to turn up for subsequent meetings with the British and American representatives. When Bevan complained, it was explained that the delay was caused by the absence of Stalin at the front. It was essential to consult him before the negotiation could be taken any further.[17] When the Ambassador, accompanied by the American Counsellor, called at the Foreign Ministry to try to find out what was happening, they were assured that, in spite of all that had been said, the Bulgarian threat had not been rejected. It was still under consideration by the highest military authorities, and the official who received the Ambassador said *he* thought the Bulgarian deception made sense. A decision was promised as soon as possible.[18]

Bevan was nonplussed by the way the discussions were being conducted. His own explanation of the delays was that the representatives they had met at the beginning were too junior (which suggests that the Embassy had failed to find the right contacts in spite of the Foreign Office's request), and he guessed that the proposals were now being considered behind the scenes on a much higher level.[19] On 29 February, he sent another plaintive telegram to London: 'Have had no meeting since 14 February. However, now that Stalin is back from the front am hoping for a decision soon.'[20] The same day he and Baumer had a short informal interview with the Russians, the first for a fortnight. They were assured that the deception plans were still under consideration, and that a decision was expected shortly, although it could not be said what it would be. Bevan took the opportunity to say yet again that the western Allies regarded the threat to Bulgaria as crucial.[21]

On 3 March he sent another report to London. There was still no hard news, but Molotov had told the Ambassador that a decision was imminent. The next day, the Russians simply announced that they had officially approved the whole of the *Bodyguard* plan as it had been handed to them by Bevan when he arrived in Moscow. A protocol was signed on 6 March in which the three Governments agreed that the overall deception scheme should come into effect forthwith. As Bevan recorded bitterly, this meant that all the many exchanges between Moscow, London, and Washington, the argument about the pretended dates of the Russian and Allied offensives and the relative merits of the threats to Bulgaria and Romania, had been a waste of time.[22] With the benefit of hindsight it seemed that there had been no need for his visit – the Embassy could probably have done all that was necessary.

This sudden somersault by the Russians may be explained in various ways, in the absence of documentary evidence on the Russian side. It is possible that, after studying *Bodyguard* in detail, and discussing it at length at the highest level, they saw the light and decided that they must go along with every sentence in it, in spite of the fact that, so far as Bulgaria was concerned, it cut right across their accepted policy.

Alternatively, they may have decided – again after high-level examination – that their contribution to the *Bodyguard* plan would have little effect in the long run, and that the simplest thing was to agree to the plan lock, stock, and barrel, with the firm intention of doing nothing about implementing it. There is no real documentary evidence to support this cynical view, but subsequent events tended to lend colour to it.

The day after they had announced their comprehensive acceptance of *Bodyguard*, Bevan had a discussion with the Russian representatives. They now seemed to realize that there was a need for an immediate threat to the Balkans, especially Bulgaria and Romania, and they agreed that the threat should be supported by diplomatic and military activities, and by propaganda. However, they could give him no details of what they proposed to do, and they enlarged on the great difficulty of organizing deceptive activities in the Black Sea. Bevan, ever the optimist, suggested that they should call an early meeting of representatives of the three powers to discuss what could be done. In a later telegram he reported that the Russians had agreed that Dudley Clarke and 'A' Force were free to implement their intentions in the Balkans if a good opportunity presented itself; but since the Russians had not yet prepared any deceptive plans this did not amount to much.[23]

The Russians' inertia was now exchanged for great activity – or so it seemed. General Burrows of the British military mission in Moscow was told by General Slaven, the principal Russian actor in the earlier part of the transaction, that they urgently wanted maps, charts, and aerial photographs of the coasts of Norway and Finland, so that they could carry out raids there. When Burrows replied that this was a tall order, in view of the length of the Scandinavian coastlines, and suggested they specify the exact areas where they intended to operate, he was told that the Russians knew very little of the region, and that they would decide where to attack in the light of the information supplied. Burrows took the request at face value, and in passing it on to the War Office reminded them that this was the first time that the Russians had asked for operational help. He suggested that an officer should bring the material, either by

Catalina flying boat to north Russia, or by Mosquito to Moscow.[24]

As a result, a comprehensive dossier was prepared, including charts, maps, aerial photographs, information about beaches, and a list of the best targets in the assessment of Combined Operations Headquarters.[25] On 1 May the Joint Planning Staff recommended that it should be taken to Moscow by a suitably-briefed officer who would be accompanied by an expert in the interpretation of aerial photographs. It was assumed that the Russians were entering into the spirit of the thing and that they must be given every possible encouragement. The Foreign Office agreed. The Ambassador, however, should ask the Russians to make it clear to the Norwegians that the forthcoming raids on their territory were not a preliminary to permanent occupation.[25] Burrows asked for an urgent interview with Slaven to pass on the good news, but he was kept cooling his heels for a whole day – 'which indicates normal dilatoriness of Soviet general staff in receiving me even when matter is of urgent operational importance'.[26]

The dossier was ready for despatch four days later, a Flight Lieutenant was standing by to carry it, and a Mosquito from No. 8 Group had been fitted with long-range petrol-tanks to take them to Russia. Then a signal came in from Burrows. The Soviet general staff did not consider the matter urgent enough to justify a special flight. It would be enough to send the documents by the ordinary route. When it was pointed out that this would take three weeks, the Russians remained unmoved. They simply said they had no further instructions.

Burrows apologized for asking London to take emergency action. He said: 'I think that the whole affair provides an excellent example of horror with which Soviet general staff face admission of superfluous foreigners and above all foreign specialists to this country.' He had asked the Ambassador, who was seeing Molotov that evening, to complain about the dilatoriness of the Russians.[27]

Finally, on 11 May, Burrows reported to London that he had

got to the bottom of the matter. Slaven had overplayed his hand, and was shocked when he learned what had been done as a result of his request. There was no need to send a staff officer. There was certainly no need to send an expert to interpret the photographs. It would be quite enough to hand the dossier to the Soviet Military Attaché in Teheran. Burrows told him that London would not allow the documents to leave British custody, and 'to test his sincerity' suggested that a limited selection of the less technical material might be sent. 'Slaven immediately jumped at the idea ... I am now all the more convinced that Soviet general staff is out to get information and does not intend to carry out raids.' He again apologized for the false alarm.[28]

The transaction ended when a bundle of very general and in some cases out-of-date material was despatched to Moscow. Intelligence based on reports from British agents in Norway, which would certainly have been placed at the disposal of a thoroughly-trusted ally, was carefully weeded out.[29]

Nevertheless, the Chiefs of Staff continued to accept that the Russians were playing a useful part in deception strategy. A summary prepared by the Joint Staff Mission on 17 May recorded that they were co-operating keenly. The Russians had been taking full advantage of their strong position to implement threats against Norway, and to put pressure on Sweden. In fact, the Russian pressure on Sweden, which was part of Plan *Graffham*, amounted to nothing more than one or two visits by their Minister in Stockholm to the Swedish Foreign Ministry.[30]

In his account of the negotiations with the Russians, General John R. Deane, the head of the American military mission in Moscow, gives them credit for implementing the *Bodyguard* plans, but he is merely repeating what he was told in very general terms by the Soviet General Staff.[31] There is no sign in the British documents that the Russians ever carried out any deceptive threats along the lines implied by their discussions with Bevan. In fact the London Controlling Section's attempt to bring the Russians into *Bodyguard* seems to have been no more than an exercise in self-deception.

9 DIPLOMATIC DECEPTIONS

GRAFFHAM

The original Plan *Jael* assumed that the Germans would become increasingly apprehensive about closer co-operation between the Allies and the neutral countries. Sweden, Spain, and Turkey had so far been content to sit on the fence, but now that the Germans seemed unlikely to win the war these three neutrals might begin to help the Allies, in the hope of deriving some benefit post-war.

It was therefore proposed to have diplomatic negotiations with the three, to lead the Germans to think that new hostile alliances were in the offing which would increase the threat to their positions far removed from the *Overlord* assault area.[1]

The Foreign Secretary had suggested in November 1943 that it might be worthwhile asking the Swedes for operational facilities. He thought they would be prepared to go a long way towards meeting the Allies' wishes, provided they were not driven to give the Germans a *casus belli*. They were already allowing refugees from Norway to have weapons and to engage in military training as a 'police force'. Eden, was in fact more concerned with pleasing the Russians than striking a blow at the Germans: Molotov had been disappointed by Britain's negative attitude towards the acquisition of air bases in Sweden 'and it would be well to make some positive proposals'.[2]

Plan *Graffham*, however, was *not* designed to make the Germans think that Sweden was about to join the Allied cause. It was much more devious. The intention was to induce the Swedish Government, and through them the German High Command,

125

to think that the Allies were mounting a campaign against Norway. The Swedes would be faced with a number of demands which lent colour to the idea that Norway was about to be attacked, details of which would almost certainly be leaked to the Germans.

It took some time to decide what these demands should be, but finally the following were listed:

(a) the right to refuel aircraft which had made emergency land-ings in Sweden after operating over enemy territory;

(b) facilities for minor repairs to these aircraft;

(c) the right for Allied civil aircraft to land on Swedish military airfields;

(d) the passage to Britain of Norwegian troops who had escaped to Sweden [this was quickly dropped, since on reflection it was deemed to be inappropriate for the purposes of *Graffham*];

(e) permission to send an expert to consult the Swedes about transport between Norway and Sweden in the event of a German withdrawal from the former; and finally

(f) that Allied reconnaissance aircraft should be allowed to oper-ate over Sweden.[3]

Some of these concessions – the four relating to aircraft – would be welcome in themselves, although the Foreign Office did not hold out much hope that any of them would be granted. Nevertheless, they believed that a show of determination might pay a surprising dividend. The other demands were admitted to be 'pure *Graffham*': they were made simply for the purpose of effect, and the Allies had no other interest in them.

The Swedes would probably assume that the requests for air facilities were to enable Allied aircraft operating over Germany which had been damaged and forced down in Sweden to return to Britain. This in itself might be of marginal help, but the real point (which it was hoped the Swedes would take) was that the concessions would be of enormous help if Allied aircraft were based in Norway. The Allies' interest in Swedish railway trans-port was also supposed to imply that their forces were soon to be established in Norway.[4]

There had been three earlier deceptive threats to Scandinavia, and the Controlling Officer felt that this time something out of the ordinary was called for. This was a diplomatic deception, the plan for which was approved by the Chiefs of Staff on 10 February.[5]

Sir Victor Mallet, the British Minister in Stockholm, visited London at the beginning of March, which fitted in well with the deceptive plan. It was arranged that he should tackle the Swedes as soon as he got back, thus leaving them with the impression that he had been recalled for consultation about the demands. He suggested that the negotiations might be prolonged by spreading the individual requests over a period; and that he should start with those which did not imply a flagrant breach of neutrality, and which the Swedes were therefore less likely to reject out of hand. The two requests deemed to be less difficult from the Swedish point of view were to receive a transport expert, and to allow Allied reconnaissance aircraft to operate over the Swedish–Norwegian border. The more difficult requests were held over to the middle of April.[6]

It was pointed out to Mallet that since the demands would be leaked secretly to Germany it would not be essential to prolong the discussions with the Swedes; but nevertheless the longer the talks went on the better for the deceptive effect. Even if the demands were rejected out of hand and the Swedes told the Germans what had happened, Mallet should keep up the deception by paying frequent visits to the Foreign Ministry 'on no matter what business', and encourage his United States and Soviet colleagues to do the same.[7]

The *Graffham* deception was very much a team effort, in which the British, United States, and Soviet Ministers played their part. The British contribution was the most extensive. It involved the Minister himself, the Service Attachés, a transport expert who was brought to Stockholm, a fake Air Vice Marshal, an artificial increase in radio traffic between the Legation and London, and finally the successful rigging of the Swedish stock market.

The Minister's task was almost impossible, since he was required to attain two conflicting objectives. On the one hand, the aim of the *Graffham* plan was to give the Germans the impression that the Allies were about to invade Norway, so that they would hesitate to move troops from Scandinavia to Normandy. This meant putting pressure on the Swedish Government. The conflicting objective had nothing to do with *Graffham*. As far as possible, Mallet was to deny supplies of Swedish ball-bearings to the Germans and to ensure supplies to the Allies, in view of their great importance for aircraft production. This meant keeping on friendly terms with the Swedes, which would be difficult if *Graffham* looked like forcing them to abandon their neutrality, the keystone of their policy since the beginning of the war.[8]

The Special Operations Executive was asked to study the possibility of solving the ball-bearing problem by means of sabotage, which was not a very sensible idea. There were bottlenecks in the ball-bearing factories and it would have been relatively simple to reduce output through a few judicious explosions; but the idea was quickly rejected. It would be obvious who had caused the explosions, and the Swedes would then be more likely to sever diplomatic relations with the Allies than to accord them special facilities. Further, if the supply of ball-bearings was drastically reduced, the Allies might have cut off their nose to spite their face. So sabotage was out.[9]

On 8 March the State Department told Herschel Johnson, the American Minister in Stockholm, about the facilities that were to be requested, saying that if he consulted his British colleague he 'would learn something interesting'. Mallet was still in England and Johnson hesitated to ask the Chargé what this cryptic observation meant. Instead he replied to the State Department that the facilities requested seemed to be of such great importance that he suggested they take precedence over representations he was due to make about the supply of Swedish ball-bearings to the Germans. He did not realize that he was suggesting that genuine representations should take second place to a hoax, and on 13 March he was instructed to lodge the ball-bearing protest without further delay. No doubt Johnson was puzzled by the fact that the State Department seemed to have got its priorities upside down.[10]

As soon as Mallet returned to Stockholm, he went into action. He called on Erik Boheman, the Secretary-General to the Ministry of Foreign Affairs, to put forward the requests about the transport expert and reconnaissance aircraft. Thus began a bout of diplomatic fencing which was to carry on for weeks. During this period the Swedish authorities must have become heartily sick of the three-pronged assault by the British, Americans, and Russians – especially if they guessed the Allies' real purpose.

The Secretary-General, perhaps with tongue in cheek, said he was puzzled by the Allies' interest in Swedish railways. If they had in mind the re-opening of trade with Norway after the Germans had left, the existing railway system was perfectly well able to cope. Or were they seeking to use Swedish lines of communication in an operation against south Norway, or perhaps Denmark? If Denmark *was* the objective, it could be taken without Swedish help. He asked Mallet to get the Foreign Office to elaborate what they had in mind. As for using Swedish air space for reconnaissance, the answer would almost certainly be an unequivocal 'No'. In reply, Mallet argued that since all the Allies wanted to do was to photograph German positions on the Norwegian border there would be only minimal violation of Swedish air space; but Boheman pointed out that they would photograph Sweden's own defences at the same time. No government could agree to *that*. Still, he would put the request to his Minister. He concluded by hinting that the Allied aircraft would run little risk of being shot down if they went ahead with their reconnaissance. (This did not help *Graffham*. What was wanted was co-operation which would be obvious to the Germans, not unidentifiable connivance.)[11]

Mallet put Johnson and the Soviet Minister, Madame

Kollontay, fully in the picture. In reporting his meeting with Mallet, Johnson said they had decided that the 'particularly interesting aspect of the question to which the Secretary of State had referred' (i.e. that *Graffham* was a hoax) should not be put in writing or mentioned in any communication. The British Minister had told him that he had presented an *aide memoire* in which the British Government sought permission to send a transport expert to discuss with the Swedish authorities the transport problems that might follow a German withdrawal from Norway. This would cover route capacities, the supply of coal and diesel fuel, and the condition of rolling stock and locomotives. Mallet had also asked for permission to carry out photographic reconnaissance.

Thus briefed, Johnson called on Boheman on 5 April, and solemnly went over the same ground, with the same result. The Secretary-General repeated that he did not understand the Allies' interest in Swedish transport, and that it was preposterous to expect Sweden to agree to violation of her air space – especially when it was well-known that it was already happening. The Soviet representations were added next day through their Counsellor, who pursued the Secretary-General to a country house some distance from Stockholm. No doubt Boheman's puzzlement was further increased.[12]

On 6 April Mallet called on the Swedish Minister of Foreign Affairs, Christian Gunther, ostensibly to renew contact after his absence in London, but knowing full well that the Allied demands would be discussed. The Minister at once tried to draw him. Perhaps the Russians were going to attack north Norway from the Finnish side, while the British and Americans landed from the sea? If so, the operation would have to be carried out before the spring thaw. The transport expert would probably be most interested in communications between Narvik and Haparanda? Mallet said he had no idea what was planned – which must have seemed a strange admission. British envoys were supposed to know what His Majesty's Government had in mind. No doubt the expert would enlighten the Swedish authorities when he arrived. Gunther, having failed to solve the mystery, said there would be no objection to the visit.[13]

On the same day Bevan received a message from Mallet, who was anxious that the reconnaissance of the Norwegian/Swedish border (which Boheman suspected was already happening) should start at once – if it had not already started. The fact that the Allies were taking the law into their own hands would strengthen the impression that, whatever was behind *Graffham*, it was deadly serious.[14]

Johnson saw the Foreign Minister on the evening of 5 April and repeated what he had said to Boheman; and the Minister reacted just as the Secretary-General had done. He was puzzled why the Allies should want a transport expert to come to Sweden, but there was no objection in principle. The answer about the reconnaissance aircraft, which was a curious request, must be no. It was out of the question that Swedish anti-aircraft gunners should be instructed not to fire on belligerent aircraft flying over Swedish territory.[15]

The British and American Ministers kept up the pressure by calling together on the Secretary-General on 6 April, supposedly to discuss matters unconnected with *Graffham*. Boheman took the opportunity to tell them formally that the answer to the aerial reconnaissance request was no. If such a request was granted, it would mean the end of Swedish neutrality and not a single member of their parliament would agree to that. He again hinted that there was nothing to stop the Allies getting all the aerial photographs they wanted. If their aircraft were spotted they would be given the benefit of a few warning shots. It would have been much more sensible not to have asked for permission. However, the Swedish Government would not object to the transport expert's visit, though it would be a pity if he made the long journey only to find that the Swedish authorities were unwilling to discuss most of the subjects on his list. So again he wanted more background on the visit.

The American Minister reported to Washington that the

Allied requests had upset the Swedes. He believed that the further demands which were due to be made – the right to refuel aircraft which had made emergency landings on Swedish territory, and facilities for minor repairs – would certainly upset them a good deal more, and might lead to serious misunderstandings. On his part, Mallet was suggesting to the Foreign Office that they should think again about these further demands.[16]

While these exchanges were taking place (and, it was hoped, being observed by the Germans in Stockholm), the radio traffic between the British Legation and the Foreign Office had been artificially increased. The Germans monitored this traffic, and although they were unable to read the messages – because of the use of one-time pads – they could still deduce something from the volume and nature of the signals. A Royal Navy signals expert was sent to Stockholm to organize the increase in traffic, which was achieved partly by sending many dummy messages, and partly by reporting at great length every discussion with officers of the Ministry of Foreign Affairs. The Military and Air Attachés played their part in this game, but the Naval Attaché, whose reports in the ordinary course of events were few and far between, was not required to increase them. Instead, he was inundated by fake messages from the Admiralty. Air Commodore Thornton, who had come to Stockholm to support Mallet on the technical aspects of the requests for aircraft facilities, and to encourage the Swedish air staff to believe that Norway was about to be invaded, also made his contribution; but he feared that his studied verbosity would be deprecated by the Air Ministry, and he sent a special request that the reasons should be explained to them.[17]

Thornton had been given the fictitious rank of Air Vice Marshal for the purposes of *Graffham*, and had been almost smuggled into Sweden. He had obtained a diplomatic visa on the ground that he was going to inspect the Air Attaché's office – in spite of the fact that the Air Attaché, who would normally be present during such an inspection, had suddenly been recalled to London – but as soon as he arrived in Sweden it became obvious that he had other fish to fry. He spent his time meeting senior Swedish air force officers, who were intrigued by the presence of such a senior British officer, and he had little difficulty in leaving the impression that there was more to his visit than met the eye. He found an ally in the Commander-in-Chief of the Swedish air force, General Nordenskiold, who was satisfied that the Allies intended to invade Norway. Mallet told the Foreign Office that Thornton had proved to be a trump card. He remained in Sweden until 29 April, but when he left he let it be known that he would be coming back in the middle of June – by which time great events would be taking place in Norway.[18]

The transport expert, Brigadier Manton, arrived at the end of April and played his part skilfully. He had several discussions with the management of Swedish National Railways, when he duly enquired about the state of the track, rolling stock, and locomotives. He had been instructed to make no commitment of any kind without reference to the Foreign Office; but in fact his talks were purely exploratory.[19] They raised no problems for anyone – except possibly for the United States Minister. Although Johnson was well aware that a British transport expert was due to visit Sweden, and indeed had made representations on his behalf, he sent a telegram to the Secretary of State on 31 May which disclaimed all knowledge of these facts. He said he had just been informed by Mallet that a British transport expert had been in Stockholm for three weeks. He had not met him, nor had there been any effort on the part of the expert or the British Minister to arrange a meeting. Mallet had told him that Manton had confined his contacts to transportation officials and that he had gathered useful information. 'Mallet has also given me rather sketchy information from voluminous exchanges of telegrams between himself and London on the subject matter of this series. He did not offer to let me see the messages but I gather that the British consider the purposes of his mission to have been partly fulfilled. I suppose that the Department is kept fully informed from British quarters in London of various suggestions and counter-suggestions which have passed between Mallet and the British Foreign Office.'

It is difficult to know what to make of this. It was clearly in the interests of *Graffham* that the transport expert should be seen to have the support of the United States Mission in Stockholm, yet Mallet seems to have regarded him as private British property. This is curious. Even more curious is the American Minister's disclaimer that he had any prior knowledge of the transport expert's visit, when he had been personally informed of it by his Secretary of State and had made representations about it to the Swedish Foreign Ministry. It looks as if he was being kept at arm's length by Mallet and that his *amour propre* was not unreasonably upset.

The longer *Graffham* went on, the more difficult it became to reconcile it with the ball-bearing problem. Mallet felt that the Swedes' reaction to the first of the *Graffham* demands had been so unsatisfactory that it might do more harm than good to proceed with the others. The threat of an Allied attack on Norway might be established at the cost of a serious breach of relations with Sweden, which might reduce the supply of ball-bearings to the Allies. On the other hand, Major Derrick Morley of the London Controlling Section, who had gone to Stockholm to help stage-manage *Graffham*, was more concerned with the effect on the deception if the Swedes were confronted with further and stiffer demands. It would strike a note of unreality, and *Graffham* would suffer as a result. In any case, he thought the first demands, helped by the other elements in the deception, were producing the right effect. There may have been some wishful thinking in this. It was not unusual for the deceptionists to decide that whatever happened to their plans was all for the best.[20]

Both Mallet and Morley began to favour a drastic change in

policy. Morley told Bevan that it could be more profitable to stop trying to frighten the Swedes with stiff demands, and instead to offer to sell them a dozen Spitfires, without asking for a *quid pro quo*. It would worry the Germans – but only if the aircraft were actually sent. Promises would not be enough. Bevan should get the Foreign Office to persuade the Air Ministry that Plan *Graffham* was worth a dozen Spitfires. Mallet went still further and suggested offering as many as two hundred.[21] This idea had already been floated by the Air Ministry themselves at the beginning of March, when they had suggested that the best way to convince the Germans that the Allies intended to carry out military operations in Scandinavia would be to offer the Swedes fighter aircraft, which they badly wanted, and aviation spirit. This would probably lead the enemy to believe that Sweden had secretly offered something in return.[22]

But this idea was a non-starter. The Foreign Office told Mallet that whether or not it would be a good idea to sweeten the Swedes with an offer of fighter aircraft was now beside the point. The United States Secretary of State had made it very plain in a speech on 9 April that the United States Government intended to take a tough line with the neutrals in general, and with Sweden in particular. Therefore there was no question of offering a sop in the form of Spitfires or aviation spirit: rather it would be necessary to put a pistol to the head of the Swedish Government in the matter of ball-bearings and iron ore.[23]

In the event it was decided not to press the other demands. Mallet and Morley both continued to press for a few Spitfires without *quid pro quo* 'for *Graffham* account', but the American Secretary of State had spoken – and that was that.[24]

An unusual element in the *Graffham* deception was the rigging of the Stockholm stock-market to bring about a rise in the price of Norwegian securities, which would imply that the liberation of Norway was imminent. This idea was first considered by the London Controlling Section in January 1944. The Treasury were not too enthusiastic at first, but they had not rejected the ploy out of hand, for it was known to British intelligence that their German opposite numbers watched the stock-markets. When the idea was put to the Treasury again for the purposes of *Graffham*, they agreed to provide the funds needed for the manipulation.

It was first intended to carry out the rigging in London, but the relevant bonds were not quoted in the principal British financial papers. A suggestion that they should suddenly be included in *The Times* (which would have been much too obvious) was rejected. It was decided on reflection – and after consultation with a leading merchant banker who held a senior position in the Special Operations Executive – that it would be more sensible to manipulate the market in Sweden. Suitably heavy purchases were made in London on the Stockholm stock-market. The results were very satisfactory. Of the ten issues attacked, six went up, one showed no change, and three went down. The sudden movement would have been enough to catch the eye of the Germans in Stockholm – if in fact they were watching the market. The principal increases were in the Oslo City 1937 loan, and the Norwegian *Kommunalbank* (1935), both of which rose in the week between 9 and 15 May by just under twenty per cent.[25]

Graffham was kept going in a half-hearted way until the middle of June, partly by pressing the Swedish air force for particulars of their secret airfields, and partly by the three Allied Ministers' seeking an assurance that the Swedes would resist a German invasion following the notional Allied occupation of Norway. The main effort to keep the threat alive was carried on outside Sweden, however. It included increased naval activity against the Norwegian coast, possible Russian raids in north Norway (Bevan apparently continued to hope that the Russians would help, in spite of the discouraging news from Burrows in Moscow), and further leakage through the double agents about the supposed preparations in Scotland.[26]

It was accepted at the time that Plan *Graffham* produced no dramatic results, although it did have some effect. Mallet collected some pointers in a round-up telegram in the middle of April. The Soviet Legation had found out that Swedish intelligence believed there was a plan to fly Norwegians from Sweden to Britain, so that they could take part in the 'forthcoming' Allied attack on Norway. The wife of the Swedish Minister of Foreign Affairs had told a friend that her husband believed the impending Allied attack would be on a grand scale, and would include Norway and Denmark. A Swedish intelligence officer had informed the British Naval Attaché that German diplomats in Stockholm thought Thornton's visit was in connection with the American Flying Fortresses which had force-landed in Sweden. There was a rumour in Swedish social circles that Thornton had come to Sweden to arrange for the reception of British squadrons in the event of an emergency. It was certain that this rumour would reach German ears.[27]

There was other evidence that *Graffham* had made its mark. The Swedish Minister to Denmark, who was in Stockholm on leave, told Mallet that the Germans expected the Allies to invade Denmark round about 30 April, when the moon was full. He added that the Swedish Government also regarded this as the likely date. The British Legation Press Attaché, who was not in the know about *Graffham*, reported that there was gossip in Swedish journalistic and junior military circles that the Allies intended to invade Norway. It was being said that the interruption of air services between Sweden and Britain was due to the large concentration of troops in Scotland.[28]

It is impossible to say what the effect of all this was on the Germans. They cannot have failed to observe the gyrations of the three Allied Ministers, the visits of Thornton and Manton, and the increase in signals traffic between Stockholm and London. The war diary of the German High Command records that there were signs of a possible Allied attack on Denmark and Sweden, but concludes that it was probably no more than a diversion.[29] This may have discouraged them from moving troops from Norway to France; but in fact it is more likely that they were already so stretched in all theatres that only sheer military necessity would make them move large formations.

Mallet feared that the whole *Graffham* plan might be blown after Thornton's return to London, when he lost his fictitious promotion to Air Vice Marshal; and he asked the Air Ministry to allow Thornton to retain the higher rank for the duration of *Graffham*. His letter reached the Air Ministry some little time after Thornton had returned to London, and had already run the risk of being seen in uniform by his contacts in the Swedish Legation. The Director of Plans was unsympathetic. He wrote: '... if it was part of the requirement that Thornton should have retained his rank and remained mysteriously in London, it is somewhat late in the day to think of that now.' The fault, if any, did not lie with the Air Staff – a fact which must be placed on record. If it was essential that Thornton should visit London, and perhaps be spotted by his Swedish friends, he could come in mufti – when he would be indistinguishable from an air marshal.[30]

There was another loose end, which illustrates the risks which the deceptionists ran. The Air Ministry Pay Branch, which was of course unaware of Thornton's supposed promotion, refused to sanction his claim for expenses at the Air Vice Marshal rate – until a member of the Air Staff came to his rescue.[31]

ROYAL FLUSH

Royal Flush was a plan to support the earlier *Bodyguard* threats against the south coast of France, the Balkans, and Scandinavia, by taking advantage of the changed military and political situation after the successful invasion of Europe. It was believed that when the neutral countries saw that the Allies had gained a firm foothold in France, the most important of them – Spain, Turkey, and Sweden – would decide that they had little to fear from German reprisals. They might even help the Allies by some 'unneutral action'.[32] So in March 1944, while the principal deception officer was busy in Moscow being deceived by the Russians, his deputy Wingate put forward ideas for using Sweden, Spain, and Turkey to make the Germans think there were certain courses which the Allies would *not* follow. For example, there could be negotiations about restricting the supply to Germany of iron ore from Sweden, wolfram from Spain, and chrome from Turkey. The enemy would not expect the Allies to try to stop Spain from sending wolfram to Germany if they were about to invade France, which would have cut off Spanish overland exports to the Reich anyway. Therefore pressure on Spain to halt wolfram supplies to the Nazis would lead them to believe that the invasion of France was not imminent.

Such is the versatility of the deceptionist that the neutrals could equally well be used to put across the opposite idea – that there were enterprises to which the Allies were committed. For example, a demand that Spain should provide air bases would imply an attack on the south of France; and in fact this ploy was later included in Plan *Vendetta*.

Wingate's ideas provided the basis of Plan *Royal Flush*, drafted by the Controlling Officer on his return from Moscow. He rather allowed his pen to run away with him, which was perhaps forgiveable. Deception plans were fiction, and even a member of the War Cabinet Office occasionally had to be given his literary head. The entire world, and in particular the enslaved countries, had been waiting for years for liberation from the Nazi yoke. When D-Day came, Europe would be in a ferment. Communications in the occupied territories would be interrupted, rumours would be rife, confusion widespread. New hope would be kindled among the forces of the resistance. Neutrals might then allow transit facilities, which could greatly increase the threats to the south of France, the Balkans, and Scandinavia. The movement of even token forces could change the picture overnight. To this end it was decided to make a diplomatic approach to the principal neutrals about four days after the Normandy landings.[33]

This elaborate exploitation of the machinery of diplomacy

did not meet with universal approval among Bevan's colleagues; and it was felt that his picture of a Europe rallying to the Allied cause after D-Day was too optimistic. Nevertheless, the Chiefs of Staff approved *Royal Flush* insofar as it applied to Spain and Sweden. The plan was blessed by the United States Chiefs of Staff on 25 May, and General Eisenhower and General Wilson were asked to consider the implications it would have for their own cover and deception plans in northern Europe and the Mediterranean area respectively.[34]

(a) Spain

In 1943, the Chiefs of Staff had weighed the pros and cons of invading Spain, which some thought would provide an easier return to Europe than a cross-channel expedition. Alternatively, the Germans might somehow be induced to invade Spain, enabling the Allies to come to her rescue and thus gain a foothold in Europe without all the hazards of an amphibious attack. Thirdly, it might be possible to engineer a revolution to restore the Spanish monarchy, which would probably be more favourable to the Allies than Franco's regime. However, even if the Allies had succeeded in invading Spain they might have been held at the Pyrenees. In the end all these ideas were dropped.[35]

Nevertheless, the mere fact that they had been considered suggested to the Controlling Officer that a simulated invasion of Spain was plausible. He proposed that immediately before the Normandy landings the Spanish Government should be asked to allow the evacuation of casualties from a supposed invasion of the south of France, and the sending of food through Barcelona. When the Allies were established in Normandy they should demand the right to send troops through Spain and to operate aircraft from bases in the north-east of the country. Leaflets should be dropped urging the Spanish Government to co-operate in these plans.[36]

The Joint Planning Staff thought this was going too far. There was a difference between an approach to a neutral country merely to assist in a deception plan, and one crucial to the plan's success. For example, there was no danger in a request to evacuate wounded. If it was refused, it was (in theory) too bad on the wounded, but the plan would not be ruined. If, however, the Spanish turned down a request for the passage of troops, the plan would be seen to have failed and the deception would evaporate. Further, the dropping of leaflets was bound to antagonize the Spanish Government. A deceptive threat implying military action within Spain was therefore abandoned.[37]

Instead, the Spanish would be asked for facilities indicating an Allied seaborne invasion of the south of France – for example, permission for the evacuation of casualties and the supply of food through Spain. The British Ambassador in Spain, Sir Samuel Hoare, came to London to be briefed in person – a move which helped to build up the deceptive threat. It was left up to him to explain to his American opposite number, Mr Carlton Hayes, the purpose of the requests they were to make of the Spanish authorities.[38] The State Department had instructed Hayes to leave the Spanish Government in no doubt about the importance which the Allies attached to their requests. Without waiting for a reply he was to arrange for enquiries to be made in Barcelona. Until Hoare put him in the picture Hayes had no idea that he was engaged in a deception.[39]

Hayes put forward the Allies' requests on 3 June, just before the Normandy landings. The Spanish Foreign Minister, Count Jordana, told Hayes that he fully accepted the urgency of the matter. He could not give an immediate answer, but he undertook to consult General Franco. The Allied requests, which might have to be discussed in Cabinet, would of course be kept secret. When Hoare saw Jordana on 5 June, he was promised a favourable reply shortly.[40]

Meanwhile the British Consul-General and his American colleague in Barcelona had called on the Civil Governor and put similar requests to him, laying stress on their confidential nature. They reported that 'Governor Corre assured them of the amplitude of port and warehouse facilities and of his desire to assist in this humanitarian project.' Although the hospitals were under the control of the military authorities, he was sure that 2,000 beds could be provided. He showed no surprise at the diplomats' visit, which suggests that he had already been told by Madrid what was in the wind.[41]

On 19 June Count Jordana told Hayes that the Allies' requests had been discussed with Franco. They would be granted, but only after the military action had begun. Spain was anxious to provide humanitarian facilities, but she must also preserve her neutrality. It would therefore be left to the Spanish Red Cross to look after the Allied casualties from France. Food sent through Spain would be reserved for civilians, and distributed through the Spanish Consuls in France, or the International Red Cross.

The Spanish element in *Royal Flush* was rounded off in the middle of July when the British and American Consuls-General told the authorities in Barcelona that the success of the Normandy campaign made Spain's help unnecessary.[42]

(b) Turkey

Bevan hoped that Turkey could be used to contain enemy forces in the Balkans. He proposed that Plan *Hardihood*, which in 1943 had envisaged substantial military aid to Turkey, should be revived, and that a military mission should be sent to the country. Then, 4 days after D-Day, the British, American, and Soviet Ambassadors should demand immediate facilities for Allied aircraft to operate from Turkish bases, and for troops and supplies to move through Turkey to the Bulgarian frontier. He reckoned that this would discourage the Germans from weakening their forces in the Aegean and southern Greece.[43]

However, the Air Ministry was against reopening the *Hardihood* negotiations, which they thought would simply lead to further endless argument with the Turks. It would be better for the British Ambassador to drop a few ominous hints and follow them with an outright demand for co-operation. The Joint

Planning Staff feared that Bevan's proposals might land the Allies with unacceptable commitments, but they did agree that it might be worthwhile sending a mission with instructions to spin out their discussions as long as possible. 'If we can get a mission into the country with lots of brass hats and gold braid, the Turks and the Germans will really feel there is something in the wind.'[44] But the Foreign Secretary decided that to send a mission to Turkey would humiliate Britain and weaken her standing *vis-à-vis* the Turks. Even a trickle of military supplies would be hailed by the Turks as a triumph for their policy of non-cooperation and positive proof that Turkey was indispensable to the Allies. It would make more sense to keep up economic pressure on the Turks, which the Germans believed was an attempt to force them into the War on the Allied side. The idea of sending a military mission was therefore abandoned. The Allies would rely on the Germans' existing apprehensions about possible threats from Turkey to keep powerful enemy garrisons pinned down in the Balkans.[45]

(c) Sweden

So far as Sweden was concerned *Royal Flush* was a continuation of Plan *Graffham*: the objective was still to contain enemy forces in Norway and Denmark.

Immediately after D-Day, the Allied Ministers in Stockholm would demand assurances from the Swedish Government that they would resist German violation of their territory. If these assurances were forthcoming, the Swedes would be invited to agree to staff talks. The Germans were well aware that the Swedes had given way to Allied pressure to reduce exports of iron ore and ball-bearings to them, and they could not disregard the possibility that if *Overlord* went well they would be much more willing to help the Allies.[46]

On 5 June Mallet was instructed to join with his United States and Russian colleagues in making oral representations to the Swedish Government. They were asked to make their approach to the Swedes sometime between 7 and 11 June. On 9

June Mallet asked the Swedish Foreign Minister for an assurance that a German attack would be resisted, which was given without hesitation. The next step, however – that the Allies should ask for staff talks – was abandoned. The Joint Planners' scepticism about the Controlling Officer's assessment of the position after D-Day had proved to be justified. Neutral reaction to the invasion had at first been favourable, but it had cooled rapidly. There was no sign that *Overlord's* success would lead the Swedes to depart from their position of strict neutrality.[47]

At this point a divergence between the British and American attitude to Sweden's relationship with the Nazis endangered the deception plans. The Americans wanted to take a much tougher line with the Swedes, and threaten sanctions if they did not break off economic relations with Germany. These would include the freezing of Swedish balances in the United States, the black-listing of all Swedish firms trading with Germany, and even the cutting off of the 'basic rations' which the Allies allowed into Sweden.[48] This worried the British Chiefs of Staff, who commented: 'In our view the formal and official expression of these threats would have the worst possible effect on Sweden. It has been our experience during the past two years that while it is possible to obtain substantial concessions from the Swedish Government, a great deal depends on the way in which our requirements are sought. The Swedes have invariably reacted badly to a full-dress demand, particularly if coupled with threats.'[49] If the Americans went ahead with their threats the deception plan would be wrecked. Its objective was to contain German troops in Norway and Denmark by indicating Allied landings there. If the landings were genuine, the Allies would be able to control Sweden's economic policies. Therefore *Royal Flush* would be undermined if an issue were made of Sweden's economic contacts with Germany. Moreover, the Swedes were now helping the Allies by discouraging their ships from visiting German ports.[50]

These arguments induced the State Department to drop the

idea of sanctions; but the point very soon became academic. The Germans were so short of men on the real operational fronts that they could not avoid thinning out their forces in the other areas, including Scandinavia and the Balkans. It was decided that *Bodyguard* had run its course, and that henceforth it would be left to General Eisenhower and General Wilson to prepare deception plans to cover their immediate operational requirements.[51]

The Swedes had the last word on *Royal Flush*, and on the Allies' attempt to exploit them. Mallet reported from Stockholm that they 'particularly resent the idea of our foreign policy being dictated by the United States Government, who until they became victims of aggression at Pearl Harbor ostentatiously clung to theoretical neutrality'. The Swedes now claimed that in practice they were adapting their neutrality to help the Allies every bit as much as the Americans had done before Pearl Harbor.[52]

10 THE EASTERN MEDITERRANEAN

The aim of Plan *Zeppelin* was to prevent the transfer of enemy troops from the eastern Mediterranean to northern France in time to oppose the Allied landings in Normandy. This would be done by mounting threats against Greece, the Dalmatian coast, the Bulgarian/Romanian coast (by the Russians), the Aegean Islands (using Turkish aerodromes with or without Turkish consent), and eventually by a threatened advance into Istria by the Allied Armies in Italy. The Allies' strength in the Mediterranean was to be exaggerated. This had already been done with remarkable success through Plan *Cascade* in 1943, which had led the Germans to believe that the Allied armies contained many more divisions than they actually did.

Zeppelin was executed in four stages, which were evolved by 'A' Force after the most painstaking efforts to divine the enemy's appreciation of future Allied strategy. To convince the Germans that the Balkans were to be attacked on three fronts, certain preliminary steps were essential. The Russians must have regained the Crimea; and the British must have entered Turkey. However, the British could land on the west coast of Greece, on the Dalmatian coast, and on Crete with very little preparation. So these objectives were to be threatened first, and the Black Sea coast and the Greek mainland left for later threats. The deceptive plan would have to reach a climax in the middle of March if enemy forces were to be kept away from Normandy during the crucial period, but it would also have to be kept going after that, to prevent the Germans from correcting their faulty dispositions. This would be done by including two notional changes in the plan, to explain away the fact that the assault had not taken place on the due date.

A further element in the highly-complicated reasoning process was 'A' Force's assumption that the Normandy landings would take place during a full moon period – which in fact it did. It would be helpful if *Zeppelin* could be used to fool the enemy into thinking that the Allies preferred to carry out amphibious operations on dark nights. This meant that *Zeppelin* would have to begin in the middle of March, when there would be no full moon.

The time-table suggested by this reasoning was as follows:

Stage 1: attack Crete and/or western Greece and the Dalmatian coast on 23 March. Further attacks on Greek mainland, and Russian attack in the Black Sea on 21 April;

Stage 2: attacks on Crete, western Greece, and Dalmatian coast postponed to 21 April. Black Sea assault and attack on Greek mainland postponed to 21 May;

Stage 3: attacks on Crete, western Greece, and Dalmatian coast postponed again, to 21 May. Black Sea assault and attack on Greek mainland remain at 21 May;

Stage 4: all preliminary threats cancelled. Balkan assaults now to take place on 19 June without previous seizure of Crete, western Greece, and Dalmatian coast.

Most of the notional assaults would be carried out by the notional Twelfth British Army. This comprised five real divisions, three real brigades masquerading as divisions, and four wholly fictitious divisions. Of these the 15th British Motorized Division (bogus) and the 34th British Infantry Division (also bogus) would land on Crete between Canea and Heraklion. They would be followed by the 8th British Armoured Division (bogus) from Tobruk. There would be four simultaneous landings elsewhere in the Mediterranean. The IIIrd British Corps headquarters (real), including the 1st Greek Division (half bogus), would land at Kalamai from Alexandria and Tobruk, to establish a bridgehead in the south Peloponnese. The 10th Indian Division (real) from the Levant ports would seize the Islands of Cephalonia and Zante. The IIIrd Polish Corps (bogus), comprising the 2nd Polish Armoured Division (half bogus) and the 7th Polish Infantry Division (bogus), would use south-east Italy as a staging-post to establish a bridgehead at Durazzo, with a view to the eventual capture of Tirana, capital of Albania. The United States Seventh Army (real, but including several bogus formations) would land at Pola in the Istrian peninsula. All these operations would in theory begin on 23 March.[1]

There was a problem over the notional use of Polish troops in the threat against Albania. The partisans in Yugoslavia refused to accept Poles in the Balkans. General Wilson directed that they should be removed from the plan; but Dudley Clarke said that there were no other forces, real or notional, for the threat on Albania. If the Poles could not be used, the threat must be abandoned – which might free a whole German division for transfer to France, even before the *Overlord* critical period had been reached. In any case, the story of the pretended Polish assault had already been planted on German intelligence. 'A' Force would ensure, however, that no rumours about the Polish presence would reach the Yugoslav partisans – a tall order, given the nature of the rumour weapon.[2]

The fictional background to *Zeppelin* was carefully composed, so that 'A' Force planners would all be working along identical lines. This was no less essential than it is for an impostor to make himself believe that he is the man whose character he has assumed. The story ran as follows:

At the Teheran Conference, Stalin had asked that the Allies' first main effort in 1944 should be an advance into the Balkans from three sides to force the satellites out of the war, to deprive Germany of vital raw materials, and to threaten communications with her troops in south Russia. It had therefore been agreed to defer the invasion of Europe to the late summer of 1944. For the time being in the West the Allies would rely only on the combined bomber offensive.[3]

The go-ahead for *Zeppelin* was given on 10 February 1944.[4] The programme included virtually every known deceptive ploy, and

Dudley Clarke manipulated all branches of the Allied forces in the Mediterranean like a master puppeteer. Navy, army, air force, administration, camouflage experts, propagandists, saboteurs, even the Commander-in-Chief himself, were all expected to play their part. GHQ, Middle East Forces, took administrative measures to lend colour to the idea that Tobruk was to be used as an advance base for an attack on Crete. Port facilities, railhead, and roads leading to the harbour were visibly improved. Red Cross markings on the hospital roofs were repainted. Pamphlets describing the various threatened regions were prepared for the benefit of the invading troops, and printed by Middle East printers chosen for their known insecurity. Guides were called for. Maps were provided 'for a selected distribution' – which meant that a few copies would find their way into the hands of agents and from them to the Germans. The enemy would expect Greek troops to be included in any assault on their homeland, so they were given concentrated training. Stationery and office supplies which would be required by an Allied administration in Greece were ordered 'in a scheme of calculated insecurity'. There were as many exchange visits between Russia and the Middle East as possible, to show how closely the Allies were co-operating. General Wilson paid a visit to Cairo to suggest that the Allied centre of gravity was further to the east than it really was.

Although half the British Twelfth Army was a figment of Dudley Clarke's imagination, real forces nevertheless played an important part in *Zeppelin*. There was a noticeable and regular increase in the bombing of Balkan targets. Naval and air operations against shipping in the Aegean and Ionian Seas was carried on to the greatest possible extent. There were beach reconnaissances in Crete, the south Peloponnese, Cephalonia, Zante, and near Durazzo; and there was also to be air reconnaissance in these areas, with particular attention being paid to Canea and Heraklion in Crete, where the bogus 34th British Infantry Division was due to land. Wireless telegraph activity in Tobruk was stepped up; and special United States naval equipment was used to simulate the passage of landing-craft through the Straits of Gibraltar into the Mediterranean.[5]

Visual deception played its part. The genuine landing-craft at Tobruk were supplemented by dummies, so that by 10 March there were at least 100 in Cyrenaican waters. Tobruk's anti-aircraft defences were also increased.

The propagandists were asked to suggest that the second front in north-west Europe would be preceded by operations in southern Europe, with a view to the early liberation of the Balkans.

The dropping of propaganda leaflets designed to undermine the morale of the German forces was increased in Crete, the Peloponnese, Istria, and Albania; although this could not be fully carried out because of a shortage of aircraft. Newspaper articles emphasized General Wilson's close association with the Balkans in general and with Greece in particular, and other articles proclaimed the eagerness of the Greek troops to return to their own country. The Special Operations Executive and the Office of Strategic Services were asked to give priority to the supply of equipment to the resistance groups in Crete, the Peloponnese, and Albania: this was intended to convey the idea that they were being prepared to co-operate with Allied invasion forces.

General Wilson made his own contribution to the deception plan by suggesting that a recent transfer of air force training establishments to Palestine should be used to make the Germans believe that the Allies intended to fly aircraft into Turkey without Turkish agreement. There was, however, a technical difficulty. The RAF Operational Training Units' (OTUs) radio telegraphic traffic was so characteristic 'that the Hun is bound to appreciate from Y [the monitoring service] what and where they are'. The only way of putting across Wilson's idea was to let it be known precisely where the OTUs were, and to publicize their presence, which could be done by placing an article in the *Palestine Post* on 'Palestine, the public school of flying'. The story could then be spread that the OTUs were really cover for a fly-in of operational squadrons. Airfields in the neighbourhood of Aleppo could be made ready for use as staging-points for the fly-in.[6]

The postponement of the various threatened attacks which ended Stage 1 of Plan *Zeppelin* (which was of course legislated for at the outset) was for the purposes of the deception attributed to the Allies' failure to make satisfactory headway in Italy, which had thrown their whole strategic time-table out of gear. It meant that operations against Istria would not now be possible before May; and so the whole Balkans programme was put back a month. The Allies' pretended intentions remained the same. The landings in Crete, the Peloponnese, and Albania were now timed for the original 'revised' date, and the moves against Istria and the Black Sea coast would come a month later. The British forces would be ready to move into Turkey at the beginning of June.

Stage 2 ended on 14 April. Stage 3 followed the original plan, except that a new fiction was added. The Russian General Staff had made the unexpected request that Allied operations in Greece and Albania be delayed, so that they would coincide with the entry of Russian troops into Bulgaria in May and thus cause the maximum distraction to the Germans. In fact – so the story was developed – this request came at an opportune moment, for feeling was running high about the form of government which the Allies wanted to see in liberated Greece. Moreover, it gave the British the chance to withdraw the genuine 46th and 56th Infantry Divisions from Italy to refit for the pending operation in the Balkans. (In fact these two divisions were withdrawn from Italy, but their genuine destination was Egypt.) The decision to postpone the assaults was supposed to have been taken at the last minute, when General Wilson visited Cairo on 10 April. The new date would be 21 May – again as provided for in the original plan.[7]

By the time Stage 4 was reached, it was felt that the deception was wearing rather thin, and it was considered necessary to change the cover story. The continuing postponement of the assault on Greece was now attributed to trouble with the Greek Goverment and forces. It was noised abroad that early in April the disputes about the form of government which the Allies intended to set up in Greece, and which had already been the subject of rumours, had reached dangerous proportions. There had been a series of political crises. The Greek armed forces had been seriously affected by these developments, and when they learned that the operation that would take them back to Greece had been postponed, they had mutinied. The mutiny was under control by the end of April, but it left the troops in no condition to take part in operations for some time. Indeed (so it was rumoured), most of the 1st Greek Brigade had had to be demobilized. This ruled out the assaults on Crete and the Peloponnese timed for 21 May, so they were now abandoned in favour of an attempt to accelerate a Balkan collapse by a giant pincer movement. The story was now that the British Twelfth Army would enter Istria in the middle of June, and on the same day the Russians would enter Bulgaria. This would maintain the threat in the eastern Mediterranean well beyond *Overlord* D-Day, and SHAEF asked that it should be kept going even longer, into July. But on 28 June Wilson told the Chiefs of Staff that *Zeppelin* should now be allowed to die a natural death, partly because the genuine troop formations which had been taking part in the deception were required for real operations.[8]

The successive *Zeppelin* stories were backed up more thoroughly than many of the earlier deceptive plans, although it was physically impossible to do everything the planners wanted. Aerial attacks on Balkan targets were carried out during the whole of the plan, and Istria was added to the bombing programme half-way through: however, the attacks were on a smaller scale than had been hoped for. To support the idea of an impending attack, 100 gliders appeared on airfields near Tobruk, and 150 Mosquitos, 60 Lightnings, and 200 other fighters were displayed on aerodromes within range of the Balkans. Every day when the weather was suitable there was aerial reconnaissance of Durazzo, the Peloponnese, and Crete. Aerial attacks of shipping on the routes to Crete were conspicuously successful.

The number of landing-craft in the area, real and dummy, was steadily increased. In Tobruk berths for 70 were provided, and tugs and motor-boats were assigned the task of moving them to give them life. Landing-craft in Egypt put on a fine deceptive performance. A dozen of them sailed through the Suez Canal to Port Said and Alexandria by day, and then returned to Suez under cover of darkness – this suggested that there was a constant stream of craft entering the Mediterranean. However, the hoped-for display of dummy craft at Bizerta was delayed because the canvas for their manufacture did not arrive in time.

Radio made its usual contribution. The naval radio station at Tobruk was re-opened to simulate preparations for an amphibious assault against the Balkans. The stations at Port Said, Alexandria, Benghazi, and Bizerta also helped in this aspect of the deception.

One part of *Zeppelin* which it was not possible to implement fully was the increased supply of arms and equipment to the resistance groups in the threatened areas, because there were no aircraft to spare for the delivery of these supplies. There was also a special problem in Greece, where the delivery of arms had to be suspended because of dissension between rival resistance groups. Partisan and commando raids were carried out on the Dalmatian coast, according to plan.

The propagandists' contribution was less than perfect. The directives on which the Political Warfare Branch of Allied Forces Headquarters was supposed to act came from the Political Warfare Executive in London, which did not understand the subtleties of Plan *Zeppelin*. These directives made too much of Allied strength in the West, whereas what *Zeppelin* needed was the maximum build-up of apparent Allied strength in the eastern Mediterranean.

Genuine military formations were used on a considerable

scale. Tobruk was reinforced by the 27th Lancers, as well as three heavy anti-aircraft regiments and one light. Vehicles of the 1st Armoured Division, a genuine formation which had been in Egypt and the Western Desert since 1942, and which had taken part in the Battle of El Alamein, were displayed in Cyrenaica. New camps with ammunition and stores dumps were built in Cyprus.

The principal physical deception was the subordinate Plan *Turpitude*, which was based on a pretended improvement in the Allies' relations with Turkey as the invasion of Europe drew near. Large army and air forces, including the 87th Armoured Brigade (Dummy Tanks), the 31st Indian Armoured Division, and other genuine formations of the Ninth Army, were built up in Syria. These troops then moved through Syria and concentrated in the north, ostensibly waiting to be reinforced from other theatres before proceeding through Turkey – with the supposed blessing of the Turks – to attack eastern Greece.[9]

All these activities, which involved many thousands of real troops and were spread over the whole of the eastern Mediterranean area, confirmed the Allies' intention to mount the various assaults contained in Plan *Zeppelin*. They did not, however, enlighten the Germans as to why the threatened assaults never took place. This could be done only through 'special means', the secret channels which were used to convey information directly to the enemy. The agents controlled by 'A' Force passed on the key points in Dudley Clarke's stories – how the assaults had to be postponed, first because the Allied advance in Italy had been held up, then because the Russians had asked them to stay their hand, and then because of the mutiny among the Greek troops. Carefully edited fragments of 'intelligence' were leaked to the Germans to enable them to build up the overall picture invented by 'A' Force, which was confirmed by the activities their own agents observed, and by the reports of their air reconnaissance.

That the Germans believed much of Plan *Zeppelin* was supported by feedback picked up by 'A' Force agents. It was generally believed that the threatened assaults were genuine. It was 'common knowledge' in Alexandria that the invasion of Crete was due very soon. A Greek lady said at a society sewing-party that the Greek troops at Tobruk were destined for Crete. Another lady remarked that the reason for the sudden departure from Alexandria of British naval officers was that they had all gone to Tobruk in connection with operations that were planned there. These rumours were so widespread, and so generally was it believed that Greece was about to be liberated, that in the middle of March the stock of the Bank of Athens rose from 126 to 150.

In his summing-up, Dudley Clarke said that *Zeppelin* and the deceptive plans for the western Mediterranean had compelled the Germans to keep substantially the same number of troops in the Mediterranean theatre from the beginning of February 1944 onwards. During the preparatory period for *Overlord* not one division had moved from the Mediterranean to north-west Europe, and none had arrived in time to influence the battle during the *Overlord* critical period. German sources reveal that they were indeed worried by the possibility of limited Allied operations in the Balkans, in particular an attack on the Peloponnese, on the eve of the invasion of France.[10]

The most striking evidence of the success of 'A' Force's deceptive planning was found in captured German documents, which proved that the enemy had been completely taken in by the consistent exaggeration of Allied strength in the Mediterranean theatre.

The fake order of battle (code-name *Wantage*) was a subtle blend of genuine formations, formations created for deceptive purposes, which were of course simply a nucleus, and formations which did not exist at all. The Germans were induced to build up the order of battle by the systematic planting of scraps of false information over a long period through secret intelligence channels; by the display of bogus divisional signs on vehicles in areas where they would be seen and reported by enemy agents; and by the use of the names of bogus formations in signals and official documents.

The order of battle was worked out in great detail. A single flaw or inconsistency could easily have given it away. For example, the non-existent XIVth British Corps, which was allotted to the United States Seventh Army, was presumed to have arrived in North Africa during December 1943, complete with its insignia – a black wolf's head, with a red tongue lolling on white square. It comprised two divisions, the 42nd Infantry Division which had in fact ceased to exist in 1941 (divisional sign; a small white diamond on a red diamond), and the 57th Infantry Division which had been invented for deceptive purposes out of the headquarters of the 42nd Infantry Brigade in November 1943.

In turn, 42nd Infantry Division comprised 133rd Brigade (disbanded in January 1943) and 142nd and 149th Brigades, which were never formed. By contrast, 57th Infantry Division had three brigades (170th, 171st, and 172nd), which had been formed in 1943 purely for deception.[11]

The *Wantage* plan would have been even more effective if it had included United States formations, but to do so was considered to be impossible because of the procedures for activating divisions in theatres overseas. This could be done only by the War Department in Washington, and 'to devise a similar system in the U.S. Forces so much explanation and so many changes in custom and procedure would be required as to "blow" the scheme pretty thoroughly before it could be put into effect'.[12]

Nevertheless, the exaggeration of the British forces was enough on its own to make the combined Allied threat significantly greater in German eyes. The first *Wantage* plan, which was prepared in February 1944 (as a successor to Plan *Cascade*, which used the same techniques), provided for 18 bogus divisions. A further 8 were added during March and April. Of this total of 26 imaginary divisions, no fewer than 21 were shown in the German intelligence papers as genuine. At the end of May, there were in reality 38 Allied divisions in the whole Mediterranean theatre. According to the fictitious *Wantage* order of battle, the number was 64. The Germans actually credited the Allies with 71, an overestimate of about 85 per cent, although they were uncertain about the genuineness of 11 of these. If the latter are discounted, there nevertheless remain 22 non-existent divisions in the German estimates, or nearly a quarter of a million men. Most of the 22 had been planted on them by 'A' Force, but some were figments of the Germans' own imagination. For example, the 18th British Infantry Division, which appears in the German version of the Allied order of battle (which in fact had been taken prisoner in Malaya during 1942 and had never reformed), was not included in the *Wantage* order of battle, so 'A' Force could take no credit for this element in the deception.[13]

The *Wantage* plan was remarkably successful, and it seems that it more than anything else discouraged the Germans from moving troops from the Mediterranean area to north-west Europe during the run-up to *Overlord*. No doubt the threats in the Balkans played some part, but they would have been meaningless had the Germans not believed that the Allies had the massive strength needed to carry them out.

11 THE WESTERN MEDITERRANEAN

The problem which General Wilson had to solve in the western Mediterranean was more complex. His main aim, as in the eastern Mediterranean, was to help Operation *Overlord* by using deception to keep the maximum number of German troops away from the Normandy beaches. This could be done by staging a threat to the south of France; but if that was too successful the Germans might move troops there which would still be manning the defences when in due course Wilson launched Operation *Anvil*, the genuine Allied invasion of southern France. The deceptive operations which Wilson used in this tightrope-walking act were *Ironside*, *Vendetta*, and *Ferdinand*.

IRONSIDE
As *Overlord* D-Day approached, reports from agents in France suggested that the Germans were coming to believe, correctly, that the main Allied assault would be launched against the Channel coast somewhere between Brittany and the north of Belgium. They thought an invasion of the south of France was less likely, and they had virtually written off the idea of an attack on the west coast of France. If they continued to think on these lines, it meant that they would not hesitate to move reserves either north or south, depending on where the Allies chose to land, knowing that these reserves would not be needed to deal with an attack from the Bay of Biscay. It would therefore help both *Overlord* and *Anvil* if a threat to the Biscay coast could be successfully simulated. This threat was given the code name *Ironside*.

The threat implied that an operation would be launched against the Bordeaux area from west coast ports in Britain and from the United States. Its immediate objective would be the port of Bordeaux, to enable American troops to enter south-west France. Three days after the Normandy landings, a brigade group would supposedly attack in the neighbourhood of Royan on the north bank of the Gironde estuary, in order to capture the airfields at Medis and Cozes a few miles inland. A division would attack Le Verdon and Soulac on the opposite bank of the estuary, to establish a beachhead there. A second division would go in further south at Arcachon, to gain control of the main road to Bordeaux. Three follow-up divisions would sail from the United States – one for each beachhead; and the force would eventually be built up to a total of ten divisions, which would then advance along the Garonne.[1]

An elaborate but entirely fictitious naval programme was worked out, requiring personnel ships, landing-craft, merchant transports, and mine-sweepers. Naval forces would bombard the coast. Once the two airfields were secured, aircraft from carriers and from British bases would be established there, to provide cover for the next stages of the operation.

This ambitious fiction was doomed to failure almost before it was drafted. The only physical evidence possible to support the deception was a bombing programme of the type that would precede a genuine invasion. When the air forces were asked to help, their reply was no, although they found it difficult to say so in a single word. 'A study of the air bombardment involved in consummating the Plan indicates that vital commitments at a very critical time will not permit of the diversion of a suitable force without prejudicing the successful fulfilment of existing programmes.' It would have taken a minimum of 840 heavy bomber sorties to lend colour to *Ironside*.[2]

Since the naval element in Plan *Ironside* was pure fiction, and since there were no spare aircraft for bombing, it meant that the deception had virtually no chance of success. There was some Allied aerial reconnaissance of the threatened area, but it did not cut much ice. The Germans would hardly believe that a major attack was in prospect without physical confirmation. The double agents could have been used to help, but their credibility would have suffered when the deception was seen through. 'A' Force were asked to use their agents to put *Ironside* across, but they were prepared to give the plan 'only very light treatment'. There was no point, they said, in wasting scarce resources in backing a lost cause.[3]

Shortly before this, Hitler himself believed that there was a distinct possibility of an Allied attack on the French Atlantic coast.[4] Perhaps if *Ironside* had been more energetically pursued it would have confirmed his belief.

VENDETTA

Plan *Vendetta* had more hope of success. It involved mounting a positive threat to the south of France, which would culminate shortly after *Overlord* D-Day. The backbone of the threat was the training and embarkation of the 91st United States Infantry Division, so that it would appear to be preparing for an attack on southern France round about 19 June. The order of battle provided for *Vendetta* also contained large numbers of entirely fictitious troops, which were ostensibly part of the United States Seventh Army.

All the usual deceptive ploys would be used; but the Combined Chiefs of Staff had specified a positive threat. Dudley Clarke took this to mean that there must be large numbers of men and landing-craft on display, genuine shipping movements, and troops going through the motions of embarking. He devised a plan beginning with real operations which the enemy could not fail to notice – the bombing of routes in north Italy and the Rhône valley which the Germans might have used to move reinforcements to the battle zone in Normandy. Communications in the Montpellier and Carcassonne Gaps were sabotaged by the Special Operations Executive and the American Office of Strategic Services. The area selected for the notional assault – between Sète and Agde – was raided and reconnoitred. It was hinted to the resistance groups that a genuine assault was due shortly. General Patch, supposedly in command of the expedition, was given a good deal of newspaper publicity.

Like almost every deception plan, *Vendetta* erred on the side of optimism. It was easy enough to sit at an office desk and pluck from thin air all the ingredients of a massive deceptive operation, but when it came to the crunch many of them had to be done without. There was no problem about marking out transit camps in Oran, where the 91st Division was to embark, but a stipulation that all units must be brought up to strength was wishful thinking. All that could be done under this heading was to instruct units to submit deficiency returns, with the inference that the next step would be to bring them up to strength. Although it had been intended that all courses of instruction should be suspended, it was realized that this might not be feasible. The planned-for increased anti-aircraft protection at the ports would have to be simulated.[5]

The biggest blow, however, came when it was suddenly decided that the 91st Infantry Division would be sent to reinforce the Allied Armies in Italy at the beginning of June. At a stroke, this demolished the idea of a visible threat. Without actual troop movements, *Vendetta* would become impossibly thin. Even if only part of the 91st Division went to Italy and was identified by the enemy the deception would be blown, since it had already been leaked that the Division was destined for France. The planners urged that the Division's move should be postponed until the middle of June. So strongly did they argue that it was agreed to keep the Division in North Africa long enough to make its contribution to *Vendetta*. The Division would therefore undertake amphibious training at Oran, and embark for Italy on 16 June – the date on which the *Vendetta* force would have embarked for France, had it been going to France. Its training programme would include the study of maps of France and aerial photographs of the French coastline, and there would be classes in the French language – which probably led to some unflattering remarks about the brass hats when the 91st Division found that its actual destination was Italy.[6]

Dudley Clarke was very much afraid that *Vendetta* would fail through lack of resources, and Wilson appealed to the Chiefs of Staff for reinforcements to make good the deficiencies. The Joint Planning Staff agreed without hesitation that his Command was stretched, but there was very little they could suggest to help. Wilson had all the aircraft he needed, so there was no point in sending him more. There were certainly no land forces to spare. A suggestion of his that the 2nd British Division should be transferred from India to the Mediterranean was impracticable. There were no spare landing-craft. In general, he would simply have to make do with the resources he already had.

He could be helped with ships, however. The convoy programme could be juggled to give the impression that an unusually large concentration of shipping was passing through the Straits of Gibraltar round about the time when ships were supposed to be loading for the *Vendetta* expedition. The Admiralty contrived that three convoys containing about 130 ships entered the Mediterranean at the end of May in broad daylight. The last of the three joined a westbound convoy under cover of darkness and retraced its passage to Britain.[7]

Administrative measures did not call for ships or troops, and if properly misinterpreted by the enemy they could be very effective. One such measure, which was belatedly thought up to make good the weaknesses in *Vendetta*, was the closing of the frontier between French and Spanish Morocco: it was hoped this would confirm in the Germans' mind that something was afoot. The closure had to be carefully timed. If the Germans were convinced that the south of France was about to be invaded from Mediterranean bases, they might jump to the conclusion that the north was to be attacked simultaneously, and the vital element of surprise would be removed from the Normandy landings. Thus instead of closing the frontier just before *Overlord* D-Day, as originally planned, the date was put forward 7 days, by which time the assault would have succeeded – if it was going to succeed. Cipher and bag facilities were withdrawn from neutral consuls in North Africa, to enhance the idea that military operations were being prepared.[8]

It was necessary to go through the motions of supplying the *Vendetta* troops. Otherwise casual observers in Oran – and perhaps professionals observing on behalf of the enemy – would see through the deception. On 16 May, the North African Theater of Operations, United States Army, complained that they had been given no troop, vehicle, or weapon lists; and that it was therefore quite impossible for them to put on a convincing display. Time was so short that they would simply go ahead with the provision of supplies on the basis of the information they already had.[9] Stores were set aside and suitably marked for the 91st United States Infantry Division and a French formation, which was the only other genuine component of *Vendetta*. Stores had already been prepared for the 91st Division on the assumption that it was joining the Allied Armies in Italy; but since *Vendetta* was supposed to be a beach assault they now had to be specially packed and waterproofed. In all, ten thousand tons of stores were provided, including petrol and on-board rations for a week. The 91st Division arrived at the staging-area between 5 and 9 June – 500 officers, 14,000 men, and nearly 3,000 vehicles.[10]

Meanwhile, targets in the south of France were attacked in accordance with a priority list mainly designed to help *Overlord*, but which was also intended to support the *Vendetta* threat. The principal railways, which the Germans had staffed with their own railwaymen and over which they were likely to move reinforcements to Normandy, were identified for the benefit of the Allied bombers. There was a Panzer division in the Toulouse area, and therefore the highest priority was given to the line running north from Montauban to Vierzon, which that division would have to use. It was bombed for three days after the Normandy landings. Next came the line from Bordeaux to Tours, which was attacked between 10 and 13 June, to hamper the movement of a training division which was in the process of converting itself into a Panzer. The line running north up the Rhône valley from Nîmes through Lyons to Dijon had third priority. It was attacked between 14 June and 1 July, to contain two divisions in the neighbourhood of Avignon. Finally, the line from Modane on the Italian border to Lyons was bombed from 14 June onwards. In all cases the road networks associated with the railways were also attacked, to deny the enemy an alternative form of transport.

The pattern of these attacks made it obvious that the Allies' main objective was to restrict the northerly movement of German forces towards the Normandy bridgehead. Unless something was done to imply support for an invasion of the south coast it seemed very likely that the *Vendetta* threat would be written off by the Germans. So the railway from Bordeaux to Narbonne on the south coast (which ran through Toulouse), the road which ran alongside it, and the road from Severac to Nîmes, all of which were important only in the context of an assault on the south coast, were also bombed, simply to keep the Germans guessing.[11]

The movement of German reinforcements from the south of France to Normandy was further hampered by resistance groups under the direction of the 'Jedburgh' teams – a British or American officer, a French officer, and a radio operator – which were dropped into France to organize the sabotage of road and rail communications. These teams also contributed to the *Vendetta* fairy-tale by paying particular attention to the Narbonne–Bordeaux road and railway.[12]

The *Vendetta* threat was wound up at the end of June. This meant that the French authorities could reopen the frontier with Spanish Morocco. It would also be possible to reveal the fact that the 91st United States Infantry Division, which had embarked at Oran to take part in the invasion of the south of France, but had mysteriously been diverted to Italy, had been engaged in the fighting there. The Allied Armies in Italy had been urging that the division should be given credit for its genuine services, and at last this was now possible.[13]

FERDINAND

Wilson's third plan relating to the western Mediterranean, *Ferdinand*, was approved by the Chiefs of Staff on 8 July. *Vendetta* had been intended to convince the enemy that an Allied invasion of the south of France was imminent. One of *Ferdinand*'s objectives was to establish that it was not, and thus to reduce the enemy's strength and vigilance in the south of France, where a genuine attack (*Anvil*) was now due shortly. It was also hoped to draw German forces away from the centre of the Gothic Line in Italy – which ran from Pisa to Rimini – before the Allied Armies launched a genuine attack against it in the direction of Bologna.

The story invented by 'A' Force to make *Ferdinand* plausible was one of the most elaborate to come from the fertile imaginations of the planners. It was based on a pretended difference of opinion between the British and American commanders – a plausible starting-point. The matter on which they were supposed to differ was what to do next in the Mediterranean. The British were made out to be strongly in favour of a major attack in Italy, rather than the alternative of a difficult amphibious operation against the south of France. The French forces in Italy which were supposed to have been assigned to the still notional attack on France had suffered heavy losses, and (for the purposes of the deception story) were in no state to take part in an operation. The Combined Chiefs of Staff were supposed after much high-level discussion to have accepted the British argument that the next move must be in Italy, and to have rejected the Americans' plea that France must be the target. The forces which had been standing by supposedly to attack the French Mediterranean coast would now go to Italy. It was also to be pretended that General Eisenhower was renewing the threat to the Biscay coast.[14]

Eisenhower – that is, the genuine Eisenhower – was unhappy about the *Ferdinand* plan. In particular, he wanted to know how Wilson would be able to keep German troops stationed in the south of France away from the battleground in the north if the main Mediterranean threat was now to be in Italy. He accepted that the genuine invasion of the south of France would eventually take the pressure off the Allied Armies in the north; and that the enemy must not be allowed to increase his strength along the French Mediterranean coast. It was, however, essential to keep those German divisions which were inland from the *Anvil* assault area anchored where they were – suspended between the battle-zone in the north and the pending battle in the south. This was asking rather a lot.

Eisenhower was also opposed to carrying on the deceptive threat to the Biscay coast which had been written into *Ferdinand* without his blessing and which his forces would have to carry out. Wilson, however, was adamant. He insisted that *Overlord* and *Anvil* would have the best of both worlds if a strong deceptive threat was mounted against the Biscay coast. It could well attract German reserves to the benefit of both operations.[15]

The Chiefs of Staff asked Bevan to adjudicate in this gentle tug of war between Eisenhower and Wilson, in which each wanted to keep enemy forces away from the immediate area of his operations. The Controlling Officer thought the Germans would continue to be apprehensive about an invasion of the south coast of France; but more important, the *Ferdinand* deception was based on a pretended increase in Allied pressure in Italy. Since it was planned that a major new genuine offensive would be launched there shortly, there was a danger that the deceptive plan would induce the Germans to strengthen their defences, and thus find themselves better able to withstand the real attack. Nevertheless, he considered that on balance the help which *Ferdinand* would give to *Anvil* and *Overlord* would outweigh any harm done in Italy, and that the deception should go ahead. He also supported the Biscay threat in spite of Eisenhower's objections to it.[16]

The Chiefs of Staff agreed about *Ferdinand*, but not about the Biscay threat. They were satisfied that it would help neither *Anvil* nor *Overlord* on the ground that the Germans now had no spare reserves to move to the Biscay area. Moreover, the threat would be unconvincing for military and geographical reasons. It could not be supported by real troop movements, and would probably turn out to be a dead letter – just as *Ironside* had been.[17]

In spite of these powerful arguments, Wilson refused to budge. Eisenhower then claimed that it was dangerous to make too many threats – it might compromise *Fortitude*, the continuing threat to the Pas de Calais, which was the one that really mattered. He would agree to no more than a latent threat to the Biscay coast – by which he meant that there should hardly be a threat at all.[18] The British Chiefs of Staff suggested a compromise, in which Eisenhower would be instructed to meet Wilson's wishes, without detriment to *Overlord*. The Combined Chiefs of Staff agreed, and then told Eisenhower and Wilson that there would be only a latent threat, which was rather less than the British side had proposed. So Eisenhower got his way without appearing to do so.[19]

All that could be done to implement the Biscay threat was to increase supplies to the *Maquis* in the Gascony region to such an extent that they would be able to control the area without the help of large-scale amphibious operations. This idea would be spread through diplomatic means and agents. When the plan was submitted to General Bedell Smith at SHAEF on 5 August, he commented 'Pretty thin! But probably the best possible.' At least Wilson had been given the plan he asked for. Eisenhower's point was also met. The London Controlling Section regulated the flow of intelligence both through diplomatic channels and through agents, and could ensure that the continuing threat to the south of France did not loom large in the enemy's mind.[20]

The simulation of a threat in Italy had a much greater chance of success than the Biscay threat, if only because of the Allied Armies' presence in the country. The principal means of implementing the deception plan, which was intended to convince the Germans that there was to be a major Allied assault on Genoa, was leakage through agents. The confidence which 'A' Force now felt in its ability to manipulate the German Secret Service is reflected in the simple statement: '"A" Force will arrange to plant the story on the German SIS.' There also had to be visible evidence to support the scraps of information trickled through to the Germans via many channels: an all-out air attack on Genoa and its communications two days before *Anvil*; photographic reconnaissance, and probing of the defences of the port by light naval craft; the issue of maps of the Genoa area; increased encouragement of the Italian resistance movements; and an increase in the number of leaflets dropped to the German forces in Genoa.

While the maximum heat was thus turned on Genoa, the Allies' interest in the south of France, where the *Anvil* assault was due, was played down as far as possible. There would still be some mild effort against the region – it would arouse suspicion if it was left completely in peace; but there would be the minimum display of Allied naval and shipping strength in the western Mediterranean. Concentrations in the Naples–Salerno area where the genuine *Anvil* forces were being assembled would be concealed. To reinforce the idea of an attack on Genoa, there might be negotiations with Switzerland about the early resumption of trade through the Simplon tunnel – and the evacuation of Allied prisoners-of-war by the same route. The Republic of San Marino might be warned of the probable influx of large numbers of German troops retreating about the end of August, and told what she must do to claim the benefits of neutrality.[21]

Anvil – which had now become *Dragoon*, because it had been discovered that the Germans knew the code-name, although they did not know what it stood for – was duly launched on 15 August 1944. In spite of the fact that the shore defences were strong, the invaders had relatively little difficulty in overcoming them and making progress inland. This was principally due, not to the success of the deception plan, but to the Allies' overwhelming air superiority. In the inquest on *Dragoon*, it was accepted that the concentrations in the western Mediterranean ports must have made it perfectly clear to the Germans that an invasion was being prepared. The most that could be said was that the enemy had not known precisely when or where the assault would be.

A good deal of the credit for this belongs to the United States Eighth Fleet, which mounted diversionary operations to threaten in succession the Genoa area, Nice–Cannes, Sète–Agde, and Marseilles–Toulon, to keep the Germans guessing as to where the genuine assault would come. Motor-launches were used to simulate large convoys. They carried equipment to jam enemy radar, and towed reflector balloons which showed up as warships on enemy radar screens, some of which were left unmolested so that the movement of the simulated convoys – one of which was 12 miles long by 8 miles broad – could be tracked. The enemy reaction was most satisfactory. Much of the German coastal battery fire was directed at the imaginary convoys; and the presumed widespread movement of shipping compelled the Germans to retain forces all along the south coast of France, which reduced the opposition at the actual points of landing.[22]

12 THE CRUCIAL DECEPTION

Fortitude South, which simulated a massive attack on the Pas de Calais two hundred miles east of the chosen landing-places in Normandy, was the largest, most elaborate, most carefully-planned, most vital, and most successful of all the Allied deceptive operations. It made full use of the years of experience gained in every branch of the deceptive art – visual deception and misdirection, the deployment of dummy landing-craft, aircraft, and paratroops, fake lighting-schemes, radio deception, sonic devices, and ultimately a whole fictitious army group. It was protected by the strictest security measures, without which the most brilliant deceptive scheme could do more harm than good.

If the enemy knew the time and place of the assault it was unlikely that the Allies would be able to fight their way into Europe through the forces which the Germans could mass against them. Since the invasion forces and their landing-craft could not be hidden indefinitely from aerial reconnaissance, it seemed inevitable that as *Overlord* D-Day drew near German intelligence must become more and more certain about the Allies' intentions. The enemy would have time to locate his reserve divisions so that they could be moved swiftly to engage the Allied forces as they landed. If the Allies failed to establish a bridgehead quickly, the second front would be put back a year. Much worse, the surprise factors on which the success of the invasion largely depended – for example, the Mulberry harbours* – would be revealed to the enemy. It would be danger-

* These artificial harbours were made up from hollow concrete units, which were

170

ous to use them again, just as it is asking for trouble to do the same conjuring trick a second time before the same audience.

The first deception plan for Operation *Overlord* proposed that the Normandy landings should be helped by a genuine diversionary operation, on the lines of the ill-fated *Starkey* plan; but this was ruled out on the ground that the Luftwaffe would not be brought to battle without an actual landing in France. In any case there would only be enough landing-craft to send one division to the Pas de Calais, and it would quickly become obvious to the Germans that an assault of that size was no more than a diversion. From which it would follow that the Allies had staked everything on the Normandy assault, and that all available German reserves could safely be transferred to the battle there. Therefore any attempt to land in the Pas de Calais would be disastrous. Instead of sending a small genuine expeditionary force as a diversionary operation, preparations for a vast assault at the eastern end of the English Channel would be simulated.

The story on which this deception was founded was simple – unlike many of the fictions which the London Controlling Section and 'A' Force had invented in the past. All that was needed now was to put over one lie successfully. This was that the main Allied assault would be launched against the Pas de Calais six weeks after the Normandy landings which, it would be pretended, were no more than a diversion to take the enemy's eye off the supposed later main attack.

The naval forces allocated to the Normandy assault were originally assembled in widely-separated areas round Britain – from Invergordon in the Moray Firth to Milford Haven – which simply implied a threat to some point on the coast of Europe anywhere between Brittany and Norway. It was believed that when the ships began to move south, about a fortnight before

---

towed to the assault beaches and assembled there. Because of their great size (230 feet long by 60 feet broad and 60 feet deep) it was impossible to conceal them while they were being built. The story was put out that they were 'boom defence units' for the protection of harbours (WO 219 2237, 4C).

D-Day, the Germans would deduce that the area threatened was between Ostend and Brest; and when they took into account such factors as the suitability of beaches, the location of ports, and the strength of their own defences, they would guess that the chosen objective lay between Cherbourg and Le Havre. If this dangerous idea was to be played down, the real preparations in the west and south-west of England pointing to an attack in the region of Cherbourg must be hidden as far as possible, while deceptive measures made it appear that the centre of gravity of the Allied preparations was in south-east England. Substantial assault and follow-up forces would be simulated in the Dover and Nore Commands, together with the necessary landing-craft. The threat to the Pas de Calais would be reinforced by the presence in the south-east of genuine formations due to take part in the Normandy assault. When they had to leave the area they would be replaced by United States divisions not immediately required overseas, by British troops not forming part of the expeditionary force, and by the simulation of additional divisions.[1] Although it was evolved many months before the invasion, this plan was carried out almost to the letter. The deception lasted much longer, and was much more successful than the planners had anticipated.

It was a condition of the plan that there should be perfect security along the south coast of England. A ten-mile strip running from Land's End to the Wash was designated a restricted zone, which visitors would not be allowed to enter. Although the Services and the Secret Service considered this move to be vital, the Home Office, Ministry of Home Security, and Ministry of Health all objected to it. Even Churchill, in Cairo at the time, was not in favour: 'we must beware of handing out irksome for irksome's sake'. He asked that his view should be put to the War Cabinet, but later changed his mind and said that the forces must believe that everything possible was being done to ensure the success of the invasion of Europe. It was finally agreed that the coastal strip should be closed from 1 April 1944.[2]

So many exceptions were allowed – visits for business purposes, weddings and funerals, to see people over 70 who were dangerously ill, for example – that the ban lost much of its value. The visits had to be made by train so that they could be readily policed, but it would have been easy enough for an enemy agent to enter the restricted zone, even if he did not have a sick grandmother. Once inside, he would have spotted that the preparations in the east were as fictitious as those in the west were genuine. A simple message to German intelligence – sent perhaps by homing pigeon – would have blown the whole of the *Fortitude South* deception.

There were also bans on uncensored diplomatic communications and on the departure of foreign diplomats from Britain. The Foreign Secretary objected to these measures. He claimed that earlier Allied military operations had been helped rather than hindered by foreign diplomats. Information which they sent on their own initiative might confuse the enemy, and false intelligence could be planted on them. Of course, Eden was merely trying to avoid trouble with the diplomatic corps, but even the Prime Minister was doubtful about the wisdom of interfering with normal diplomatic practice. However, General Eisenhower, who well knew how precariously balanced Operation *Overlord* was, insisted on the muzzling of the diplomats and their confinement in Britain. After 17 April 1944 no foreign diplomat was allowed to send or receive any uncensored message, or to leave the country.[3]

Hardly had this been decided when the Foreign Secretary was asking that the restrictions on diplomats should be lifted after D-Day. Presumably he was under the impression that all need for deception would disappear when the Allied forces set foot on the Normandy beaches. Against this it was argued with great force that continued security measures were absolutely vital. To remove them, as Eden was demanding, would leave a gaping hole for the leakage of information, which the Supreme Commander had urged must be kept closed for a month after D-Day. Eden continued to insist that the restrictions should end after D-Day, and it was eventually agreed that they should be lifted on 19 June.[4]

The ban on visits to the restricted zone was said to be an intolerable interference with the liberty of the subject, although it is more likely that it was unpopular because the departments administering it found it an intolerable nuisance. Eisenhower and Montgomery pointed out that if the security measures in the south of England were swept away it would become obvious to the enemy that the Allies had no intention of invading the Pas de Calais. In the light of their arguments, the War Cabinet agreed to keep the coastal restrictions in force until 25 August, by which time *Fortitude South* had run its course.[5]

It is surprising that these security measures, which were so obviously of the greatest importance, were not accepted without question by everyone from the Prime Minister downwards. It can be said in defence of the civil servants who advised the Ministers concerned that they were for the most part unaware of the implications of *Fortitude South*, and its dependence on perfect security. Even if they had been aware of the part deception had played in getting the Allied forces safely into France, they would have assumed that after the Normandy landings it was simply a question of pressing on to Berlin. But there is little to be said in defence of the responsible Ministers, particularly the Foreign Secretary, who wanted to put their departmental interests ahead of those of the invasion forces.[6]

The press was another threat to security which it was difficult to cope with. It was, of course, the job of censorship to prevent the publication of information which would be of value to the enemy; but it was always possible that speculation in a newspaper article might seem to contain a clue about the Allies' intentions. Churchill was upset in December 1943 by a newspaper report that Eisenhower had completed 'his massive invasion plans'; and a week or two later by an article in the *Sunday Times* which purported to give the month in which the assault on Europe would take place. He instructed the Minister of Information to consider whether there was a case against the newspaper – which there was not. The Controlling Officer was equally alarmed by news items printed at this time – accounts of Montgomery's visits to the embarkation ports, a story that actors had signed 'post-invasion contracts' to entertain troops on the continent, an announcement by the American Under Secretary for the Navy that the invasion date had been set, and so on – which might give the enemy ideas about the timing of the invasion. All that could be done to stop this sort of thing was to tell newspaper proprietors and editors the types of article which were considered to be dangerous. There must be no attempt to forecast dates, even in general terms; there must be no discussion of the merits of possible targets for the Allied assault; and above all there must be no estimate of the scale of the attack.[7]

Churchill wrote to Eisenhower on 28 January to tell him that the War Cabinet had taken steps to deal with press speculation; but he was still worried about correspondents accredited to the Supreme Commander's headquarters. He asked that a strict line should be taken with them. Eisenhower replied that he would feel very disturbed if he was held as anything but a friend of the press. This did not mean that the correspondents would be told anything dangerous. Churchill accepted his assurance, but when he heard that Eisenhower proposed to call up the accredited newspapermen six days before the invasion he pointed out that it would indicate the imminence of forthcoming operations. Nothing must be allowed to prejudice the security of *Overlord*. He begged the Supreme Commander to delay calling up the newsmen as long as possible, and to ensure that they sent nothing to their papers until after the landings, which Eisenhower agreed to do.[8]

SHAEF considered that the concealment of camps and other installations would be one of the major problems to be overcome if the enemy was to be deceived about the time and place of the invasion. Many of the camps would have to be built in the winter and early spring, before the trees were in leaf, and they would be easily seen by enemy air reconnaissance. The broad formula for visual misdirection to take care of the problem was worked out at the end of 1943. Since the genuine target was the Normandy beaches, and the supposed target somewhere between the Pas de Calais and Belgium, it followed that visible preparations in the south-east of England, opposite the Pas de Calais, must be seen to threaten the supposed target. On the other hand, visible preparations in the south-west for the genuine assault must as far as possible be made invisible. It was accepted, however, that it would be impossible to hide all activity there. Long before D-Day, troops and landing-craft would be undergoing intensive training. Their movement into the assembly areas would give the enemy clues about the time and place of the assault.

At first the coast from the Wash to the Severn was divided at a point just east of Portsmouth. West of this point there was the maximum concealment of all invasion preparations compatible with the movement of the troops. To the east there was discreet display of camps by means of 'neglect of concealment'. This work was left to the Commands in which the camps, etc., were being built. In Southern Command, for example, which lay to the west of the dividing line and was therefore a maximum concealment area, the rule was that camouflage for completed or nearly-completed works should not be further developed, since the improvement of schemes which the enemy had already observed from the air would arouse his suspicion. All new works, however, would be hidden as far as humanly possible. In both old and new installations – camps, embarkation hards, assembly areas, and the like – the maximum would be done to hide signs of occupation. Tents must be darkened, smokeless stoves used in the cookhouses, khaki towels issued instead of white.[9]

The problem in the east was different. It was hoped that the enemy would take note of the activities there, many of which were genuine, since most of the troops physically in the east would eventually be transferred to France as part of the *Overlord* build-up; but care would have to be taken to ensure that the camouflage was not too bad to be true. Camps were sited without regard to the need for concealment – so long as the chosen sites were not completely inappropriate. It was believed that the degree of camouflage which would catch the enemy's eye without making him smell a rat would be achieved by simply failing to achieve the highest standards of camouflage which the latest techniques made possible.[10] It so happened that several areas in Eastern and South Eastern Command where it was logical to erect camps helped the plan of poor camouflage. Concealment was difficult in the neighbourhood of Yarmouth because of the relative absence of woods, and it was virtually impossible at Tilbury because of the wide open spaces there. Nor could large numbers of troops be readily concealed at Dover and Folkestone.[11]

When the implementation of the *Overlord* cover plan was taken over by 21st Army Group there was a good deal of criticism of what had been done so far. It was believed that the enemy would base his conclusions about the direction and scale of the coming assault not on the camps and kindred evidence, but simply on the shipping in the ports. The experts of 21st Army Group thought that too much stress had been put on the need for elaborate visual deceptive measures; and Morgan, Eisenhower's Chief of Staff, had to point out to them that they were still considered to be essential. Although it was true that there had been no significant aerial reconnaissance since 1941, the fact remained that given ten days of fine weather the enemy could easily photograph a coastal belt fifteen to twenty miles deep from the Wash to Land's End. Morgan thought that the absence of visible preparations in Kent and Suffolk amounted to an unacceptable breach of security. The policy of the Supreme Commander would be carried out – whatever ideas 21st Army Group might have.[12]

The six principal elements in the *Fortitude South* deception were code-named *Quicksilver*. *Quicksilver I* was the fiction that the main Allied assault would be directed at the Pas de Calais area several weeks after the Normandy landings.

Most of the troops which found themselves in south-east England in the period before D-Day belonged to the First United States Army Group (FUSAG). FUSAG had been activated on 18 October 1943 with headquarters in Bryanston Square, London. In May 1944, it comprised the Third United States Army, with nine divisions, and the First Canadian Army, with two. The location of these formations added plausibility to the idea that they were being prepared for a cross-Channel attack on the north-east coast of France. The 2nd Canadian Infantry Division was at Dover; the 4th Canadian Armoured Division at Aldershot; and most of the United States Third Army in Suffolk and Essex. Their locations were leaked to the enemy through the double agents, and through radio signals traffic between them and their headquarters.[13]

As the FUSAG formations were transferred to France after D-Day, the threat to the Pas de Calais presented by the army group naturally diminished. This was a gradual process, since the transfers were spread over a period of several weeks; but it was inevitable that sooner or later the Germans would identify units in the Normandy battle zone which their intelligence had taken to be in south-east England. The more this happened, the more they would realize that they had nothing to worry about in the Pas de Calais.

To disguise the fact that FUSAG was gradually moving to Normandy, and that south-east England was being steadily denuded of troops, balancing notional formations were established in the mind of German intelligence. Thus the two Canadian and three United States divisions which FUSAG had lost by 16 June were replaced by the notional IInd British Corps, XXXVIIth United States Corps, and 59th United States Division. (The technical difficulties which had prevented the activation of United States formations overseas for deceptive purposes had now been overcome.) This process of substituting

First United States Army Group (FUSAG) order of battle,
showing real and false (in bold) formations,
June–August 1944.

1st June 1944

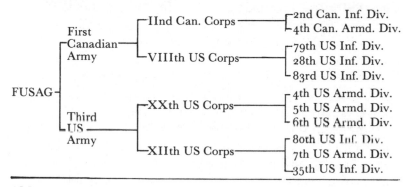

```
                              ┌─IInd Can. Corps ────────┬─2nd Can. Inf. Div.
              First           │                         └─4th Can. Armd. Div.
            ┌─Canadian────────┤
            │ Army            │                         ┌─79th US Inf. Div.
            │                 └─VIIIth US Corps─────────┤ 28th US Inf. Div.
  FUSAG─────┤                                           └─83rd US Inf. Div.
            │                 ┌─XXth US Corps───────────┬─4th US Armd. Div.
            │ Third           │                         │ 5th US Armd. Div.
            └─US──────────────┤                         └─6th US Armd. Div.
              Army            │                         ┌─80th US Inf. Div.
                              └─XIIth US Corps──────────┤ 7th US Armd. Div.
                                                        └─35th US Inf. Div.
```

16th June 1944

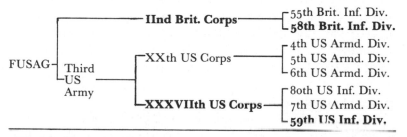

```
                              ┌─ IInd Brit. Corps───────┬─55th Brit. Inf. Div.
              │               │                         └─58th Brit. Inf. Div.
  FUSAG──────┤ Third          │                         ┌─4th US Armd. Div.
            └─US──────────────┤ XXth US Corps ──────────┤ 5th US Armd. Div.
              Army            │                         └─6th US Armd. Div.
                              │                         ┌─80th US Inf. Div.
                              └─XXXVIIth US Corps───────┤ 7th US Armd. Div.
                                                        └─59th US Inf. Div.
```

26th August 1944

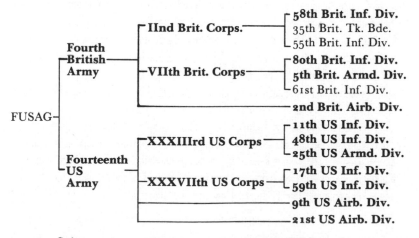

```
                              ┌─ IInd Brit. Corps.──────┬─58th Brit. Inf. Div.
              Fourth          │                         │ 35th Brit. Tk. Bde.
            ┌─British─────────┤                         └─55th Brit. Inf. Div.
            │ Army            │                         ┌─80th Brit. Inf. Div.
            │                 ├─VIIth Brit. Corps───────┤ 5th Brit. Armd. Div.
            │                 │                         └─61st Brit. Inf. Div.
            │                 └──────────────────────── 2nd Brit. Airb. Div.
  FUSAG─────┤
            │                 ┌─XXXIIIrd US Corps───────┬─11th US Inf. Div.
            │ Fourteenth      │                         │ 48th US Inf. Div.
            └─US──────────────┤                         └─25th US Armd. Div.
              Army            ├─XXXVIIth US Corps───────┬─17th US Inf. Div.
                              │                         └─59th US Inf. Div.
                              ├──────────────────────── 9th US Airb. Div.
                              └──────────────────────── 21st US Airb. Div.
```

Sources: WO 219 2223, 9A, 13C; WO 219 2225 (26.8.1944).
Note: the Ninth US Army was also associated with FUSAG in August 1944.

notional for real continued until at the end of August virtually the whole of the original FUSAG was fictitious. The notional Fourth British Army had been brought from Scotland, where it had been threatening Scandinavia, to join the notional Fourteenth United States Army and make up a total of eleven fictitious divisions. The only real formations were the 35th British Tank Brigade, and the 55th and 61st British Infantry Divisions – except that the real Ninth United States Army was temporarily shown as part of the FUSAG order of battle.[14]

If the shadow forces threatening the Pas de Calais were to be made fully credible in German eyes, they had to have commanders whose names could be leaked. The enemy would of course have no problem in finding out the names of genuine army commanders and would hope to identify corps commanders, and even some divisional commanders; and if he failed to identify a single name in the whole of an army group it would seem very strange. Therefore real individuals had to be appointed to the principal FUSAG commands – men who would plausibly have been appointed had the posts been genuine – and a suitable selection of their names passed by secret channels to the enemy.

In the peculiar circumstances of the *Fortitude South* deception, however, this presented difficulty. It was first proposed that General Omar Bradley, who had been given command of the army group in 1943, should be established as the commanding general; but it was then realized that when Bradley went to France he was bound to be identified. His presence overseas would throw doubt on the Allies' intention to use FUSAG as the main assault force, weeks after the 'diversionary' attack on the Normandy beaches had attracted German reserves from the Pas de Calais. A substitute had to be found.

The choice fell on General Patton – plausible, in spite of the fact that his indiscretions in recent months had convinced Eisenhower that he should be sent back to the United States. Patton was in command of the United States Third Army, which was not due to go to France until more than a month after

D-Day, by which time it was assumed that the Pas de Calais threat would have been played out. The double agents told the Germans that Patton was FUSAG's commanding general; and they also leaked the names of some of the subordinate commanders.[15]

The FUSAG threat fooled the German High Command longer than had been expected, so Patton in turn had to be replaced. Eisenhower told General Marshall, the United States Chief of Staff, that *Fortitude South* had led the enemy to prepare to meet a decisive Allied threat in the Pas de Calais under Patton. This threat would disappear when the Germans knew that Patton was in France, unless he was succeeded by an equally well-known commander. 'I cannot overemphasize the great importance of maintaining as long as humanly possible the Allied threat to the Pas de Calais area, which has already paid enormous dividends, and with care will continue to do so.'[16]

Eisenhower's new choice was General McNair, who took over the FUSAG 'command' on 14 July. SHAEF suggested that he should be used as an observer in France, since his only duties in England would be to show himself in public, but he was warned not to overdo his visits. Unfortunately on one of these visits he was killed by an American bomb which dropped short during a close support operation, and FUSAG was yet again faced with the problem of finding a commanding general, and telling the Germans who he was. The fourth commanding general was General De Witt, who was brought from Washington, and his name was duly passed on by the double agents – two of whom were used, so that their stories would corroborate each other.[17]

Quicksilver II was the radio deception through which the many component parts, first of the genuine, and then the fictitious FUSAG, communicated with each other for the benefit of the eavesdropping Germans. The simulated signals traffic was handled by the United States 3103rd Signals Service

Battalion, which arrived in Britain in February 1944. The Battalion at once began to analyse traffic between the United States units already in Britain so that it would be able at short notice to mount a convincing imitation of normal radio traffic within an army group. The fake signals would of course be designed to support the idea that the formations communicating with each other were preparing themselves for a cross-Channel assault in the east. If the picture presented by the radio signals was to carry conviction, there must be notional brigade and divisional exercises, for however fully-trained the new American troops were they would require some exercising with the naval forces assigned to carry them to France. There must be a credible interval between the various exercises, which should, for example, allow two or three days for probable bad weather.[18]

The networks which were set up to carry the fake radio traffic were extensive and complicated. At the peak there were 22 fake formations supporting the existence of FUSAG, starting with the headquarters of the army group at Wentworth, the Fourteenth United States Army at Little Waltham, the Fourth British Army at Chatham, and the various divisions supposedly scattered round the country at Leicester, Ipswich, Newmarket, Folkestone, Canterbury, and a dozen other places.

There is little doubt that the simulated radio traffic, most of which was carried on within a very short distance of the enemy and was therefore very easy to monitor, was – after the contribution of the double agents – the most important factor in the overall deception.

Quicksilver III – the display of landing-craft round the east and south-east coasts of England, to demonstrate that the means existed to carry the assault divisions of FUSAG to the Pas de Calais – was an elaborate failure. South Eastern Command, responsible for the 'Bigbob' launching programme, complained that 21st Army Group had no interest in the dummy craft. Eventually the programme got under way, and followed the pattern established in Operation *Starkey*. On 20 May four Bigbobs were launched at Yarmouth. Next day four appeared in the River Deben, north of Harwich, having supposedly made the trip from Yarmouth under cover of darkness. The game was repeated daily until more than two hundred and fifty dummy landing-craft had taken up station all round the coast.

The negligible weight and great surface area of the Bigbobs put them at the mercy of the merest breeze – a fact which had been established in Exercise *Harlequin* in 1943 when the great majority of the craft had been smashed or blown ashore. It might have been expected that a year later the handling problems would have been solved – but they had not. The inquest decided that only two of the places chosen to display the landing-craft were suitable. At all the others they dragged their moorings – 1½ ton concrete blocks – and many of them finished up high and dry on the shore in a torn and battered condition. If the enemy had had even a brief look at this trail of disaster it would have been abundantly clear that *Quicksilver III* was a purely deceptive operation.

It was not only the design of the dummy craft that was faulty. There were not enough launches to tow them into position, to retrieve them when they broke adrift, and to carry out repairs. There had been virtually no attempt to breathe life into them – which became apparent on 1 June when they were studied from the air. Measures were then quickly taken to make good the deficiencies – galley fires were simulated by burning tow, oil was spread around, clothes lines were put up and washing hung out – the last being a practice which was forbidden in the camouflage manuals.

The transparent fiction was kept up to the bitter end. On 15 June Montgomery ordered that the dummy craft must be maintained as long as possible. The men responsible for them must work long hours and make as much effort as they would do on the field of battle. They should live on site and ensure that there were signs of movement on the craft during the hours of daylight. No doubt Montgomery's order was carried out to the letter, but no German aircraft came to see the result – which was probably just as well.[19]

Quicksilver IV and *V* were, respectively, the bombing of the Pas de Calais beaches and of communications in the region to suggest that an attack from the sea was imminent, and an increase in activity at Dover, which included the apparent setting-up of new radio circuits as well as general bustle to indicate embarkation preparations.

Quicksilver VI covered the misleading and protective lighting-schemes along the South Coast – misleading displays in the east to persuade the enemy that there were large concentrations there; and protective decoys in the west to divert bombing attacks from the troops and vehicles at the assembly points. All the schemes were completed by the middle of May, in spite of many problems, which, according to Colonel Turner, who was in charge of the deceptive lighting, ranged from working in mined areas to combating 'pedigree cows who do not behave like ladies and stamp on all the equipment they cannot eat'. Turner was horrified to find that in their exercises the troops were using every form of intense lighting. His complaint eventually reached Sir Trafford Leigh-Mallory, who 'bit Montgomery'. This woke the army up and thereafter all lighting in the exercises was reduced to hooded lamps and torches.[20]

Turner's programme had been seriously hampered by the Admiralty's slowness in deciding what lighting should be used on the genuine embarkation hards. Eventually they chose a system in which the lights were so effectively screened that they were almost invisible. By this time Colonel Turner's Department had prepared much stronger deceptive lighting-schemes to protect the embarkation hards, which now bore no resemblance to the real thing. However, with the resilience common to all deceptionists, the Department decided that their too-powerful schemes would simulate a hard under attack. In the excitement vehicle lights would be left full on, torches would be used indiscriminately.[21] This is yet another example of how the deceptionists cut their coat according to the cloth – and then pretended to themselves that the inferior product was as good as the original design.

Much ingenuity went into the decoy lighting-schemes. For example, the display at Menabilly in Cornwall was sited in a valley specially dammed and flooded. Lights played on the water to simulate the nearby Fowey harbour, which was crowded with genuine landing-craft. At Cuckmere Haven the lights were an exact replica of the port and railway lighting at Newhaven. In all there were 65 deceptive lighting-schemes, 12 to protect the genuine embarkation hards, 11 to protect ports, 30 decoys along the south coast, and 12 misleading displays in the east and south-east.

Alas, the many displays were never given a real chance to prove their worth. There were some raids on Portsmouth and Plymouth in the latter part of May, which according to Turner's reports were drawn off by the protective decoys. After D-Day, however, the lighting schemes might just as well not have been there.[22]

The overall enemy reaction to *Fortitude South*, on which the success of the Normandy landings largely depended, was almost exactly what it was supposed to be. This was in spite of the fact that the elaborate visual misdirection measures played a negligible part in the deception. It had been assumed by the planners that aerial reconnaissance of the dummy landing-craft and fake lighting systems on the east coast would help to establish the threat to the Pas de Calais; but the enemy paid virtually no attention to them. This meant that the deceptive processes could safely have been confined to simulated radio traffic and the leakage of information through the double agents; but of course, when the plans were laid it was not known that the Germans would carry out so little aerial reconnaissance.

It is interesting to speculate what would have happened if the enemy had taken a close look at the south-east corner of England. It might have confirmed that a major assault force was being prepared there, making the German High Command even more convinced that the Pas de Calais was the Allies' principal objective; or it might have revealed the shambles in which many of the canvas and string dummy landing-craft found themselves, and thereby dissipated the threat at the eastern end of the Channel. The latter seems much more likely. That the Luftwaffe did not carry out even minimal reconnaissance of the east coast must rank as a miracle of the same dimensions as the destruction of the Armada in 1588.

German records of April, May, and June 1944 show how the assessment of the threat from England gradually changed. On 29 April the intelligence section of Foreign Armies West decided that the Allied invasion forces must already be assembled and ready to embark. There was not yet enough information about shipping and landing-craft, but it seemed likely that they were in position. Pointers to imminent invasion which the intelligence section took into account included the ban on diplomatic movement and communications, the cancellation of airmail services between Britain and Europe (including prisoners-of-war), the restrictions on civilian travel, and increasing attacks by Allied air forces on Luftwaffe installations and on communications along the Channel coast and into west Germany. The broad conclusion was that the Allied forces were concentrated in the west rather than in the east. Aerial reconnaissance had established that there were focal points at Portsmouth, Salcombe, and Dartmouth. This did not bode well for the success of the deceptive plan.[23]

A fortnight later – on 15 May – the Germans decided that new formations, including United States forces, were appearing in south-east England. 'A good *Abwehr* source' (meaning a double agent whom German intelligence thought was loyal to them) reported that the 79th and 83rd United States Infantry Divisions were in Yorkshire and Norfolk; and that the XXth United States Corps and 4th Armoured Division were in the Bury St Edmunds area. The 6th Armoured Division was near Ipswich. The VIIIth United States Corps and 28th Infantry Division had been transferred to the neighbourhood of Folkestone.

All these formations were genuine, although they were not all where they were reported to be by the double agents. The XXth Corps and 4th Armoured Division were 200 miles south-west of Bury St Edmunds, getting ready to go to Normandy; the VIIIth Corps was 250 miles north of Folkestone; and the 28th Division was 100 miles to the west. Their locations in the south-east had been confirmed in the Germans' minds by a judicious blend of false radio traffic and leakage through the double agents.

Against this, however, aerial reconnaissance between 25 April and 8 May suggested that ships and landing-craft were in position in the ports between Southampton and Falmouth in the west to carry 14 assault divisions. It was assumed that large numbers of landing-craft were probably hidden from the air, so that the total capacity must be much greater.[24]

In his report for the week ended 21 May, von Rundstedt, Commander-in-Chief, West, included south-east England as an area from which the invasion might be launched – further confirmation that the FUSAG deception was gaining strength. There had been no reconnaissance during the period covered by the report and he had to rely partly on information from agents who had put forward many new dates for the assault (some of which had already passed by the time they reached von Rundstedt) and on the German radio monitoring service which revealed a great deal of training activity in southern England. There was still no sign of all-out preparation for a large-scale attack, but he thought that when the Allies did commit themselves they would try to establish a series of bridgeheads rather than to attack on a broad front. They would probably use new types of weapons, and possibly gas. The transfer of the 19th Panzer Division to the Netherlands, to increase security there, was a further indication of the growing belief that the main Allied attack might come at the eastern end of the Channel.²⁵

In a report despatched on 5 June, the eve of the Normandy landings, von Rundstedt said that it was his considered opinion that the invasion was not imminent, although the marked increase in aerial attacks suggested that the Allies were ready to make the Channel crossing at a moment of their choosing. The heavy bombing of coastal defences between Dunkirk and Dieppe might indicate the area of the assault and the attacks on the Seine and Oise bridges might also point to this area (another success for *Fortitude South*); but they might equally well be designed to hinder the movement of reserves to Normandy and Brittany. The Luftwaffe had spotted that the number of landing-craft at Dover had increased by 20 between 24 and 30 May – Operation *Quicksilver III*'s single recorded success. The photographs must have been taken at a moment when the craft were not bouncing about Dover harbour like table-tennis balls – a lucky escape.²⁶

Almost before the ink of von Rundstedt's signature had dried, the Allies' first move had been revealed, but so well was the FUSAG myth now established that the German High Command believed that the Normandy landings were a diversion, and that the main Allied attack was still to come further east. In his weekly situation report on 25 June – three weeks after D-Day – von Rundstedt said that the enemy had still not committed the American army group assembled in south-east England, although it was ready to embark. The army group, stronger even than Montgomery's 21st Army Group, might be stiffened by battle-tried units now in Normandy, including airborne formations. He thought it possible that FUSAG would be used for landings at points between the right bank of the

Somme and the mouth of the Seine, with the objective of encircling and capturing Le Havre. Then it would join up with 21st Army Group to carry out a pincer attack on Paris. 'Our forces behind the 15th Army are not sufficient, particularly for repelling the large-scale air-landings that must be expected. Nor are the mobile units behind the 15th Army enough for a powerful counter-offensive.'[27]

The threat to the Pas de Calais had of course to be maintained as long as possible. Even if the German reserves in the area were insufficient to deal with a full-scale assault in the east, they could cause problems if they were transferred to support the forces opposing the Allied breakout from the Normandy beaches. The double agents continued to report substantial Allied formations in East Anglia and the German High Command continued to believe what they were told. At the end of June they put the strength of the Allied Armies in the east of England at 30 divisions. At this time there were no more than 12 combat divisions left in England, which meant that enemy intelligence was overestimating the Allied forces in Britain by more than 200 per cent. What was more disastrous from the Germans' point of view was that the bulk of the fictitious divisions were supposed to be located where they posed the greatest threat to the Pas de Calais, which forced them to continue to anchor in the east thousands of men who might have turned the scales in the battle of Normandy.[28]

13 DECEPTION IN THE FIELD

By the beginning of 1944, deception in the field of battle had become highly organized. It had helped to win the desert campaign, and it became a routine activity for the Allied Armies in Italy. As they fought their way up the country, they made good use of experience gained since the early days in the desert. No major operation was undertaken without a carefully-calculated attempt to deceive the enemy. Indeed, there may have been a tendency to resort to deception too readily. Very minor operations were sometimes given the benefit of a deception plan, with the consequent danger of debasing the currency. The greater opportunity the enemy was afforded to evaluate deception ploys, the more difficult it would become to put them across successfully in the future.

Field deception had a good deal in common with strategic. Most of the principal gambits were used in both. Their importance in the two sorts of operation varied considerably, however, mainly because of the differing time-scales. Whereas a strategic deceptive plan could be developed over a period of months, there were only days, or at most weeks, to prepare a tactical plan. The tide of battle moved swiftly, and deception in the field had to keep up with it.

Radio signal-traffic was perhaps even more important on the battlefield than in the wider arena. Fake radio messages originated in Britain were assiduously monitored by the Germans. They added an essential piece to the total jigsaw-puzzle dropped into the enemy's lap. In the field the Germans listened with infinitely closer attention to what the Allied formations were saying to each other, knowing that the outcome of the next battle – and perhaps even their own lives – might depend on their accurate interpretation of the messages.

Visual display on the battlefield also had a much more immediate significance. Dummy aircraft set out on airfields in the north of Scotland, to hint at a forthcoming invasion of Norway, were one thing. If there was no enemy aerial reconnaissance they might never be seen. Dummy tanks poised for an attack through an Italian valley were quite another. Patrols were bound to spot them, and if they were taken to be real it could have a direct bearing on the fighting. Given the time-factor, the desired visual effects had to be established much more quickly than in strategic deception – and there was also much less time for the enemy to observe the display and decide what it implied.

The techniques first used in the desert continued to play their part. In Italy, for example, large quantities of stores had to be concealed where they would be readily accessible before the assaults on the Gustav and Gothic lines. One way of achieving this was 'ribbon stacking': petrol drums and jerricans were stacked along the roadside in long thin lines, so that from the air they looked like walls. Shells were stacked round olive trees and concealed by their branches. Advanced landing-grounds were hidden by elaborate camouflage schemes. In one such the two crossing runways were broken up, by using camouflage netting to extend an adjoining wheat-field into one runway, and by simulating on the other both a hockey and a football pitch, which were surrounded by 'ditches' made of steel wool and scrub. Football matches were held daily for the benefit of German reconnaissance.[1]

The part played by agents in the two forms of deception was very different. In strategic deception the Allies' control of the double agents meant that they could plant a story in the enemy's mind with a good deal of confidence that it would be accepted as the truth; and indeed the continuing dialogue between the double agent and enemy intelligence often established beyond doubt that the story had been swallowed. This sort of facility was simply not available in the field. The average agents in Italy were 'local inhabitants actuated by monetary reward or spite'. The Eighth Army's experience was that information received from these people was seldom accurate. They tended to tell the story they thought would most please their paymasters, based on superficial impressions derived from formation signs and shoulder flashes, vehicle-markings, noticeboards, and so on. In France, where 'R' force was to 21st Army Group what 'A' Force had been to the Eighth Army in the desert, the position was even more unsatisfactory. There large numbers of people were prepared to work for the Germans behind the Allied lines, including double agents recruited by the Germans before the invasion. Because of this danger the Allies were chary of using agents for deceptive purposes in the field. However, it was possible to make use of this sort of agent to put over a tactical deception plan without his knowing it, provided that his character and abilities had been accurately evaluated; but there would usually be some delay before the information which he was 'accidentally' given would bear fruit. After he had been allowed to get hold of something he would need time to get through the enemy lines to make his report, and enemy intelligence would need more time to evaluate his contribution and pass such of it as they accepted to the local commander. It might then be too late for the information to have any significance. These casual agents could also be used to confirm a radio deception in the area where a fictitious display was being made; but it was a dangerous game. Great care had to be taken to ensure that they saw only what they were meant to see. Otherwise it would be very easy for them to blow a tactical deceptive operation – and then they would have earned their keep.[2]

The Germans knew that aerial and artillery bombardment preceded every genuine major attack, so a credible deceptive operation would need to be heralded in the same way. Unfortunately the RAF did not like bombing for purely deceptive

purposes, and as a rule insisted on targets which had a real
military significance. This was perhaps a narrow point of view
since it was entirely possible that 'deceptive' bombing would
pay a better dividend. The threat of artillery bombardment, on
the other hand, could be enhanced by the preparation of
dummy gun positions, simulated arms dumps near the false
gun sites, and the trial registration of targets to establish that
there were live guns in the chosen area.

The Eighth Army believed that if the same ruses were used
over and over again, their deceptive effect was bound to dimin-
ish. The planting of false orders and maps to suggest a certain
false target-area, considered a convincing ploy when carried
out at leisure in a strategic deception operation (especially
when backed up by the report of a double agent), was of
relatively little value in the field. As the War went on this type of
gambit was used less and less. Another gambit – the bombardment of a stretch of coastline to imply that it was about to be
attacked – was also beginning to lose its effect. It had been used
ad nauseam, and by the beginning of 1944 the Eighth Army
experts believed that it would always be discounted by the
Germans. Finally, beach reconnaissance had been used so often
in the Mediterranean deception plans that it had ceased to
serve any purpose 'To be convincing it must be well-staged,
and a freshly-drowned body left on the beach with the remains
of his rubber boat is considered the minimum show likely to be
effective.'

Perhaps the most important difference between strategic and
tactical deception was the crucial importance of concealment in
the latter. Of course, concealment was of great importance in
strategic deception, but it was relatively easy to enforce in an
island country. It was entirely different when the enemy lines
were only a few miles away. The enemy had to be allowed to see
enough of the preparations for the deceptive operation to be
convinced about them, but he also had to be prevented from
seeing a trace of the preparations for the real operation.

Security difficulties limited the scope for tactical deception after the invasion of France. The Allies' agents in France made it clear that the enemy had the most up-to-date information about Allied strength and dispositions. The movement of divisions was known almost immediately – which meant that it was positively dangerous to mount a tactical deception plan which pretended that a division was somewhere else. It was equally difficult to create notional formations which the Germans would accept as actually existing. The safest way to organize deception in these circumstances would have been to move real divisions around as part of the deceptive plan, but the Allies did not have enough reserves to make this possible. Further, most of the time the situation was changing too fast for there to be a chance of evolving satisfactory plans.[3]

Although dummy tanks, vehicles, and guns were important in both strategic and tactical deception, they had to be much better imitations when displayed in the field. A broad outline on an airfield in East Anglia was enough to deceive even a low-flying aircraft, but a patrol armed with field-glasses would find it relatively easy to identify dummies on the ground. (Of course, if the patrol did recognize a squadron of fake tanks, the possibility remained that they were part of a double bluff, and that the plan was to mount a genuine attack under cover of the dummy display.) Another difference between the strategic and tactical dummy was that the former could be made from wood or steel tubing and erected at leisure. This type would have been quite hopeless in the battlefield, given the shortage of transport and the need to mount displays very quickly.

The Directorate of Special Weapons and Vehicles in the War Office was able to offer a wide selection of dummies by the autumn of 1943. Indeed, there were so many that they had to be specially classified for the guidance of camouflage officers. There were wheeled dummies, which could move under their own power, or be towed; portable folding dummies, which were self-supporting when erected; portable collapsible dummies, which had to be supported by guy-ropes; ground mat dummies, simulating slit trenches; vertical screen dummies, carrying a representation of the equipment they imitated; and static dummies, which were heavy and slow to erect. The last included high fidelity devices – almost perfect imitations, which had the disadvantage that they were not easily transportable, for example, the 3.7 inch heavy anti-aircraft guns. There was also 'Meccano' equipment: sets of straight and curved lengths of steel tubing, which the deceptionist could use to construct shapes of his own invention.[4]

Some of the devices were available in inflatable form. One of the most popular was the Sherman tank, which was in fact produced in three versions: folding, inflatable, and mobile. Several sets of the folding model could be carried on a truck, but they took some time to assemble and erect. The inflatable dummies consisted of lengths of rubber tubing which, when inflated, took up the outline of the piece of equipment which was being simulated. The tubing in turn supported canvas, which became, as it were, the flesh of the rubber skeleton. The end-product of this improbable manufacturing process was quite a passable imitation of the genuine article. In addition to tanks, lorries, armoured vehicles, guns, and even aircraft were simulated in this way.

The mobile Sherman consisted of a light steel tubing framework clamped to the body of a Jeep, and covered with canvas, on which the essential features of the tank were painted. It could run on roads, but could not cross ditches or climb banks like a real tank. The narrow wheelbase gave it an unnatural wobble, it did not sound like a tank, nor did it send up clouds of dust. However, these defects were not serious. It was not supposed to behave like a tank in battle, but merely to get into position quickly. Without field-glasses, it was indistinguishable from a genuine tank at 350 yards.

The qualities which 21st Army Group demanded in its fake equipment were, in order of importance, that it should be readily portable, keep its shape, be easy to erect, and be a faithful imitation of the real thing. It was claimed that the only devices which came near to meeting all four points were the United States high pressure inflatable models. These were made up from thinner rubber tubing than the British versions. They could be blown up much harder, so that the dummy kept its shape better. Another advantage was that the thinner tubing was less likely to be punctured. It is true that when it *was* punctured the high pressure model collapsed more rapidly, but since both lost their identity in a matter of minutes there was little to choose between the two models on this score.[6]

The inflatable dummies were more vulnerable to gunfire than the collapsible. During an operation in September 1944, 148 inflatable tanks (Shermans and Cromwells) were erected – which gives an idea of the scale on which deceptive devices were used. Roughly half became casualties. 17 were 'destroyed' by enemy mortar and 88mm fire, 52 by Allied bombs falling short, and 3 accidentally, while they were being positioned. One tank had 200 punctures, caused by stones blasted through it. On the other hand, of 54 portable collapsible dummies, virtually all survived. Nevertheless the inflatable versions were much preferred.[7]

As late as May 1944 the War Office still had little information about the high-pressure dummies, which confirms the point made by the United States Joint Security Control (JSC) that there was inadequate liaison between the two countries in the production of deceptive devices.[8] Another example of this poor liaison was the development of sonic equipment – instruments which simulated the sounds of battle. The two countries had worked independently, the Americans producing a very sturdy article with powerful but not very convincing sound, the British a more fragile model with more faithful sound. The JSC thought that if there had been collaboration from the beginning the resulting device would have incorporated the best features of each design.[9] These sonic devices were wire recorders reproducing the sound of gunfire, motor-transport, the much greater noise of tanks, the clatter of troops disembarking from landing-craft, and the like. From the invasion of Sicily on,[10] they became a useful element in tactical deception during the later stages of the War; for example on *Overlord* D-Day, when they were dropped with dummy parachutists to simulate airborne landings.[11] If the dummies had been dropped silently into the Normandy landscape the deception would have had little effect, but when accompanied by machine-gun fire and other noises of battle it was very convincing. Dummy paratroops had been used with great success in the Middle East, and their manufacture – half-size – began in Britain in 1943. The Middle East model set fire to itself when it landed, to convey the impression that the parachutist had escaped into hiding after burning his parachute,[12] but this refinement was not needed during the Normandy landings, where it was simply a question of adding to the enemy's confusion in the twenty-four hours after D-Day. There were four separate simulated paratroop attacks for this purpose, code-named *Titanic I–IV*. British and American airborne forces were due to drop inland on D-Day, and it was considered that their security immediately after they landed would depend on spreading confusion among the opposing ground forces. This was achieved by dropping dummy paratroops, accompanied by a few Special Air Service (SAS) men, battle noise simulators, and special effects bombs.[13]

Titanic I used 200 dummies to simulate the landing of an airborne detachment at Yvetot, 30 miles south-west of Dieppe, about five hours before the first Allied troops were due on the beaches. Two parties of SAS men had already been dropped in this area, and as the dummies touched down the SAS men attacked despatch-riders and lone vehicles. They were briefed to allow enough of the enemy troops to escape to spread the news that there had been a paratroop landing. The object of this diversion was to retain enemy forces north of the Seine and, with luck, to draw reserves from south of the Seine. The second of the *Titanic* operations used 50 dummies, which were dropped east of the River Dives. It was intended to prevent German reserves from moving out of that area to join

the troops defending the beaches in the west. *Titanic III* also
used 50 dummies. They were dropped south-west of Caen, to
divert attention from the 6th United States Airborne Division,
and to draw local counter-attack troops away from Caen.
Titanic IV was dropped at Marigny in the base of the Cherbourg
peninsula, to entice German forces westward from St Lô. It
used 200 dummies, and it too relied on the SAS to give life to the
simulated attack. *Titanic IV* supported the genuine drop of the
101st United States Airborne Division.[14]

These four diversionary operations were carried out from
RAF Stations Tempsford and Methwold, by forty Stirlings,
Halifaxes, and Hudsons, from 90, 138, 149, and 161 Squadrons.
Most of the aircraft – of which two were lost – succeeded in
dropping the inanimate paratroops on target.[15]

Dummy infantrymen had been used in the desert, but they
did not have much of a part to play in the later stages of the
War. Indeed, it even seems doubtful that they made a big
contribution in the desert. The 'Chinese soldiers' were poles,
with a helmet at the top, and a suggestion of uniform beneath.
They were pivoted at one end and kept prone by strings which
ran back to the company controlling them. When the strings
were released, the men were suddenly pulled into an upright
position by a weight at the bottom end of the pole. With luck
they would draw the enemy's fire, reveal his position, and leave
him vulnerable to an accurate attack. 'Chinese infantrymen'
were used in the Battle of El Alamein, but in such small
numbers that they cannot have had much effect on the outcome.[16]

Finally, the troops were provided with advice on how to
make themselves less visible. The War Office recorded that the
application of some form of skin colouring by personnel during
active operations had long been proved advisable. The most
pleasant and safest were preparations made by the small
number of firms which specialized in this sort of thing during
normal times, but these might not always be available. A large
number of substitutes were listed for the guidance of the troops.

They included cocoa, which was satisfactory, except that it was a scarce material and not waterproof; soot, also satisfactory but not waterproof; mud, which dried too light in tone; printer's ink, which was inclined to shine and was difficult to remove; and cowdung, which did not darken very much, and carried the grave danger of tetanus.[17]

Taxable and *Glimmer* were highly ingenious combined air and sea tactical deceptive operations, carried out on D-Day at the eastern end of the English Channel. They were designed to make the enemy think that two very big assault convoys were approaching the French coast, so that he would be discouraged from moving reserves to the west. *Taxable* headed for the section of the coast between Cap d'Antifer and Fécamp, *Glimmer* for Boulogne. The operations used three devices to simulate on German radar-screens the movement of a large number of ships: 'Window', aluminium strips dropped from aircraft; 'Filbert', balloons which contained a special reflecting device; and 'Moonshine', electronic equipment which received the pulse sent out by enemy radar stations and sent it back to them in magnified form. 'Window' had been in use since the early days of the War. 'Moonshine' had been developed in 1942, but was virtually unused. This meant that the Germans were unfamiliar with the device, so it had a good chance of success.[18]

The naval element in each operation consisted of three lines of small craft. In *Taxable* (the larger of the two operations), the first line had 8 motor-launches, spread across a front fourteen miles wide. Their job was to jam the coastal radar stations, just enough to confuse their pictures. If the radar was put completely out of action the operators would be unable to see the approaching 'convoys'. The launches also carried radio transmitters, which exchanged signals simulating the preparations for a rocket barrage. This traffic would not normally be coded, so the Germans would have no difficulty in understanding it.

The operators had the usual detailed scripts, but because of inadequate rehearsal and the fact that *Taxable*'s own radar countermeasures made radio communication difficult, their performance was less convincing than it should have been.[19]

Two more lines of motor launches came eight and thirteen miles astern, each carrying a reflector balloon and towing a float with another balloon; and in line abreast with them came pinnaces equipped with 'Moonshine', which also carried balloons (9 craft in all). The total effect of this electronic armada, which advanced towards the French coast at precisely 7 knots, was to simulate a huge fleet on the German radar screens. The picture was further enhanced by 8 Lancaster bombers which flew round and round the launches dropping 'Window' from an altitude of between 2,500 and 3,000 feet. Their orbits carried them towards the French coast at 7 knots, to keep in step with the ships beneath them.

Glimmer, aimed at Boulogne, was on a smaller scale. It had 6 launches in the front line, and in the second and third lines 6 balloon-carrying launches and a single 'Moonshine' pinnace. Overhead circled 6 Lancasters, edging nearer and nearer to France. Both operations concluded when those balloons which had not been carried away by the high winds were anchored off-shore, to simulate a great fleet preparing to disgorge an assault force. A smoke-screen was laid to delay the dawn. The wire recorders were switched on to play back the noises of landing-craft approaching the shore. Unhappily the amplification was so poor that it could not be heard above the wind, and although the launches went to within two miles of the coast their performance passed unnoticed. *Taxable* and *Glimmer*, perhaps the most ingenious tactical deceptive operations in the whole of the War, made virtually no impact.[20]

On 13 June, when it was still not certain that the Allies had gained a firm foothold in France, a diversionary attack was simulated against the coast north of Granville in the Cotentin peninsula, to take the pressure off the Americans at the Omaha and Utah beaches. Code-named *Accumulator*, it was mounted at short notice, and carried out by two Canadian destroyers, *Haida* and *Huron*. So that the Germans would know that the 'attack' was imminent, it was pretended that one of the supposed landing-ships had developed engine trouble, forcing it to reduce speed when ten miles south-west of Jersey, and thereby delaying the whole assault. This was reported to base, which meant breaking radio silence. The subsequent discussion of the revised plan of attack was intended to be for the benefit of the enemy monitoring service.

The implementation of the plan was less than perfect. The two destroyers, which were supposed to represent a fleet of landing-craft and other naval vessels, were spotted by an innocent Allied reconnaissance plane which reported them as two unidentified warships. This almost certainly led the Germans to conclude that the operation was a fake. Then *Haida* discovered that her radio sets were not ready, and pulled out, leaving *Huron* to carry on on her own. This meant hasty recasting of the radio scripts, and although the performance was considered to be satisfactory, there was no sign of any enemy reaction.[21]

One of the more successful tactical deceptions in the later stages of the War helped the Allies to break through the Gothic line which ran from Pisa in western Italy to Rimini on the Adriatic coast. It was unusual in that the plan used was the opposite of the original plan, implementation of which had already begun. The original (*Ottrington*) presupposed a genuine attack in the mountains against the centre of the Gothic line, and a fictitious threat along the east coast. The latter would be supplemented by a pretended amphibious threat, mounted from Naples, against the west coast behind the Gothic line, and another against the east coast.

There was much in favour of this plan. The VIth United States Corps, which had fought at Anzio, was due for amphibious training at Naples and provided a ready-made threat against the west coast of Italy. The Germans would probably expect the Allies to attack along the Adriatic coast, to open up the northern plains where their superiority in armour would make itself felt. To support the plan the rumour was spread that General Alexander believed a frontal attack on the Gothic line would be very costly, and that it should be outflanked.

However, some factors made the plan implausible. The deception used in the final attack on Monte Cassino relied on a pretended seaborne assault against the west coast of Italy, which was still fresh in the Germans' mind. There were good lateral communications behind the Gothic line so that even if the enemy made false dispositions he could quickly correct them, especially as the Allied advance through the mountains was bound to be slow. Finally, the Allies' success in mountain warfare round Monte Cassino would suggest that they might try to repeat it in the mountains in the centre of the Gothic line.

This plan was turned upside down at the beginning of August. It was replaced by one in which the genuine attack would be along the Adriatic coast, and the fictitious one straight through the mountains. Thus everything done so far to establish the deceptive threats was exactly wrong. These activities had to be killed off by leaking to the Germans that they were for deceptive purposes – which must have caused them a certain amount of confusion.

The new plan (code name *Ulster*) simulated increased Allied strength in the centre threatening Florence and Bologna, and sought to persuade the enemy that the genuine attack was no more than a feint along the Adriatic coast in which surplus armour would be used. Points in favour of the plan were that Kesselring had located his best troops in the centre of the Gothic line, whereas the Adriatic sector was only lightly defended. This suggested that he expected to be attacked in the centre, an idea which it was hoped would be enhanced by the arrival there of the Greek Mountain Brigade and the Lovat Scouts.

There were of course factors against the new plan – everything that had been *for* the first plan, which simulated a concentration of troops precisely where the genuine attacking force would now concentrate. The movement of massive Allied armoured formations to the east would hardly pass unnoticed. The transfer of Eighth Army headquarters to the Adriatic sector would be given away by radio traffic.

A new background story had to be fabricated. This was that the original plan to attack in the east had been changed because all the landing-craft in the Adriatic (which had been earmarked for the seaborne landing behind the Gothic line on the east coast of Italy) were now needed for an attack on the Dalmatian coast. The troops assembled in the east would move to the centre to strike through the mountains in the direction of Bologna. Some armour would be left behind, thickened up with dummies, for the pretended attack along the Adriatic coast.

This story was implemented in the usual way. Radio signal-traffic in the east decreased. In the centre there was fake signalling at a level consistent with a major build-up there. Rumours were circulated that behind the Polish Corps in the east there were concentrations of dummy tanks which the Poles were supposed to resent, since it might invite an enemy attack. The air forces bombed the roads south of Bologna. The Psychological Warfare Branch encouraged partisans to harass the Germans in the same area, and arranged discreet publicity for the presence in the centre of the Greek Mountain Brigade and the Lovat Scouts.

Everything possible was done to conceal the transfer of troops from west to east. Most of the movement was made by night, under complete radio silence. Sign-posting was kept to the minimum. Staffs reconnoitring the assembly areas were instructed to make themselves inconspicuous. They did not fly flags on their cars, and wore berets 'to reduce the number of red hatbands'. Nothing was overlooked. The highly-finished noticeboards normally displayed at army headquarters, which would catch the eye of local inhabitants, were replaced with crude unimpressive signs. These comprehensive security measures played as big a part in the success of Operation *Olive*, the assault on the Gothic line, as did the efforts of the deception staff.[22]

Tactical deception was used throughout the remainder of the Italian campaign, and later during the advance through France, despite the fact that it was subject to the law of diminishing returns. One of the main deceptive purposes in France was to mislead the Germans about the Allies' order of battle. A typical example in October 1944 suggests that these later deceptions may not have paid much of a dividend. 21st Army Group were nearing the Rhine and dangerously short of reserves. Heavy wastage in nearly six months of hard fighting had led to the disbandment of divisions which could not be replaced, and it was feared that the Germans would become aware of the situation and seek to exploit it. It was therefore decided to create a notional IInd British Corps, comprising the 59th and 76th Infantry Divisions and the 79th Armoured Division, all of which were phoney. The Germans had already been persuaded that the 76th Division took part in the Normandy landings. Captured maps showed that they had included it in the Allies' order of battle – even the notional divisional headquarters were located where they were supposed to be. Therefore there was no problem about putting this division in the IInd Corps. The second candidate was the 59th Division, which had recently been disbanded. Before this it had been identified by the enemy, and there was no indication that the Germans knew it no longer existed. The fictitious 79th Armoured Division was more of a problem. 'R' Force believed that the enemy thought it was a real formation, but they were not certain. However, it was decided to take a chance and include it.

The story was that, because of supply difficulties, the 59th and 76th Divisions had been left behind during the advance, but that it was now possible to move them up to the Brussels area. The 76th Division was going to be used as a reinforcement after the heavy fighting south of Caen, but it had not been needed. 79th Armoured Division had been employed so far only in its component brigades, but it would now be used in its entirety as part of the IInd Corps – which itself had been well and truly established in the mind of the enemy as part of the Fourth British Army in the FUSAG deception.[22]

However convincing this story may have been to those who invented and put it across, there was no indication that the IInd Corps was accepted by the Germans. It seems likely that from this time onwards the impact of tactical deception became less and less. What mattered now was the relative superiority of the Allied forces in terms of weight of armour and air power, rather than in terms of cunning.

14 GERMAN DECEPTION

Deception may help the side holding the initiative, but is not much use to the side on the defensive. From 1942 onwards the Germans were on the defensive. It is therefore necessary to look at their performance in 1939–41 to determine how well they used the weapon of deception.

During their attack on Poland in 1939 they exploited false radio traffic on a considerable scale, but it was not until February 1940 that the German High Command set out the principles to be followed in making cover and deception plans. They directed that measures to deceive the enemy must stand up to intensive examination by enemy intelligence, and corroborate fake information disseminated by German counter-intelligence. They must be believed by the troops and even by the subordinate commanders taking part in the deceptive operations. The *Abwehr* should make use of people travelling abroad, who could speak with conviction of the things they had seen, to back up physical deceptive displays. Doctored information should be supplied to neutral Service Attachés in Berlin. German Service Attachés should cultivate 'drawing-room espionage' in neutral countries.[1] This document shows that the theory of deception was well understood. If the Germans had kept the initiative all through the War they might have continued to use deception with great effect. In spite of the disparaging comments made from time to time by the British about the enemy's intellectual capacity to deal with the deceptive ploys which they served up, there is no doubt that the Germans had mastered the bread-and-butter aspects of deception. Whether the individuals concerned had the lively imagination needed to invent The Man Who Never Was, or the inspired opportunism which sent the Commanding General of 21st Army Group to Gibraltar in the guise of a second-rate actor, is another matter.

They again used radio deception in their attack on France in 1940, and in the desert war. Operation *Sealion*, the proposed invasion of Britain in 1940, was supported with elaborate deception plans, which had not fully matured when the operation was called off. The main deceptive idea was to mount a fake expedition against the east coast of Scotland from southern Norway. The supposed invasion troops would actually embark, but would then disembark before the convoys sailed. The 'expedition' would head for Scotland during daylight, and would turn back as soon as darkness fell. There was a second threat against East Anglia, based in Holland; and a third, based in west France, which implied a landing in Eire. The genuine Operation *Sealion* was passed off as a cover for these three deceptive operations, which were given the overall codename *Herbstreise* (Autumn Journey). Details of what was supposed to be in the wind were leaked by the *Abwehr* to British intelligence.

'It is difficult to estimate how successful these deception measures would have been, partly because they never reached their climax. But they did not succeed in this respect. Although during July and August the main emphasis of defence in Britain was placed on the east coast between the Wash and the Thames, this was switched to the south-east in September.'[2]

By far the biggest German deceptive operation was designed to cover their attack on Russia in 1941. It was on the grand scale which became customary with the Allies, and made use of most of the multifarious techniques later developed and used by 'A' Force and the London Controlling Section. The plan was to threaten an attack on England rather than Russia, which had the incidental benefit – from the German point of view – that it might help to keep the British High Command and even the

British people under continuing strain. It was largely based on the cancelled genuine plan for Operation *Sealion*, and was rather crudely given the code-name *Albion*. Like Bevan's choice of an anagram of Oslo (*Solo*) for the North African cover plan, this choice was either stupid or clever, depending on whether it was interpreted as a single or double bluff. *Albion* had two component parts – *Haifisch* (Shark), which was to be an attack on England from the French Channel ports, and *Harpune* (Harpoon), a second attack from Norway. At first, even the most senior commanders in France and Norway were allowed to believe that the assault on England was genuine, but they were given sealed orders to be opened only on the instructions of the High Command, which in due course revealed the true state of affairs.[3]

When the *Wehrmacht* was told to prepare for *Albion* at the beginning of 1941, it found that so many agencies were competing for influence in the deception field that the operation seemed likely to be doomed from the word go. The principal competitors were the Reich Ministry for Propaganda, the Foreign Ministry, and the SS. The *Wehrmacht* decided that the only way to stop too many cooks spoiling the broth was to keep the whole operation to itself – which it did successfully.

After the beginning of 1941 it became impossible to conceal the ever-increasing build-up of troops in the East – just as it was impossible to conceal the concentration of Allied troops on the South Coast of England in 1944. The men themselves were left with the impression either that they were being assigned to frontier defence, or that they were providing cover for an invasion of England. The German people were also encouraged to believe that England was the objective. The means used to foster the deception included false radio traffic, rumour-mongering, phoney army orders, fictitious preparations for state visits to Germany, and misleading press releases.

The main radio ploy was to use the Sunday forces request programmes to broadcast messages which would lead the Allies' monitoring services to conclude that most of the best

German assault troops were in the West, and that most of the forces in the East were relatively inefficient garrison troops. Thus:

Three happy paratroopers on the Channel coast send greetings to Nurse Kaethe at Reserve Hospital III in Potsdam.

Reserve Hospital Berlin-Wilmersdorf thanks an armoured division's artillery regiment for 100 bottles of Bordeaux wine.

Members of the *Leibstandarte* [Hitler's SS Bodyguard Regiment] send their wounded commander three bottles of Hennessy and wish him a quick recovery.

Sergeant S. on garrison duty in East Prussia sends greetings to his sick mother in Kiel.

Rumours were started by a member of the *Wehrmacht* disguised as a porter in the Berlin *Markthalle*, the indoor fruit and vegetable market where hundreds of merchants came every morning. They were also spread at the newspaper distribution centre in the middle of the city, where the newsagents daily collected their supplies of newspapers. This was an ideal place for the purpose, since the newsagents had a professional interest in the dissemination of news – true or false.

These rumours had to be short and sharp, unlike the elaborate concoctions favoured by the London Controlling Section and the Political Warfare Executive, which would have been over the heads of the greengrocers and newsagents. For example:

Grain trains arrive daily from Russia.

Stalin is coming to Baden-Baden for a four-weeks' rest cure.

All leave in the West is to be stopped.

Starting next week there will be no more through trains to the West.

In spite of the fact that the *Wehrmacht* wanted to keep the Foreign Ministry and the Ministry of Propaganda at arm's length, the *Auslandpress Klub*, which was under Ribbentrop's influence, and the *Ausland Klub*, which was Goebbels' particular interest, were both used to foster the deception. These clubs were frequented by foreign press representatives, neutral diplomats, senior state officials, and army officers; and it was easy enough to plant rumours – rather more intellectual than those which were peddled to the greengrocers and newsagents.

There was a certain amount of play-acting as well. Paratroop officers would speak enthusiastically of the joys of living in France, and commanders of armoured divisions would be seen smoking Dutch cigars, all to create the impression that the main weight of the German forces was in the West, far away from the Russian border. While making an appointment for the following day, a senior officer in his cups carelessly gave away the date of the invasion of England. He failed to turn up for the appointment – having in the meantime supposedly been arrested for his criminal indiscretion.

The troops themselves were used to help the deception. An elaborate plan was worked out for the movement of large forces by rail from east to west, and in the East there were frequent entrainment exercises, in preparation for the expected sudden transfer of many divisions to the Channel coast. German headquarters in Norway, Denmark, and northern France were instructed to revive the *Sealion* preparations. Troops were assembled at ports, and detailed orders issued, some of which were allowed to fall into the hands of British agents. There was intensive air reconnaissance over the proposed landing-places in England, and the German Navy made a display of great activity in the North Sea ports. Notices went out calling for men with a knowledge of English, of England, and of the west coast of Ireland. Handbooks were printed on the British way of life, for the instruction of the invading troops.

The troops concentrated for the genuine assault in the East, even many of the senior commanders, were kept in ignorance of the true objective almost to the last moment. For example, until just before the attack the 6th Panzer Division was under the impression that it was simply on garrison duty, and was totally unaware that many other divisions were stationed in the neighbourhood. Then railway-yards were suddenly enlarged

German deception

and rail traffic increased, to such an extent that soldiers and civilians alike realized for the first time what was happening. Huge quantities of equipment arrived covered by tarpaulins, which could not disguise the shape of guns, tanks, and other vehicles.

The ultimate in deception was too much for one divisional commander. Although under orders to leave undisturbed a girls' camp in the path of the planned attack on the ground that its sudden disappearance might alert the Russians, he disobeyed orders and arranged for the girls to be smuggled away only hours before the attack started.

That an attack on Russia was unthinkable was supported by arrangements made in Berlin. The management of the *Schloss Bellevue*, the Government guesthouse in the capital, was instructed to prepare for the reception of dignatories from Russia at the end of May. The staff concerned, who among other things had to find a Red Flag, were used to publicize the pretended forthcoming visit, by being given strict orders not to talk about it. At the beginning of June, the public were excluded from the *Anhalter* Station while decorations with red banners and a huge electric star were tried out, and again the employees were sworn to secrecy.

Although Goebbels was not allowed to have a direct say in planning the deception, he was used to promote it. An article signed by him entitled 'Crete as a model' was printed in the *Völkischer Beobachter* of 20 June. The implication was that Britain was about to be captured, just as Crete had been only a short time before. The edition was confiscated at the request of the *Wehrmacht*, but not before a number of copies had been allowed to find their way into circulation.[4]

The invasion of Greece, which was forced on Hitler by the foolish ambitions of Mussolini in the middle of the planning for *Barbarossa*, was a fringe-benefit for the deception plan. The great preparations in the East might be seen as no more than a cover for an attack on the Balkans.

In the final stages of *Haifisch* and *Harpune*, controls in the

North Sea coastal areas were tightened noticeably. Hotel-keepers were asked to make special efforts to satisfy themselves about the status of their guests. Violations of the border regulations were severely punished. These measures were intended to give British intelligence the idea that they were covering up military preparations in the coastal districts.*

It is impossible to say from the available evidence how much the Russians and the British were influenced by *Haifisch* and *Harpune*, but there is no doubt that the possibility of invasion remained in the minds of the British High Command long after it had been discarded by the Germans.

* Some of the ploys attributed to the German deception staffs seem to be implausible. The alleged arrangements to receive Soviet dignitaries must have aroused the suspicions of Russian diplomats in Berlin – if they were actually carried out.

15 CONCLUSION

Before considering the success or failure of the Allied deception plans, it is worthwhile comparing the performances of the two major Western Allies in this field. Circumstances gave Britain a head start. The desert army had been compelled to resort to deception to make the best use of its limited resources. 'A' Force learned the value of visual misdirection very early on: the challenge of the empty desert was met by brilliant sleight of hand, and a network of agents and double agents was quickly established. Much of 'A' Force's expertise was absorbed by the London Controlling Section, and in the later stages of the War the two bodies acted as a team. However, 'A' Force had the advantage over their colleagues in London. They were a military unit operating in the field, and controlling their own agents. They probably had greater influence with the Allied High Command in the Mediterranean than the LCS had with the Chiefs of Staff. Furthermore, the LCS could not execute their own plans. It was MI5 who gave the double agents their orders, and the Service Commanders who were responsible for the contributions of the Army, Navy, and Air Force.

But while the art of deception was being steadily developed on the British side, there was a strange reluctance among the Americans to accept that it was part of modern warfare – all the more strange since the Japanese attack on Pearl Harbor was a successful deceptive operation of the greatest magnitude. The British did not at first encourage their allies to develop deception. As soon as the United States entered the War, Colonel Stanley suggested approaching them to co-ordinate deception plans, but this idea was not taken up by the British Chiefs of Staff, perhaps because at the time they did not have much faith in deception themselves. The LCS had achieved nothing of note, and even 'A' Force's dramatic success – at El Alamein – was still some distance in the future. It was not until June 1942 that the British Chiefs of Staff suggested that their American opposite numbers should set up an organization parallel to the LCS. In fact, the Americans did not act on this suggestion, but simply gave oversight of deception to the Joint Security Control, which, like the British ISSB, was generally concerned with security matters.[1]

The British High Command was apprehensive about the Americans' attitude to deception. In 1943 they feared that 'A' Force's contribution in the Mediterranean might be diminished when the new command structure there was headed by an American. Sir Archibald Nye, Vice Chief of the Imperial General Staff, told General Alexander, Deputy Allied Commander-in-Chief, that the Combined Chiefs of Staff had instructed General Eisenhower to prepare deception plans; but 'we have reason to believe Americans in general and General Eisenhower's staff in particular have virtually no experience of deception'. He asked Alexander to ensure that the experts of 'A' Force found their way on to the new Allied Forces Headquarters' deception staff.[2] At the beginning of 1944, the British anxiety about deception in the Mediterranean was again illustrated when they agreed to the appointment of a JSC representative there (Lieutenant Commander Douglas Fairbanks Jr.) only on the condition that there was no interference with the existing arrangements.[3]

Towards the end of 1943 the JSC had become so unhappy about the American performance on cover and deception that they felt that something drastic must be done. Of their own volition they presented a massive report to the United States Chiefs of Staff – rather late in the day, it might be thought. The report was highly critical of what the Americans had done so far, and equally flattering about the British. In the American forces there had been 'confusion and delays resulting from the uncoordinated handling of deception methods, devices, and equipment'. On the other hand the British were well-organized. They had established strategic staffs to carry out strategic deception, tactical staffs for operations in the field, dummy tank regiments, and units for manipulating deceptive devices. They had provided the United States authorities with full information about these activities, but there had been no real effort to make use of the British experience. The United States Chiefs of Staff, in spite of their feeling that the JSC might be trying to gain control of matters best left to the Services, accepted that there was a good deal in their criticism, and thereafter American deception was better co-ordinated.[4]

Nevertheless, the American forces were still slow to accept that strategic deception had much value. When required to play their part in *Fortitude North*, simulating preparations for an invasion of Scandinavia, they were very sceptical about its chances of success. It was only when they were allowed to know how the double agents were being used to mislead the Germans, and how deception had induced the enemy to include fictitious formations in their estimates of the British order of battle, that they realized its importance.[6]

If there is any doubt about the United States attitudes, it is surely dispelled by a paper written by Colonel W. A. Harris, the principal American expert on deception. During the summer of 1943, he and his two deputies were sent to Britain to carry out deceptive operations. All three had grave misgivings about the value of their assignment. Their mood was so critical that they 'successfully destroyed the first cover plan prepared for Operation *Overlord*' by preparing a staff study for General Devers, then Commanding General, European Theater of Operations, United States Army. Harris can hardly be blamed for his initial scepticism. The *Cockade* deceptive operations had achieved their spectacular failure immediately after he had arrived in England.

By the end of the War, however, the Americans' attitudes had changed.

'[They] were completely convinced of the effectiveness of strategic deception as an offensive weapon. The *Fortitude* operations had the dual mission of achieving surprise in the invasion (by concealing time and target area) and of rendering a decisive number of enemy divisions ineffective *following* the establishment of the initial beach-head – by pinning them away from the battle area for a minimum of 30 days ... the success of the *Fortitude* plans is a monolithic fact in any appreciation of the effectiveness of Cover and Deception ... credit for the basic conception of operations which led to this victory must go to the British who built on several years experience in the Middle East to achieve an organization of trained and imaginative personnel, and who worked out the command and control relationships which made it effective.'[6]

Few deceptive operations would have been effective without the help of the double agents, and that help would have been much less but for the information about the thinking of the German High Command provided by the Ultra code-breakers. The double agents moulded enemy thought about Allied dispositions and strategy. The code-breakers monitored the effect of the double agents' leakage of 'information', which in turn made it possible to feed more 'information' to the enemy.

It required great care and ingenuity to make the best use of the double agents and the intelligence coming from Ultra. There was always the danger that in trying to squeeze the maximum benefit from them MI5 would go too far and give the show away. But even the most cautious use of them gave the Allies a tremendous advantage in the game of bluff. Visual displays of real and dummy aircraft, guns, and landing-craft were needed to back up their reports, but they were really little more than an insurance policy against aerial reconnaissance. As the War went on and German reconnaissance was reduced, visual displays became less important.

In the earlier part of the War, the double agents were not allowed to play their full part, because MI5 were still working out the best way to use them. This should be borne in mind when considering the performance of the first Controlling Officer, Colonel Stanley. He claimed that opportunities for deception must be awaited, not made, which partly explains why little was accomplished while he was in charge; but the main reason was that he was not given full use of the double agents. Sir John Masterman writes in *The Double-cross System* that from the start one of Stanley's hands was therefore tied behind his back.[7]

When Bevan took over from Stanley it was mooted 'that the whole double agent system should be run as an offshoot of deception', but this would have been going too far in the other direction. 'Colonel Bevan himself had no wish for this change. He very reasonably regarded double agents as a channel through which his deception could be passed ...'[8] This was a wise decision. The exploitation of the double agents in Britain was a highly-skilled full-time job, and it was far better that MI5 should carry out the wishes of the Controlling Officer on an agency basis.

Masterman hesitates to say how effective the double agents were in comparison with the other means of deception. With equal modesty Bevan has recorded that it was largely through the double agents that the German High Command was deceived. At one time or another, there were 120 double agents under MI5 control, communicating with the Germans by means of wireless telegraphy, letters in invisible ink, micro-photography, or through contacts in neutral or enemy countries:[9] for example, *Treasure*, who spent her weekends at Bristol, and confirmed the Germans' belief that the main cross-Channel attack must come from south-east England by reporting that on her weekend visits she saw hardly any troop movements in the West Country; *Tate*, who was supposed to have become friendly with a railway clerk at Ashford in Kent, from whom he obtained details of all the arrangements for the

supposed movement of FUSAG to the embarkation ports at the
eastern end of the English Channel; *Mullet*, whom the Germans
knew had been concerned with the insurance of factories in the
Low Countries and northern France before the War, and who
told them that the British authorities were most anxious to get
information about the Pas de Calais area; and *Garbo*, who had
led the enemy to believe that no FUSAG formation was taking
part in the Normandy assault. The seemingly disconnected
crumbs of information provided by these double agents and
many others all pointed to the same fact. FUSAG was being
held in readiness to attack in the eastern Channel.

The double agents were essential tools for the deceptionists;
but a tool is only as good as the operator using it. The double
agents were not wielded as effectively as they might have been.
Their very existence was hidden from the great majority of
senior officers, many of whom would have willingly co-operated
in deceptive ploys had they known how the London Controlling
Section was able to work miracles. But it was essential to keep
secret the existence of the corps of double agents, and the closer
the secret was kept the more the deceptionists were denied the
sympathetic co-operation of many who would otherwise have
been willing helpers.

How much did deception help to win the War? There is no
precise answer to this question. It is impossible to prove that a
particular error of judgement lost a minor skirmish, which lost
the battle, which in turn lost the campaign and the war. King-
doms may have been lost for the want of a single horseshoe nail,
but the historian cannot document the process. It is equally
impossible to evaluate the part played by cover and deception
in a World War.

Tactical deception in the desert paid off. It helped the British
to win the Battle of El Alamein, which changed the course of the
War. So there is one credit for deception – tactical deception –
of enormous proportions. The invasion of North Africa

depended more on strict security than on cover and deception, although they helped. The invasion of Sicily was also helped by deception, but it was not a major factor.

The deceptive operations round Britain in 1943 – *Starkey*, *Tindall*, and *Wadham* – were an unmitigated disaster, as General Morgan freely admitted. 'The sky reverberated with the roar of great formations of American and British fighters racing for the battle that they failed to find. We were told that a German coast artillery subaltern on the far shore had been overheard calling his captain on the radio to ask if anybody knew what all the fuss was about. Were our faces red? It certainly looked as if we had played a complete air shot!'[10]

With the benefit of hindsight, it seems that the deceptionists missed a great chance of convincing the enemy that the deceptive plans of 1944 related to genuine operations. As *Starkey*, *Tindall*, and *Wadham* proceeded it became evident that they would achieve nothing. The London Controlling Section might have been expected to use these forlorn hopes to establish the future credibility of the double agents. If it had been leaked to the Germans that the failed deceptions were no more than pieces of amateur play-acting – which is what they were to 'Bomber' Harris – the enemy would have realized that they were telling the truth. This would have given their lies of 1944 great credibility. But according to Masterman, the double agent *Garbo* was used 'to pass over the greater part of the plan *Starkey*' – as if it was intended to be a genuine operation.[11]

The threat to Scandinavia from Scotland in 1944 – *Fortitude North* – retained German troops in Norway and Denmark which would otherwise have been available for the defence of France. It is unlikely that the ingenious diplomatic deceptions – Plans *Graffham* and *Royal Flush* – had much effect on German dispositions, but at least they probably contributed to the general confusion in the mind of enemy intelligence. The various deceptive plans in the Mediterranean may have had some effect on the movement of troops, but by this time the Germans were so stretched generally that it was difficult for them to make any major changes in the disposition of their forces. Any reluctance to move troops from the Mediterranean area, however, must have been greatly increased by the success of the *Wantage* order of battle plan.

It may be a fair assessment that the deception planners just about broke even before *Overlord*, but there can be no doubt whatsoever that *Fortitude South* was an outstanding achievement. The First United States Army Group, originally in the substance and later in the shadow, induced the Germans to make disastrously false dispositions in France, and it certainly made a major contribution to the success of the invasion of Europe.

However, it is too much to claim that *Fortitude South* alone gave the Allies victory in Normandy. There were other factors. The weather hindered the invasion forces as they headed for France, but it helped to conceal them. It also discouraged enemy aerial reconnaissance over East Anglia which could have revealed the flotillas of dummy landing-craft for what they were. The Allies had overwhelming strength in the air. PLUTO, the pipeline under the ocean, made it possible to keep the Allied armour moving in France. The Mulberry harbours, an inspired invention of enormous importance, were wholly unsuspected by the Germans. *Fortitude South* was only one of the factors contributing to the Allied victory.

Two final points about deception planning. First, plans were often modified to meet the circumstances of the moment to such an extent that they almost ceased to be plans. Second, the deceptionists sometimes lost themselves in the world of their own make-believe, and persuaded themselves that whatever story they put across the enemy would accept as the truth.

It was inevitable that deceptive plans should take second place to plans for real operations. The deceptionists were in the nature of things second-class citizens who had to make do with facilities not required by the other services, but they were as a rule reluctant to admit that enforced changes in their plans weakened them. The *Cockade* deceptions of 1943 are a good example. The deceptionists prescribed the scale of operations needed to produce the desired effect on German intelligence, but when for one reason or another that scale had to be drastically reduced, they continued to hope, or perhaps pretend, that the modified plans would still be effective. They might almost have taken a leaf from *Alice Through the Looking-Glass*.

'When I make a plan,' Humpty Dumpty said in rather a scornful tone, 'it means just what I choose – neither more nor less.'

'The question is,' said Alice, 'whether you *can* make plans mean so many different things.'

'The question is,' said Humpty Dumpty, 'which is to be the master – that's all.'

PRIMARY SOURCES

Public Record Office

ADM 179   Portsmouth Station Records
ADM 199   War History Cases
ADM 223   Naval Intelligence Papers

AIR 2   Air Ministry Correspondence
AIR 8   Chief of Air Staff Records
AIR 14   Bomber Command
AIR 15   Coastal Command
AIR 16   Fighter Command
AIR 20   Air Ministry Unregistered Papers
AIR 27   Squadron Operations Record Books
AIR 28   Station Operations Record Books
AIR 29   Miscellaneous Units Operation Record Books

AVIA 1   Royal Aircraft Establishment Flight Log Books

CAB 21   War Cabinet Registered Files
CAB 64   Minister for Co-ordination of Defence
CAB 65   War Cabinet Minutes
CAB 69   War Cabinet Defence Committee
CAB 73   War Cabinet Committee on Civil Defence
CAB 79   War Cabinet, Chiefs of Staff Committee, Minutes
CAB 80   War Cabinet, Chiefs of Staff Committee, Memoranda
CAB 119   Joint Planning Staff Files
CAB 122   British Joint Services Mission, Washington

DEFE 2   Combined Operations Headquarters

FO 188   Embassy and Consular Archives
FO 371   General Correspondence, Political
FO 898   Political Warfare Executive
FO 954   Avon Papers

PREM 3   Prime Minister's Office Papers

WO 106   Directorate of Military Operations and Intelligence
WO 107   Quarter-Master-General
WO 169   War Diaries, Middle East Forces
WO 199   Military Headquarters Papers, Home Forces
WO 201   Military Headquarters Papers, Middle East Forces
WO 204   Military Headquarters Papers, Allied Force Headquarters
WO 205   Military Headquarters Papers, SHAEF
WO 219   Military Headquarters Papers, 21st Army Group

National Archives of the United States

RG 59   Department of State
RG 218   Records of the US Joint Chiefs of Staff
RG 319   Records of the Army Staff
RG 338   Records of US Army Commands

SELECT BIBLIOGRAPHY

G. Barkas, *The Camouflage Story* (Cassell, 1952)

Ralph Bennett, *Ultra in the West* (Hutchinson, 1979)

Anthony Cave Brown, *Bodyguard of Lies* (W. H. Allen, 1976)

Sefton Delmer, *The Counterfeit Spy* (Harper & Row, 1971)

Ladislas Farago, *The Game of the Foxes* (McKay, 1971)

M. R. D. Foot, *SOE in France* (HMSO, 1966)
  Resistance: an Analysis of European Resistance to Nazism (Eyre Methuen, 1976)

Clifton James, *I Was Monty's Double* (Rider, 1954)

R. V. Jones, *Most Secret War* (Hamish Hamilton, 1978)

David Kahn, *The Codebreakers* (Macmillan, 1967)

Ronald Lewin, *Ultra Goes to War: the Secret Story* (Hutchinson, 1978)

Sir John Masterman, *The Double-cross System in the War of 1938–45* (Yale University
  Press, 1972)

Ewen Montagu, *The Man who Never Was* (Evans, 1966)
  Beyond Top Secret U (Peter Davies, 1977)

Sir Frederick Morgan, *Overture to Overlord* (Hodder and Stoughton, 1950)

David Muir, *Practise to Deceive* (William Kimber, 1977)

Alfred Price, *Instruments of Darkness* (William Kimber, 1967)

Ronald Wheatley, *Operation Sealion* (Clarendon Press, 1958)

Sir Ronald Wingate, *Not in the Limelight* (Hutchinson, 1959)

F. W. Winterbotham, *The Ultra Secret* (Weidenfeld and Nicolson, 1974)

NOTES

Introduction pp. xi–xiii
1. *The Second World War* (Cassell, 1948–54),
    vol. v, p. 126.

CHAPTER 1

Deceiving the invader pp. 1–17
1. WO 219 2246, 7A.
2. AIR 2 2878, 9A, 9B, 15A–C.
3. Ibid., 20A.
4. Ibid., 25A.
5. Ibid., 30A.
6. AIR 2 3180, 1A, 6A, 12A, 143A.
7. AIR 2 8021, 8A.
8. AIR 2 2878 (12.10.1939); AIR 20 4354.
9. AIR 2 3180, 41C; AIR 2 3213, 138A.
10. AIR 2 4579, 70C; AIR 14 3340 (28.7.1941).
11. AIR 14 3340 (28.7.1941; 2, 4.8.1941); AIR
    15 320, 40A.
12. AIR 2 2878 (12.10.1939; 31.3.1940).
13. AIR 2 3213, 2A.
14. AIR 15 320, 5B, 5C, 17A.
15. AIR 2 3213, 47A, 138A; AIR 15 320, 33A;
    ADM 199 69. f. 37.
16. AIR 2 2878 (14.9.1938); AIR 2 3447
    (13.10.1938).
17. AIR 2 3447 (26.9.1939); AIR 2 3705, 2A.
18. AIR 2 3705, 81A, 87A.
19. AIR 20 964 (19.7.1943).
20. AIR 2 3180, 26A.
21. PREM 3 118, f. 5.
22. AIR 20 5213 (20.11.1940).
23. AIR 20 4354.
24. AIR 20 5213, 1A; AIR 15 320, 8B.
25. AIR 2 4708, 68A; AIR 20 5213 (16.12.1940).
26. AIR 14 2780 (7.5.1942); ADM 199 69, f. 38B.
27. AIR 14 2780, 51B; AIR 15 320, 8B;
    AIR 20 4354.
28. AIR 2 4708, 10A.
29. PREM 3 118, ff. 6–8.
30. CAB 80 31, f. 85.
31. AIR 20 4259 (29.2.1944).
32. AIR 2 3180, 42A; AIR 20 5213, 1A;
    AIR 2 6016, 4A.

33. ADM 199 69, ff. 99b, 101.
34. Ibid., ff. 99b, 101.
35. Ibid., f. 149.
36. Ibid., f. 149.
37. Ibid., ff. 110, 152–3.
38. AIR 20 5238 (26.10.1940); AIR 29 868 (10.11.1943); AVIA 1 13 (27.10.1940).
39. CAB 21 1477 (29.7.1940).
40. CAB 80 20, ff. 47A, 48.
41. CAB 80 25, f. 45.
42. CAB 80 18, ff. 17–27; CAB 80 25, f. 49.
43. CAB 80 21, ff. 34–5.
44. PREM 3 81/4, ff. 43, 148, 154–6.
45. PREM 3 118, f. 9.
46. CAB 80 18, ff. 80–3.

CHAPTER 2   Deception in the desert pp. 19–33
1. AIR 20 2497 (5.2.1944).
2. WO 201 772.
3. WO 169 3976.
4. Ibid.
5. WO 201 2025.
6. WO 204 4814 (24, 27.1.1943).
7. The following paragraphs are based on reports in WO 201 2023.
8. WO 201 434.
9. WO 201 2023.

CHAPTER 3   The North African landings pp. 34–49
1. CAB 80 60, ff. 80–3.
2. AIR 20 3693 (21.4.1942).
3. Ibid. (20.6.1942); AIR 20 2508 (15.12.1942).
4. AIR 20 4504 (1.8.1942).
5. AIR 20 2508 (26.11.1942); AIR 20 4504 (6.10.1942).
6. AIR 20 2508 (26.11.1942).
7. WO 106 2778 (4.9.1942).
8. WO 106 2714 (20.9.1942; 2.10.1942).
9. Ibid. (8.9.1942).
10. AIR 20 4504 (31.7.1942).
11. AIR 20 2508 (26.11.1942).

12. WO 106 2778 (4.9.1942).
13. AIR 20 2497 (8.1.1944); AIR 20 4504 (9.8.1942).
14. AIR 20 4504 (17.8.1942).
15. WO 106 2778, 6A.
16. RG 338, Records of US Army Commands, Foreign Military Studies, MS P–041h.
17. WO 106 2771, 105A.
18. AIR 20 2508 (26.11.1942).
19. AIR 20 2497 (8.1.1944); WO 106 2714, 15A.
20. AIR 20 2508 (26.11.1942).
21. RG 218 CCS 385 Cover and deception plans. (7–20–1942).
22. RG 59 811.3338/187A.
23. Ibid., 188.
24. Ibid.
25. Ibid.
26. AIR 20 4504 (8.10.1942); AIR 20 2508 (26.11.1942).
27. CAB 122 1206 (8.1.1944).
28. *The Double-cross System in the War of 1939–45* (Yale Univ. Press, 1972), pp. 109–10.

CHAPTER 4   The invasion of Sicily pp. 50–60
1. CAB 79 86, ff. 43–9, 53–4, 58–9.
2. CAB 69 2, ff. 59, 61.
3. PREM 3 227/1, f. 4.
4. AIR 20 4535 (30.1, 1.2.1943).
5. WO 204 1561; FO 898 398 (24.5.1943).
6. WO 204 211 (1.6.1943).
7. CAB 79 60, f. 138; WO 204 1561 (10.4.1943); see Ewen Montagu, *The Man Who Never Was* (Evans Bros., 1953).
8. WO 106 3867 (28.3, 30.4.1943); WO 204 211 (7.5.1943).
9. WO 204 211 (7.5.1943).
10. WO 106 3867 (18.6.1943); WO 204 6589–90; AIR 20 4535.
11. WO 106 3867 (30.4.1943); FO 898 398 (24.5.1943).
12. FO 898 398 (29.6.1943).
13. AIR 20 3696 (9.4.1943).

14. FO 898 398 (28.4.1943).
15. AIR 20 4535 (2, 3, 4.7.1943).
16. FO 954 23, f. 202.
17. Ibid., f. 203.
18. WO 106 3867 (20, 25.6.1943).
19. CAB 79 62, f. 44.
20. WO 204 211 (7.5.1943).
21. CAB 80 78, no. 16.
22. F. W. Winterbotham, *The Ultra Secret* (Weidenfeld and Nicolson, 1974), p. 107.
23. WO 204 758 (24.6.1943, 1.7.1943, 12.8.1943).

CHAPTER 5

Deceptive operations, 1943 pp. 61–84
1. WO 106 4223, 2A, 4A, 14A.
2. Ibid., 18A.
3. CAB 122 1293 (23.6.1943).
4. AIR 20 4547 (17.6.1943).
5. WO 106 4241 (26.6.1943); AIR 20 4547 (7.6.1943).
6. CAB 79 62, f. 273; DEFE 2 458 (13.7.1943).
7. DEFE 2 458 (17.7.1943); AIR 8 1202 (15.6.1943).
8. AIR 8 1202 (9.7.1943).
9. AIR 2 1202 (25.8.1943).
10. CAB 80 73 (20.8.1943); AIR 2 1202 (28.8.1943).
11. CAB 79 61, f. 236.
12. Ibid., f. 324; WO 106 4241, 4A; PREM 3 333/17, f. 691.
13. CAB 122 1293 (23.6.1943).
14. CAB 80 71, no. 386; WO 106 4223, 39C; RG 331, SHAEF G–2 Ops. 200 DX/Int. 1A.
15. FO 898 398 (11, 27.8.1943).
16. AIR 20 964 (14.7.1943); WO 199 184, 5B.
17. WO 199 184, 16A; ADM 179 272 (9.2.1943).
18. FO 898 373.
19. AIR 16 766, 91A; DEFE 2 458 (5.7.1943); WO 219 1858 (8.9.1953).
20. PREM 3 333/17, f. 687; AIR 8 1202 (30.8.1943).

21. ADM 179 271 (9.9.1943).
22. ADM 179 270 (28.7.1943; 7.8.1943); ADM 179 271 (9.9.1943).
23. FO 898 373, ff. 122–5.
24. CAB 80 71 (12, 20.7.1943); CAB 80 73 (3, 9, 16, 24, 31.8.1943).
25. CAB 80 74, f. 28; WO 106 4241, 32A, B, C; FO 954 32, f. 268.
26. PREM 3 333/17, ff. 678–9.
27. AIR 20 4801 (16.9.1943); WO 205 449 (10.9.1943).
28. WO 205 449 (10.9.1943); ADM 179 275; WO 106 4241, 38A.
29. ADM 223 8 (6.9.1943); PREM 3 333/17, f. 677.
30. WO 106 4241 (29.9.1943); AIR 20 4841 (16.9.1943); WO 219 1856, 7A, 8A, 9A, 24A, 42A.
31. CAB 80 74, f. 270.
32. Ibid., no. 514.
33. CAB 80 70, no. 288; DEFE 2 458 (30.6.1943); WO 199 464 (30.6.1943).
34. CAB 79 61, f. 324.
35. DEFE 2 458 (30.6.1943); AIR 20 4550.
36. DEFE 2 458 (30.6.1943).
37. WO 199 464, 1C.
38. DEFE 2 458 (30.6.1943); WO 199 464, 1C.
39. WO 106 4223, 42B.
40. AIR 20 964 (14.7.1943).
41. CAB 80 71, no. 388.
42. AIR 20 4550 (21.7.1943); WO 199 464, 15A.
43. WO 199 464, 36A, 51A.
44. Ibid., 79A; WO 205 440, 16A.
45. WO 199 464, 57A.
46. Ibid., 79A.
47. WO 106 4223, 32B; RG 331 SHAEF/203/DX/Int. (*Wadham*); AIR 20 4547 (17.6.1943).
48. FO 898 373, f. 158.
49. WO 106 4227.
50. AIR 20 4547 (9.9.1943); FO 898 373 (31.7.1943).

51. WO 219 1851, 3B; RG 331
SHAEF/203/DX/Int. (*Wadham*).

CHAPTER 6   The overall deception plan, 1944
pp. 85–98
1. RG 218 Records of the Army Staff CCS
(6–25–43) Secs. 1 and 2.
2. WO 219 307 (14.7.1943).
3. Ibid. (16.7.1943).
4. CAB 122 1272.
5. WO 219 307 (20.7.1943).
6. CAB 80 75, no. 615.
7. WO 106 4165, 6C.
8. CAB 80 75, no. 651.
9. WO 219 307 (22.7.1943).
10. WO 219 2204A, 16A.
11. CAB 80 76, no. 695.
12. Ibid., no. 701; WO 106 4165, 9A.
13. WO 219 308 (7.10.43).
14. CAB 80 76, no. 735; PREM 3 342/4, ff.
195–201.
15. CAB 122 1251, f. 2.
16. Ibid., no. 6.
17. Ibid., no. 25.
18. Ibid., no. 42; CAB 80 77, no. 779.
19. CAB 80 77, no. 779.
20. Ibid.
21. WO 219 2206, 3A.
22. Ibid., 3B, 5B.
23. RG 331 Allied operational and occupation
headquarters: SHAEF G–2 00/11
DX/INT.

CHAPTER 7   The threat to Scandinavia pp. 99–113
1. WO 219 2220, 13G.
2. CAB 122 1251, 47A; WO 219 309
(23.2.1944).
3. WO 219 2220, 3D, 14B; WO 219 2221, 25A.
4. WO 219 2221, 20B.
5. WO 199 1378 (26.3.1944).
6. WO 219 2221, 22A.
7. Ibid., 1A.
8. AIR 2 6022 (30.12.1944).

9. WO 219 2221, 6A.
10. WO 219 2220, 13F.
11. Ibid., 20A.
12. WO 219 2244, 3A.
13. WO 219 2221, 32B.
14. Ibid., 42A.
15. Ibid., 44A, 47A.
16. Ibid., 15A.
17. Ibid., 8A.
18. WO 219 309 (24.3.1944); WO 219 2220.
19. WO 219 2214, 15A.
20. WO 219 309 (18.7.1944).
21. WO 219 2222, 2A.
22. Ibid., 4B.
23. WO 219 2224, 1A.
24. RG 319 Army Staff G–3, Cover and deception: Folder 8.
25. RG 319 Army Staff G–3, Cover and deception: Folder 12.
26. *Kriegstagesbuch of OKW 1940–44*, p. 298.

CHAPTER 8

Russian charade pp. 114–124
1. CAB 79 87, f. 1; AIR 20 3693, f. 2.
2. CAB 79 18, f. 342; AIR 20 3693, f. 4; FO 954 23, ff. 107, 109, 110.
3. FO 954 23, f. 204.
4. WO 106 4165, 21A.
5. CAB 122 1251 (15.1.1944).
6. Ibid. (21.1.1944); FO 954 17, ff. 47, 49; 32, f. 452.
7. FO 954 17, f. 50.
8. AIR 20 4548 (14.2.1944).
9. Ibid. (14.2.1944).
10. Ibid. (14.2.1944).
11. FO 954 17, f. 55.
12. AIR 20 4548 (17.2.1944).
13. FO 954 17, f. 56; WO 106 4185, 61A.
14. FO 954 17, f. 61.
15. Ibid., f. 64.
16. Ibid., f. 65.
17. Ibid., f. 67.
18. Ibid., f. 68.
19. Ibid., f. 69.

20. Ibid., f. 71.
21. Ibid., f. 73.
22. Ibid., ff. 76, 78; WO 106 4165, 85A.
23. FO 954 17, ff. 77, 80; WO 106 4165, 86A.
24. AIR 20 4548 (28.4.1944).
25. Ibid. (30.4.1944; 1, 2.5.1944); CAB 79 74, f. 16.
26. AIR 20 4548 (4.5.1944).
27. Ibid. (5.5.1944).
28. Ibid. (11.5.1944).
29. Ibid. (25.5.1944).
30. CAB 122 1253 (17.5.1944).
31. John R. Deane, *The Strange Alliance: The Story of Our Efforts at Wartime Cooperation with Russia* (Viking, 1947) pp. 147–9.

CHAPTER 9   Diplomatic deceptions pp. 125–145
1. CAB 80 75, no. 615(0).
2. CAB 80 76, no. 716(0).
3. FO 954 17, ff. 271–4; FO 188 446, nos. 4, 9, 26A.
4. FO 188, 446, no. 29.
5. CAB 80 80, no. 126(0).
6. FO 188 446, no. 7; FO 954 17, f. 281.
7. FO 954 17, f. 274.
8. FO 188 446, no. 104.
9. WO 106 4158, 90A, 94A.
10. RG 59 740.0011/33492A, B, 1/2.
11. CAB 122 1252 (4.4.1944); FO 188 446, no. 32.
12. FO 188 446, no. 40; RG 59 740.0011/33858 1/3.
13. CAB 122 1252 (8.4.1944).
14. FO 188 446, no. 34.
15. RG 59 740.0011/33858 2/3.
16. CAB 122 1252 (8.4.1944); RG 59 740.0011/33858 2/3.
17. FO 188 446, nos. 20, 21, 30, 36, 43.
18. AIR 20 3694; FO 188 446, no. 128.
19. FO 188 446, nos. 51, 78, 85.
20. Ibid., no. 35.

21. Ibid., nos. 35, 39.
22. AIR 20 3694 (7.3.1944).
23. FO 188 446, no. 46.
24. Ibid., nos. 81, 91.
25. Ibid., no. 127.
26. Ibid., no. 123.
27. CAB 122 1252 (19.4.1944).
28. Ibid. (23.4.1944).
29. *Kriegstagesbuch of OKW 1940–44*, p. 297.
30. AIR 20 3964 (16.5.1944).
31. Ibid.
32. AIR 20 4548 (28.4.1944).
33. Ibid. (28.4.1944).
34. CAB 122 1253 (26.5.1944).
35. CAB 79 62, f. 192.
36. CAB 122 1253 (16.5.1944); AIR 20 4548 (11.5.1944).
37. AIR 20 4548 (3, 11.5.1944).
38. CAB 122 1253 (29, 31.5.1944); AIR 20 4548 (18.5.1944).
39. RG 59 740.0011, 34436 1/4.
40. RG 59 740.0011, 34436 1/4.
41. Ibid., 3/4.
42. RG 59 740.0011, 34436, 1/2, 3/4; RG 165 a.b.c. 385, Spain; Sweden (19.5.1944); RG 331 SHAEF 381, *Royal Flush*.
43. AIR 20 4548 (28.4.1944).
44. Ibid. (2, 11.5.1944).
45. CAB 80 83, f. 183.
46. AIR 20 4548 (28.4.1944).
47. AIR 20 4549 (22.7.1944); CAB 122 1254 (26.7.1944).
48. CAB 122 914 (8.8.1944).
49. CAB 122 915 (18.8.1944).
50. Ibid. (19, 22.8.1944); CAB 119 109 (22.8.1944).
51. AIR 20 4549 (25.8.1944).
52. CAB 122 915 (9.9.1944).

CHAPTER 10   The Eastern Mediterranean pp. 146–157
1. WO 204 1795, nos. 42, 44; WO 204 1920 (22.2.1944).

Notes

2. WO 204 1795, no. 33.
3. Ibid., no. 44.
4. Ibid., no. 7.
5. Ibid., no. 7.
6. Ibid., no. 14.
7. Ibid., no. 44.
8. Ibid. (26.6.1944); WO 106 3944 (28.6.1944).
9. WO 201 1196 (22.5.1944; 13.7.1944).
10. *Kriegstagesbuch of OKW 1940–44*, p. 297.
11. WO 204 1795 (7.6.1944).
12. WO 204 1561 (10, 12.2.1944).
13. WO 204 1795 (25.6.1944).

CHAPTER 11

The Western Mediterranean pp. 158–169
1. WO 219 2218, 7B, 7C.
2. Ibid., 8B, 8C, 9A.
3. Ibid., no. 1A; WO 219 317 (8.5.1944).
4. *Kriegstagesbuch of OKW 1940–44*, p. 297.
5. WO 204 218 (6.5.1944).
6. Ibid. (22.5.1944).
7. CAB 80 83, f. 83; AIR 20 4548 (12.5.1944).
8. WO 204 759 (14, 16.5.1944).
9. WO 204 4270 (17, 18.5.1944).
10. WO 204 759 (10.6.1944).
11. WO 204 4270 (20.5.1944).
12. Ibid. (26.5.1944).
13. WO 204 759 (2.7.1944).
14. WO 204 1913 (28.7.1944).
15. WO 106 3944, nos. 22, 23; WO 219 306 (3, 5.7.1944).
16. WO 106 3944, no. 23A.
17. Ibid., no. 34.
18. Ibid., nos. 35, 36.
19. Ibid., nos. 37, 40.
20. WO 219 317 (5.8.1944).
21. WO 204 1913.
22. ADM 199 909: United States Eighth Fleet report on the invasion of the south of France, pp. 177–9.

CHAPTER 12

The crucial deception pp. 170–189

1. AIR 20 4849 (20.11.1943).
2. CAB 64 45, ff. 83–4; PREM 3 345/5, f. 293.
3. CAB 65, 46, ff. 13–14; FO 371 41980 (5.7.1944).
4. CAB 80 83, no. 457; WO 219 2238, 2A.
5. CAB 65 43, f. 101.
6. WO 219 2238.
7. CAB 80 78, no. 68; PREM 3 345/5, ff. 258, 293, 299–300.
8. PREM 3 339/13, ff. 77–9.
9. WO 219 2210, Ap. D.
10. Ibid., f. 8.
11. Ibid., f. 8.
12. WO 219 309 (4.3.1944); WO 219 2246, 10A.
13. WO 219 2217, 5B; WO 219 527 (21.10.1943).
14. WO 219 2223, 9A, 13C; WO 219 2224, 5C, 12E; WO 219 2225 (26.8.1944).
15. WO 219 2217, 1A, 2A, 6A, 7A, 13A; WO 219 309 (4.5.1944; 13.6.1944).
16. WO 219 2226, 1A, 5A.
17. Ibid., 12C, 12D, 14B, 19A; WO 219 2217, 38A.
18. WO 199 1377, 99A; WO 219 2223, 3G; WO 219 2227, 3D.
19. WO 219 2215, 57B; WO 199 2629 (18.9.1943); WO 199 2630 (24.4.1944; 15.6.1944).
20. AIR 20 4259 (16.5.1944).
21. AIR 2 6017, 47A.
22. AIR 2 6022, 67A.
23. RG 319 Records of the Army Staff, G–3, Cover and deception: Folder 28. (OKH: Report of *Abteilung Fremde Heere* West III/v, 29 April 1944).
24. RG 319 Records of the Army Staff G–3, Cover and deception: Folder 28. (OKH: Report of *Abteilung Fremde Heere* West III/v, 15 May 1944).
25. RG 319 Records of the Army Staff G–3, Cover and deception: Folder 28.
26. Ibid.

27. RG 319 Records of the Army Staff G–3, Cover and deception: Folder 28.
28. Ibid.

CHAPTER 13

Deception in the field pp. 190–205
1. WO 204 8107.
2. WO 204 8013.
3. WO 219 2246, 43A, B.
4. WO 205 606 (7.1.1943); WO 205 611 (19.10.1943).
5. WO 205 611 (9.3.1944; 10.12.1944); WO 205 612 (5.1944).
6. WO 205 611 (10.12.1944).
7. Ibid. (29.9.1944).
8. RG 319 Records of the Army Staff G–3, Cover and deception: Folder 11.
9. RG 218 CCS 385 (4–8–43) (2) Sec. 1.
10. ADM 199 1595, f. 27.
11. RG 319 Records of the Army Staff, G–3, Cover and deception: Folder 11.
12. AIR 20 3693 (9.2.1943).
13. AIR 14 725, 21A.
14. RG 319 Records of the Army Staff G–3, Cover and deception: Folder 11; AIR 14 725, 21A.
15. AIR 20 820, f. 85b; AIR 27 732; AIR 27 1004; AIR 27 956; AIR 27 1068.
16. WO 201 2023.
17. WO 205 606 (7.1.1943).
18. AVIA 7 1544–5.
19. WO 219 2214, 13A, 17A; RG 319 Records of the Army Staff G–3, Cover and deception: Folder 11.
20. ADM 199 1595, ff. 611–8; AIR 14 2041, 2C, 2B; AIR 27 2129 Ap. 10.
21. WO 219 2214, 16A.
22. WO 204 8010 (20.10.1944).
23. WO 219 2247 (9.10.1944; 5.11.1944).

CHAPTER 14

German deception pp. 206–212
1. RG 338 Records of the Office of the Chief of Naval Operations: Espionage, sabotage, conspiracy. Report by the Office of Naval

Intelligence, p. 109. (The contribution
made by the wife of the Swedish Minister
of Foreign Affairs when she told what her
husband thought about the Allies' deceptive
Plan *Graffham* is a good example of the
success of drawing-room espionage. See
Chapter 9.)

2. Ronald Wheatley, *Operation Sea Lion:
German Plans for the Invasion of England
1939–42* (Clarendon Press, 1958), pp. 162,
162n.

3. This description of the cover plan for
Barbarossa is based on accounts written
after the War by General Hans von
Greiffenberg, *Generaloberst* Erhard Raus,
and *Oberstleutnant* Harald Weberstadt (RG
338, Foreign Military Studies MS. P–044
a, b, and c.)

4. The only copy of the *Völkischer Beobachter*
for this date which I have seen is on
microfilm in the Library of Congress and
contains nothing by Goebbels. It may be
that no copy of the fake issue survived. A
similar ploy was used by the Americans in
1942 when the Office of War Information
(OWI) instructed Major Fielding Elliot to
write an article for the *New York Herald
Tribune*, emphasizing the Allies' interest in
Norway. U.S. censorship then prevented
the issue from leaving the country, and
when Elliot made his regular weekly
broadcast he pointedly made no reference
to Norway. This unilateral deception by
OWI upset General Eisenhower, with
whom it had not been cleared. (RG 218 CCS
385 [7–20–1942]).

CHAPTER 15

Conclusion pp. 213–221
1. AIR 20 3693 (29.8.1942; 2.9.1942).
2. AIR 20 4535 (30.1.1943); WO 106 2778
(1.2.1943).
3. WO 204 1562 (18.4.1944).

4. RG 218 CCS 385 (4.8.43) (2) Sec. 1.
5. RG 319 Records of the Army Staff, G–3, Cover and deception: Folder 1.
6. RG 319 Records of the Army Staff, G–3, Cover and deception: Folder 1.
7. *The Double-cross System*, p. 160.
8. Ibid., p. 162.
9. In *The Double-cross System* (published in 1972, but for all practical purposes an official document written in 1945), Masterman lists 39 of the 'more interesting' double agents who played a vital part in deception.
10. Sir Frederick Morgan, *Overture to Overlord* (Hodder and Stoughton, 1950), p. 108.
11. *The Double-cross System*, p. 207.

INDEX

(showing contemporary rank and style)

Index

Index